MW00638245

SLAVES TO RACISM

SLAVES TO RACISM

AN UNBROKEN CHAIN FROM AMERICA TO LIBERIA

Benjamin G. Dennis

and

Anita K. Dennis

Algora Publishing
New York

© 2008 by Algora Publishing.
All Rights Reserved
www.algora.com

No portion of this book (beyond what is permitted by
Sections 107 or 108 of the United States Copyright Act of 1976)
may be reproduced by any process, stored in a retrieval system,
or transmitted in any form, or by any means, without the
express written permission of the publisher.

Library of Congress Cataloging-in-Publication Data —

Dennis, Benjamin G.
  Slaves to racism: An Unbroken Chain from America to Liberia / Benjamin G. Dennis
and Anita K. Dennis.
    p. cm.
  Includes index.
    ISBN 978-0-87586-657-4 (trade paper: alk. paper) — ISBN 978-0-87586-658-1
(case laminate: alk. paper) — ISBN 978-0-87586-659-8 (ebook) 1. Racism—Liberia. 2.
National characteristics, Liberian. 3. Liberia—Race relations. 4. Racism—United States.
5. National characteristics, American. 6. United States—Race relations. I. Dennis, Anita
K., 1945- II. Title.

    DT630.D46 2008
    305.80096662—dc22

                          2008033512

Front Cover:

Printed in the United States

To all who long for freedom from racism

"Oh would some power the gift to give us,
To see ourselves as others see us."
— Robert Burns

TABLE OF CONTENTS

INTRODUCTION

In the spring of 1980, in Flint, Michigan, I received two phone calls in the middle of the night that drastically altered my life and signaled a lasting change in Liberia. At the time, I was preparing to return there to live. In several trips to Liberia during the 1970s, President William R. Tolbert, Jr. had convinced me I could better serve at home. He was a good friend, having done much for my Mende people. I had just signed a purchase agreement to sell our house. Everything seemed in place.

This return would add another chapter to my Liberian saga, since my arrival in America in 1950. As a boy, I learned that my last name "Dennis" stemmed from the transatlantic slave trade. My father told me that some of our Mende people in West Africa had been taken into slavery in America. In Richmond, Virginia, the two Dennis brothers became Free Negroes, each owning three or four slaves themselves. During the 1800s, they returned to Liberia, freeing their slaves and taking them with them. One of the brothers remained on the coast in the capital, Monrovia, as an Americo-Liberian. The other, knowing his Mende ancestry, traveled to the area where the Mende live in Liberia. There, he was accepted as a descendant of someone taken into slavery from the line of the great Mende chief, Ngombu Tejjeh.

In 1976, I discovered my American roots. One morning, when I walked into my office at the University of Michigan–Flint, I saw a young black woman sitting at my desk. After she explained that her name was Vicki and she was taking a make-up exam, she said, "Is that your name on the door — Dr. Dennis? That's our family name."

I said, "Are you a native of Flint?"

"No, we come from Virginia."

"From Richmond, Virginia?"

"Yes! How'd you know? My mom told me some of our relatives way, way back joined a group of black people going to Africa before the Civil War."

Several days later, Vicki's mother Juanita, visited our home. During the conversation, Anita, my white American wife, said, "I've noticed that the Dennis men have a ridge of skin at the lower back of their head. My husband's got it." Juanita simply took Anita's hand and put it in her hair. When Anita felt the ridge, she got goose bumps. Later that summer, we visited the Dennis' in Richmond and presented them with country cloth from my father's village of Vahun.

Those two phone calls in the spring of 1980 wiped out my plans to return home. In the first call, I learned that President Tolbert, of the Americo-Liberian ruling elite, had been assassinated in the Executive Mansion by a group of security guards who were African-Liberians — Liberia's disenfranchised majority. I was devastated. To learn more, I kept trying to tune in the BBC on my shortwave radio. Ten days later, in another call, I heard that African-Liberian soldiers had tied thirteen Americo-Liberian government officials to poles on the beach and machine-gunned them. One was a cousin, Cecil Dennis, the Minister of Foreign Affairs. Another was a former brother-in-law, Richard Henries, the Speaker of the House of Representatives. My uncle C.C. Dennis, a prominent newspaper publisher in Monrovia, had been chained to the back of a pickup truck and dragged to his death.

Two weeks later, a parcel of Liberian newspapers arrived. In gruesome photos taken at the beach, bullet-riddled bodies were slumped over the ropes that tied them to the poles. One of the articles said that Senator Frank Tolbert, the president's older brother, spit at the soldiers just before they shot him.

Liberia's Coup of 1980 overturned one hundred thirty-three years of Americo-Liberian rule established solely for their benefit. And Liberia has never been the same. Samuel Doe, the Krahn master sergeant who led the group that shot Tolbert, took control and later became president in 1986.

During the 1990s, Liberia descended into civil war and anarchy. African-Liberian rebel groups roamed the countryside randomly killing as they vied for power. Doe was killed by a segment of these rebel groups and warlord Charles Taylor eventually became president in 1997. In 2003, Taylor was deposed by rebel groups and is now on trial at The Hague for war crimes. Despite Ellen Johnson-Sirleaf's democratic election in 2005, Liberia remains in ruins as a classic failed state in Africa. The obvious question is: Why did the Negro experiment planted in Africa in 1822 fail so miserably?

This account of the social and cultural forces that destroyed Liberia is based on social psychology — how people think and act as a group. In every society and nation, while every individual may not exactly fit the mold, there are cultural similarities that lead to groupthink — an essential element of national character.

America and Liberia are very different countries on very different continents. They have different cultures and racial combinations. And yet they have striking parallels of racism. Why is this? First of all, racism and its effect are universal. Since they are based on emotional need, they make us all captive and similar. Secondly, Liberia's cultural racism stemmed from America's racism. The effect of slavery and racism in America had a huge impact on Liberia's ruling class and thus Liberia's destiny. Liberia's story begins with America's story.

Racism is a group phenomenon. Whites in America were faced with a conflict between their ideals of freedom and democracy and the profit of slavery. Despite their freedom and independence as Americans, they were compelled to rationalize their behavior to maintain their self-esteem and status. They justified themselves by perpetuating and augmenting racism.

Racism displays the power of the group. While the North and South were divided on slavery, whites shared racist attitudes as a racial group. Negroes faced slavery and lynching alone because of white racial unity. Today, racial attitudes continue to grant every white American racial advantage in some way or another.

The need to rationalize made whites racially consistent. Whites' perception was culturally controlled. Exceptions to Negro stereotype were ignored. Peer pressure punished "Nigger lovers." Racial assumption became reality as Negroes were made inferior in slavery.

The effect of racism is also a group phenomenon. White racial consistency led to Negro racial consistency. Racism generated a common experience among Negroes as a racial group — whether slave or free, North or South, urban or rural. Their common longing for status rendered them fundamentally and perpetually insecure — not only as individuals but as a people.

The effect of racism ensured its compulsive perpetuation. In a white/black nation, race superseded culture. During the 1950s, upper and middle class Negroes weren't assimilated no matter how culturally "American" they were. Since they couldn't transcend race, light-skinned mulattos "rose" by considering themselves superior to dark-skinned Negroes. In Negro racism, "superiority" was based on a racial similarity to whites — soft hair and a lighter skin tone.

Liberia is a classic example of the effect of racism and its perpetuation. The Free Negroes and freed slaves who went there thought they were free. Instead, as Americo-Liberians, they remained captive to the effect of slavery and racism. In their longing for success and status, they "rose" by exploiting the natives and justifying it on the basis of cultural inferiority. In an all-black nation, culture superseded race. The Americo-Liberians saw themselves as a superior cultural group. They saw natives as a collective inferior cultural group.

Under the influence of Americo-Liberian oppression and white missionary and business activity, natives were gradually made socially and culturally insecure. To fit into Americo-Liberian society, they had to follow Americo-Liberian ways. Even so, they were exceptions to the rule, that didn't change the rule. Uncivilized or illiterate natives remained inferior. Like Negroes in America, Westernized natives/African-Liberians learned the wrong lessons from their masters. They essentially replicated the destructive cultural mentalities of the Americo-Liberians.

When Westernized African-Liberians overthrew the Americo-Liberians in the Coup of 1980, they thought they were free. Instead, they remained captive to Americo-Liberian and white influence. Again, and even in an all-black nation, culture superseded race. In a *modern tribalism* based on Western values, Westernized African-Liberians "rose" by discriminating against and oppressing traditional African-Liberians.

Racism can only end in futility for all concerned. It made Americans and Liberians image, rather than reality. As a group phenomenon, racism has the power to destroy not only individuals, but societies and nations. For example, what would Liberia be today if the Americo-Liberians had garnered the cooperation of the natives and enrolled them in nation building? What would the United States be if Negroes had been fully assimilated?

This description of the principles of racism is based upon my life in Liberia and America from the 1930s until now. While I have seen great social change, I have also experienced the resilience of racism and its effect since they are based on emotional need. This is a cross-cultural, cross racial view of racism — an eyewitness account from both sides of the racial and cultural fence. As a classic marginal man, I have a unique perspective. I am the son of a Liberian diplomat in Berlin, Germany, during the 1930s and early 40s. My childhood consisted of three influences — the German Western culture, the Americo-Liberian Western culture, and traditional native culture. While I was included in all of them, I didn't fully belong in any of them. My Mende father, Ngombu Tejjeh Dennis, was a middleman himself. He not only moved easily within and between native and Americo-Liberian circles but within traditional and Western culture as well.

My winters were spent in the Liberian consulate in Berlin. My summers were spent in Liberia — both in Monrovia and in my father's Mende village of Vahun and my mother's Gbande village of Somalahun. As an African boy in Nazi Germany, I spoke German and thought I was a German. When my father stopped me from marching for the Fatherland with my German playmates and told me I wasn't a German, I ran and asked my mother.

I said, "Papa says I'm not a German."

She said, "He's right."

"But then, what am I?"

"You are an African."

"You mean the place we go for vacation?"

Because of my ties to one set of the Dennis' in Monrovia, I am an Americo-Liberian. As a Mende and Gbande, I am a native/African-Liberian. In America, I was equally socially and culturally marginal — accepted and rejected by both Negroes/blacks and whites. As "everyman," I belong nowhere and yet, everywhere. I'm at home in both African traditional culture and modern Western culture.

This is the viewpoint of a participant as well as a scholar. I am a black sociologist who has lived racism — an anthropologist who is a hereditary Mende chief. My training and cross-cultural experiences made me an observant outsider. My personal connections made me a trusted insider with access to confidential racial and cultural attitudes. Since social scientists can't put people in a lab and test them, my evidence of racism and its effect is largely anecdotal.

While my aim is to tell the truth, not criticize, every racial and cultural group mentioned here is negatively affected by racism. The impact of racism is generalization — making these groups more alike than they are different. When I say "Americo-Liberians," "African-Liberians," "whites," and "blacks," I'm referring to commonalities of viewpoint and attitude. At the same time, because of individual differences, I am not referring to every Americo-Liberian, African-Liberian, white, or black.

The most difficult thing for any of us to do is to examine and understand why we think and act as we do. This is especially true in the area of race and culture. What you are about to read is an intimate look at racial and cultural groups impacted by racism. I hope it serves as a catalyst, not only for self-examination, but for social change — to bring about a world where everyone is judged by the content of their character, not race or culture.

PART I. RACISM'S IMPACT ON NATIONAL CHARACTER IN LIBERIA

Emancipate yourselves from mental slavery.
None but ourselves can free our minds.
— Bob Marley, "Redemption Song"

CHAPTER ONE: IDENTITY

The Inferiority/Superiority Complex

> "The Love of Liberty Brought Us Here"
> —The National Seal of Liberia

Liberia was a conflicted nation because it was ruled by a conflicted people. The Americo-Liberians were a classic marginal people — socially and culturally. As a displaced people with no pride, they never found the self-worth they were looking for in Africa. "With God above, our rights to prove," they re-invented themselves in a myth of glory.

In 1943, as a teenager, I asked one of my Americo-Liberian uncles, "Old Man Dennis, why don't you talk about something new? Why do you always bring up those old times in Virginia?"

He said, "Well, our history is dead if we don't keep tellin' it. No one will write books about these things. Our forefathers worked hard to be here in Liberia. They never thought they'd ever come back to Africa. Our people were stolen from here and taken to that cold, cold country. It was God who brought us here — the same God who took the Israelites outta Egypt. They had only a small body of water that God dried up so they could walk through. But God brought us in ships over the wide, wide ocean. When the Jews reached the Promised Land, they crossed over another body of water we just sang about in church, remember?"

"I don't remember all the songs."

"You oughta be listenin'. That was a good song."

He sang in his rich bass voice, "Roll Jordan Roll, Roll Jordan Roll, I wanna go to heaven when I die, to hear ole' Jordan roll." Then he said, "B.G., we were home, no problems. We didn't have to go hungry anymore. We could eat paw paw, banana, and cassava and sleep all day if we wanted to. Our ancestors had no choice but to get up before daybreak and work, work, work till sundown. I tell you, they carried a heavy burden. That's why they sang, 'Nobody knows the trouble I've seen.' That's why we became Christians. No human being could have ever saved us from those people. You know what, B.G.? It was God. It's mind-boggling. You can't even imagine."

He pounded his fist on the table for emphasis as he continued, "Liberia is the land of God! God preserved this place and brought us here! Look all over Africa. When we were freed in America, they chased us into Africa. Whites took every little bit of African land except our little country here. God planted us here. That's why Liberia is God's land. Nobody's gonna evict us from our home. The white man can't take it because God has preserved the Lone Star of Africa for his people. We're God's chosen people too. Has He done that for any other African group? No, B.G., this is the history of Liberia. Don't you forget it."

Liberia was founded in 1822, by the American Colonization Society, a combination of Northern philanthropists and Southern slave masters. According to society records, approximately 12,000 Negroes were shipped to the West coast of Africa from 1822-1867. Of this, approximately 4,500 were born free; 350 purchased their freedom; and 6,000 were slaves freed on the condition they leave America. Since the importation of slaves into America was abolished in 1807, approximately 6,000 slaves recaptured on the high seas were dumped in Liberia in one year, 1860. The recaptives, unable to speak the local languages, were civilized by the Americo-Liberians. Although the Americo-Liberians tried to recruit intelligent and industrious Negroes to join them, Liberia's record gave no incentive. After the Civil War, only a thousand came since Emancipation brought greater hope in America.

The real goal of the society was to rid America of Negroes. Liberia was the solution to the "Negro problem." Free Negroes threatened slavery and were thought to instigate slave revolts. If they became successful, they might marry white women. Slave masters and widows of such got rid of old or unwanted slaves by paying their war to Liberia, thus freeing them and America from any further obligation.

Africa was the "Dark Continent," no glorious place to go to. Northern Free Negroes refused to be banished. Southern Free Negroes were escaping from something worse. Liberia's Declaration of Independence states, "...we were debarred by law from all rights and privileges of man....We were excluded from all participation in government. We were made a separate and distinct class and against us every avenue of improvement was effectively closed."

For the most part, it wasn't the talented or successful that went to Liberia. Only the Free Negroes, one fourth of the group, had any form of literacy or training whatsoever. Since the Americo-Liberians associated learning with whites, they were anti-intellectual.

During the 1930s and early 40s, Liberia's backwardness was legendary in European circles. The taunt was that Liberia had the "lowest form of government in Africa." When Firestone came in during the 1920s, men had to literally hack their way through the forest to survey the site. Liberia had a few rudimentary health facilities and only one Liberian doctor trained at Meharry Medical College in Nashville. Because of yellow fever, malaria, and smallpox, foreigners were concerned about the lack of sanitation and health care. Liberia's only saving grace was Duside Hospital at the Firestone Rubber Plantation.

Liberia's Frontier Force, initially trained and equipped by the British, was led by a few American Negro officers as well as Americo-Liberians. Missionaries ran the College of West Africa, a Methodist high school in Monrovia, and staffed it with white and American Negro teachers, as well as Ghanaians and Sierra Leoneans educated at Fourah Bay College in Freetown. The same was true for Liberia College in Monrovia. Although Firestone had many clerical and overseer positions open, they were overwhelmingly filled by Sierra Leoneans and Ghanaians rather than Americo-Liberians. The vast majority of nurses at Duside Hospital were native. Ninety-five per cent of all trade was in the hands of German, British, French, and Lebanese traders. In contrast, the Americo-Liberians derived their support directly or indirectly from government service.

The Americo-Liberians were powerless on the world scene. They lived on foreign loans. As masters of playing on America's guilt and Christian sympathy, they continually "carried the hat," asking for charity. As a result, there has been a tremendous private flow of money into Liberia from Christian organizations.

Those rejected by whites, rejected the natives. Caught between two very different cultures, the Americo-Liberians didn't belong anywhere. With no genuine place or roots on either continent, they were outsiders in America and Liberia. The "African" had been taken out of them in slavery. Since their access and inclusion into the American society had been severely restricted, they weren't genuinely American either.

The Africans they could easily become, they didn't want. They were in Africa, but they were loyal to anything but Africa. "Going native" was opposed from the very beginning. They never fulfilled their glorious goal to redeem Africa because they came to reform and reinvent it, not to become a part of it.

The white Americans they couldn't be, they wanted. Since they couldn't be racially white, being culturally white was the next best thing. They were "Americans" seeking the liberties and opportunities denied them in their "homeland." White culture implied power through technology — firearms and access to education, however limited. Speaking English meant they belonged with whites.

In their love/hate relationship with America, America's greatness and power was combined with the reality of their suffering. They assumed an American connection in Africa, calling themselves Americo-Liberians. They took pride in their Western names. The upriver Americo-Liberians said, "We Congo people..," which meant they were better than the natives.

The capital, Monrovia, was a small town. You could walk from Waterside at one end, to Crown Hill on the other, in twenty minutes. Where the Executive Mansion now stands, was the site of the old Frontier Force barracks, then considered the "outer limits of civilization." The campus of the University of Liberia was a field of palm trees with a road through it leading to the German Legation in Sinkor, where people made palm wine.

Streets were hard-trodden dirt with an occasional plank walk. Only Ashmun Street was paved in front of the old State Department Building, the old Executive Mansion, the Legislation Building, and the War Department, where tailors made the khaki uniforms for the Frontier Force. Mr. Dabobi, a gunsmith trained in Germany, repaired their weapons. Henry Cooper paved Broad Street as a boulevard during the 1940s, using a coal tar machine loaned by Firestone. In the center, Poinciana trees were planted and enclosed with concrete blocks.

People walked or rode bicycles. The few cars were owned by the embassies; Liberia's three former presidents; and a few other Americo-Liberians. My father's black Model T had to be cranked to start. One day, Pa Cole, a Sierra Leonean family friend, told Joe and me that he would drive us around town if we brought him the key. As he fumbled with the key, he accidentally pressed the horn. Startled, but quickly composing himself, he said, "Dennis? You think a man who no *sabe* [doesn't know] how for drive car, *sabe* how for blow horn?" Then he told us he couldn't take us after all because the Americans didn't know how to build a car. They put the steering wheel on the wrong side.

Liberia had five Americo-Liberian counties near the coast — Montserrado, Maryland, Cape Mount, Sinoe, and Grand Bassa, as well as Marshall Territory. The interior was divided into the Western, Central, and Eastern Provinces. Natives called Monrovia "Ducor" because it was located on the Du River.

The Western Province was Liberia's breadbasket. The rice farms of the Loma, Kissi, Kpelle, Gbande, and Mende provided Liberia's staple food. To a much lesser extent, this was the case with the Loma and Kpelle in the Central Province. Natives in the interior were also the source of chickens, goats, and cattle. The Kru on the coast provided fish. Five trucks traveled back and forth from Kakata, thirty miles inland, bringing bags of rice and other foodstuffs to sell at Waterside in Monrovia.

One of these trucks was owned by Old Man Thomas, a Sierra Leonean Methodist pastor and teacher at Booker T. Washington Institute in Kakata. During rainy season, when the truck was heavily loaded, car boys followed behind on foot putting wooden blocks behind the slick rear tires to keep the truck from slipping backwards as it made its way up the steep incline at Mount Barclay. One day, after it had rained steadily for two days, Thomas told his driver and carboys, "We're not making any money sittin' down here. Let's go. I'll go with you."

When the truck stopped halfway up the hill as usual, Thomas yelled, "Put Blocks! Put blocks!" He jumped out and put his foot behind one of the rear tires to temporarily hold it. But the wheel rolled over his foot and the truck slid down the hill and into a gutter by the side of the road. Thomas lay on the road crying, "Me money! Me Truck! Me Foot!"

The twenty mile path to the Firestone Rubber Plantation at Harbel was popular because natives employed there were always going back and forth to their villages. Their relatives traveled this way as well since they were also eligible for free medical care at Firestone's Duside Hospital.

Two boats traveled on the St. Paul River, as it wound inland from Monrovia. Just below the rapids, were the upriver towns of Millsburg and White Plains on opposite banks. Every day, except Sunday, the Cooper and Bulee boats left their opposite docks at 5:00 a.m. to go to Waterside in Monrovia. Each boat carried up to thirty people, as well as market produce to sell.

Cooper didn't collect the fifty-cent fare until the boat left the dock. When anyone didn't pay, he announced the next morning, "I've got my right shoe on my left foot and my left shoe on my right foot. And you know what that means! If you don't have the fare, get out right now! Otherwise, I'm in a mood to boot you into the river where the crocodiles will take you to hell in their belly!"

The journey into Monrovia took no more than an hour. It was the same for the evening trip if the tide was good. The minute the boats arrived at Waterside, people waiting there fought to buy produce, including market women buying up large quantities for resale. Shoppers at Waterside yelled, "Woloco! Woloco!" for boys or men to carry purchases on their heads. Before the ride back, the boat passengers bought rice and palm oil at Waterside and kerosene and salt in the Lebanese stores. The boat captains waited for the tide to come in before they headed up Stockton Creek and on into the St. Paul River.

The Americo-Liberians were a small, closed community of about twelve thousand. They lived in Monrovia on the coast, and in the upriver communities nearby, as well as the small towns along the coast. Although they were vastly outnumbered by a million natives, they indirectly controlled Liberia's 43,000 square miles, about the size of Ohio. The elite were descendants of Southern Free Negroes with some small means and education. They lived in Monrovia as an urban people. The elite also included prominent Americo-Liberian families living in the coastal areas and upriver settlements — as well as descendants of the three hundred West Indians who had migrated to Liberia in 1865.

The leading families in Monrovia lived in two-story brick or weatherboard Southern homes. Although they were few in number, they set the standard for Americo-Liberian society. They consolidated and retained their power through intermarriage. They maintained their status by social exclusivity — private social clubs where a "crowd o' boys" came up together.

They controlled everything through family alliances. Everyone knew every family by name. Status was based on family ties and "who you knew." Everything was a family affair, particularly politics.

The vast majority of Americo-Liberians in Monrovia were poor. They lived in houses so old, leaky, and rotting, that new paint flaked off of them. When you walked on the wood plank floors, the boards popped up. Outhouses were a stinking den of flies, where people wiped their behinds with old newspaper. Amongst themselves, the Monrovia Americo-Liberians were loving and loyal. The poor survived by working for elite families. Ingratiating with small gifts and performing services, they assumed status by association with those who were "up there."

The cash crop farms of the leading families in the coastal and upriver areas resembled a Southern plantation with a "big house," servants' quarters, and storage sheds. Their homes were surrounded by a yard and garden with fruit trees. They used glass plates and silverware. Some families had a house in Monrovia as well.

Second-class Americo-Liberians in the coastal and upriver areas were called "Congos." They were descendants of recaptured slaves thought to have originally come from the Congo, as well as descendants of freed slaves. They lived in small clapboard houses with a corrugated zinc roof. Out back was an outdoor kitchen with corrugated zinc walls and a thatched roof, as well as an outhouse. Ancestral portraits on the walls were covered with spider webs. In small adjoining rooms, beds were covered with Southern quilts made in quilting bees. At night, the wooden shutters on the windows were closed.

Like natives in the area, the upriver Americo-Liberians trapped raccoons and rats. They dried and salted meat. They cooked over a small wood fire and used a water pot and drinking gourd. Their Western clothing was so worn out, it was a conglomeration of patches. The men wore their hair close-cut. Because of their high-stepping walk, natives said, "He walks like a Congo man."

The women wore colonial-style dresses. The few women who had sewing machines made their own dresses. The others bought a ready-made dress in Monrovia or had a tailor make them one. They cooked in pots and pans and used enamel plates and wooden or rusty spoons, rarely forks.

As a boy, I visited Mr. Haskins in Careysburg a number of times. There were so many tree branches hanging over his house, I could barely see it from the main path. When I walked through the elephant grass after it rained, I was soaking wet by the time I reached the porch.

Haskins was light-skinned and toothless. I couldn't tell the original material of his clothes. When he walked, the tops of his shoes flapped. His wife, who was taller and dark-skinned, always wore a colonial dress with an apron.

I usually found him sitting on his porch with a shotgun in his lap. Whenever he got up, he put his gun down and stepped carefully over the empty spaces in the rotten wood floor.

Each morning in the creek behind his house, he collected fish, crabs, and crayfish from fish trap baskets baited with beaten palm nuts. He raised chickens in his back yard and had a large garden of tomatoes, cassava, sweet potatoes, onions, and gourds.

One day, I asked a local Kpelle man about Haskins. He told me, "He just sit there with that old, old gun. When I was small boy, that gun look like that. He never fire it, cause no trigger. He shoot monkey with bow and arrow. Those Kwii

(Western) people! His clothes be well rotten. It be his wife take old one to fix it. He no go nowhere, just for creek and sit down and eat catfish."

The Americo-Liberians were intellectually superior since they had adopted the complex white culture. They were morally superior since they adopted Christianity, the white man's religion. Because of their Western ties, they were all superior, regardless of circumstance.

They were essentially "whites in disguise" — an imaginary people of self-delusion and pretense who lived in the fear of being found out. Their self-hatred kept them from facing the truth. As they tried to be somebody they didn't really know, their white characteristics and habits made them foreign to Africa.

In 1939, the sun was hot as my brother Joe and I walked to Providence Baptist Church in Monrovia. As the tails of my black woolen tailcoat dragged behind me in the dust, its scent of stale sweat made me nauseous. The black bow tie was tight and made the starched collar scratch my neck. My hands were soaking wet in the white gloves. My top hat tilted and the small-rimmed glasses pinched my nose. At least, I had refused to wear the woolen long johns.

Everyone at church was smiling and laughing. Girls in full-skirted dresses and pantaloons stood giggling, sweat running down their faces. Their broad-brimmed hats tilted too. At least, they had parasols for the parade.

During the service, while the pastor droned on and on about the glorious pathfinders, men in woolen suits and women in hats and gloves sat sweating in the pews. Afterwards, the men sat on the church steps taking off their shoes for the walk home. We stumbled down the high steps onto Broad Street, with the congregation cheering, "Here come the pioneers!" As we marched around the block, we had the street to ourselves since there were so few cars. Later, people came out of their parties onto second floor porches to clap and cheer for us.

All over town, tables were laden with goat soup, chicken dumplings, fried chicken, barbecued ham, fried corn bread, black-eyed peas, and collard greens. For dessert, there was pumpkin and sweet potato pie. The German companies donated beer and there was plenty of wine and cane juice. Our house on Gurley Street was filled with foreign diplomats, Americo-Liberians, and natives.

Americo-Liberian status-consciousness was oriented to the West. In their desire to prove themselves worthy to a white world, they were focused on a white audience. Liberia was their stage and they were the performers. They judged their behavior in comparison with civilized countries. They preferred imported goods since they implied status. What they wanted most was status in the eyes of whites. Only secondarily, did they want status in the eyes of their peers and their status confirmed in the eyes of natives below them.

During World War II, the British Royal Navy docked in Monrovia for a few days, and Liberia's soccer team, "The Barclay Eleven," challenged the sailors to a goodwill match. As right shortstop, I knew we had to win. This was a game against civilized whites. To prepare, we split into two teams, playing each other. I knew everyone was counting on me since my twin brother Joe was sidelined with the flu.

Things were very tense that Saturday as we ran onto the field. The few bleachers were packed. Crowds lined the field.

During the first quarter, there was no score. In the second quarter, as I outran my defender and approached the goal, I used my right foot to position the ball but kicked it in with my left. The crowd went wild. So many people ran onto the field, they had to clear it before the game could resume.

The euphoria quickly dissipated when the British scored a goal in the third quarter. During the fourth quarter, I again used my kicking strategy for the winning goal. Pandemonium broke out. Everyone ran onto the field as the sailors shook our hands.

Someone lifted me on their shoulders and carried me across the field. The crowd yelled, "We beat the white people!" Everyone rushed to shake my hand. Someone said, "That's a helluva boy! He can play ball like hell!" As the crowd poured back into town, a group of Kru girls started up a chant, "Oh Yah, Oh Yah, B.G. Dennis, play your ball...Oh, B.G. Dennis play your ball, play your ball...."

The Americo-Liberians bragged, "We were never a colony." The boasted that whites couldn't become citizens or own land. In reality, Liberia was America's unofficial colony. Since America had no obligation to develop Liberia as a whole, Liberia shares the negatives of colonialism without the positives. Americans and Europeans only built infrastructure in Liberia related to business or defense interests. It was America's need for a guaranteed source of rubber during wartime that brought Firestone to Liberia. It was the need for a military base during World War II that brought about Robertsfield Airport and the Freeport in Monrovia.

The Firestone Rubber Plantation is a classic example of American imperialism — "dollar diplomacy." Since the Americo-Liberians were always in desperate need of revenue, it was easy for America and other foreigners to exploit Liberia. The Americo-Liberians essentially derived their livelihood from serving as business middlemen between foreigners and natives/African-Liberians. Foreigners easily manipulated the Americo-Liberians by catering to them and flattering them with empty praise. In deference, the Americo-Liberians said what foreigners wanted to hear.

Firestone is a classic illustration of white racism. Duside Hospital had private rooms for white patients upstairs and two large communal rooms for Liberians downstairs, men on one side and women on the other. As a teenager, I worked at Duside as a dresser and medical assistant. One day, Pa Cole, who worked there as a pharmacist, told me how two white doctors killed Mr. Laryea, a Ghanaian who was one of the best trained pharmacists there. Laryea was an alcoholic. To make his drinks, he used a certain type of alcohol from the pharmacy supply.

In time, two of the white doctors noticed that one alcohol supply ran out long before the others. Just before Liberia's Independence Celebrations on July 26, they poisoned the entire alcohol supply. When Laryea tasted his batch of drinks for the festivities, he realized he was poisoned. He tried to get back to the hospital by taking a short cut through the rubber trees. Too weak to climb a small ravine, he collapsed and died several yards away. The white doctors announced they were happy to have found the rogue. They said Laryea died because he was stealing and the same fate would apply to anyone else.

One day, a white superintendent hit and killed a native boy on the embankment of a road in Division 44. When the news reached Monrovia, Richard Henries, the top Americo-Liberian lawyer for Firestone, came to investigate.

I was chosen to participate in the investigation. Native witnesses took us to the scene. When I saw the blood on the embankment, I said, "This road is big enough to accommodate two big latex trucks passing each other. You say there was no other traffic? The superintendent had no reason to swerve all the way over onto the embankment."

The witnesses whispered to me, "You've been away too long. You don't know this country. The big people will decide."

Back at the general manager's office, Richard Henries declared it an accident. Someone in our group asked, "How's that?"

He said, "Well, the superintendent said when he opened his eyes, the little boy was in front of him."

I said, "The road was dry. The superintendent was coming up out of a small ravine with no oncoming traffic. I'm sure the boy gathering stones for his sling thought he was safe."

The superintendent said, "No, he was right in front of me. The force of the pickup must have pushed him to the side of the road."

Richard Henries said, "Obviously, it was an unfortunate accident. He's just one little boy." And that was the end of it.

One of the dressers at Duside, named Lewis, came from a prominent Americo-Liberian family in Grand Bassa County. He was tall and dressed well. When he talked with his mouth wide open and his white teeth shining, you thought he owned the world.

Dr. Dougen, one of the white doctors, walked with a limp. After he went to America and returned with his young wife, Lewis saw him in the hall the next day and said, "Hey Doc! I saw your wife!"

Dougen said, "Only my wife calls me 'Doc.' Don't call me Doc anymore. Call me Doctor from now on. Do you understand?"

Lewis said, "Yeah."

The next day, several of us dressers were in the hall when Lewis saw Dougen coming and yelled with his broad smile, "Hey Doc! Good mornin'!"

Dougen told us, "You guys were there yesterday when I told him don't call me Doc." He told Lewis, "Lewis, what's wrong with you? If you call me Doc anymore, you're fired. Do you understand that?"

Lewis said, "Yes, Doc, I understand."

"You're fired now."

"But what did I do?"

"I told you don't call me that anymore!"

"Eh yah, Doc. Don't fire me."

"You see? You did it again. You're FIRED!"

Lewis looked at us and said, "The man is vexed for nothing, oh."

Dougen said, "You're fired. Go on home. You can keep your uniform."

"No, I'm not. I can't afford to be fired. I'm comin' back."

"No pay for you from this moment on."

Dougen reported to Dr. Campbell, the head doctor, that Lewis was fired. A week later, when Campbell saw Lewis working, he called him into his office and said, "Dr. Dougen told me you were fired. What are you doing here?"

"I'm workin'."

"When you're fired, the company has no responsibility to pay you. Get out of here."

"But Sir, I need the work. I don't have anywhere to go, oh. I'm gonna work."

"Get out of here and go home."

"This is my home. I'm not goin' anywhere. I'm gonna work."

Campbell called a meeting of the dressers. We told him Lewis wasn't going anywhere. Finally, Campbell and Dougen met with Lewis. Campbell told him, "Don't call Dr. Dougen, Doc anymore! You can stay. Write 'Doctor' on a paper a hundred times. Don't call him Doc ANYMORE."

Lewis said, "Yes, Sir!"

Everyone laughed. Campbell said, "That's better." Lewis stayed.

The Americo-Liberians were classic examples of the insecure personality. In their inferiority complex, they didn't know themselves because they couldn't accept themselves. They defused the pain of their self-hatred in self-deprecating humor.

As a boy in the 1930s, I heard the story about President Arthur Barclay which circulated around Monrovia. During World War I, when a German gunboat shelled Monrovia and everyone ran for cover, Barclay ran inside some rock formations.

A little while later, a man and his wife crept into the same cave. When the man saw two eyes shining in the dark, he yelled to his wife, "Oh my god! We're destined to die! We're running from a bomb and now we've run into a baboon!"

Barclay yelled, "I'm not a baboon! I'm your president!"

The man said, "Oh, my god! The baboon can talk! We're done for!"

The Americo-Liberians were sensitive to criticism and took insult easily. *Top Hats and Tom Toms*, a book about Americo-Liberian folly during the 1940s, was banned in Liberia. In order to preserve Liberia's image abroad, no one was allowed to speak against the president. America and the West were to blame for Liberia's failures. Anyone who pointed out weaknesses was being too critical. In their fear of being shamed, they defended their honor by violence, just as Southerners in the frontier of the Old South.

As a teenager, I visited my Aunt Louise's shop on Carey Street, where I met her good friend, Willie Haines. Willie was a small man like his father. His clothes were always covered with paint since he made his living painting the houses of prominent Americo-Liberians. His teeth were so stained from chewing tobacco, they looked like foreign objects in his mouth. He always wore long pants to cover up the tropical sore on his leg that I dressed a number of times.

Because Willie's father had prestige in the old days, he focused on the past. He complained that Monrovia was getting too big and said they shouldn't have paved Broad Street. In truth, Monrovia was rural. There were mostly paths through backyards planted in cassava and sugar cane that wound their way to the main street.

One day, Willie told me, "A Congo man walked by my father's house every day. One day, my father yelled at him, and the next day, the Congo man beat him up. My father got his shot gun and waited for him. The next morning, when he saw him coming, he said, 'Look here! You beat me bad but I got up. Now I'm gonna get you and you won't get up!' And he shot him."

I said, "What happened then?"

He said, "They took him to city court but they let him go right away because it was self-defense."

I said, "How was that?"

He said, "Well, my father was an important man and the other guy was just a Congo man. The judge said the Congo man would have killed my father, if my father hadn't killed him first."

The Americo-Liberians had to be right and they had to be in control. Since they always had to win, they took things into their own hands.

As a boy, I heard the story about an American newcomer called "Sweet Candy," who had a candy shop on the way down to Waterside. People in Monrovia liked his candy better than store-bought candy. With his profits, he built a house on Crown Hill.

While the native Frontier Force controlled the interior, the upriver Americo-Liberian militia was to protect Monrovia. It was a rag tag bunch of about one hundred fifty men, who were even rougher than the Frontier Force. In their drills in Monrovia, they marched barefoot with "guns" that were mortar pestles used by native women to beat the husks off rice.

Since the militia received no salary, they regularly grabbed produce from the native market women at Waterside before boarding the boats to go back home. They also raided Sweet Candy's shop. When he reported it to the government, they ignored him. One day, when he knew the militia was coming into town, he told his wife to leave the house. He waited at his shop with two loaded rifles. As the men approached, he heard laughter and easily killed the first two or three. The others ran back to Broad Street, shouting, "Sweet Candy's killin' people!"

Sweet Candy ran to his house. The Frontier Force surrounded it and ordered him out. He yelled from an upstairs window, "No!" and shot several soldiers. As the afternoon waned and more soldiers were getting killed, the Frontier Force decided to burn him out. A soldier ran up with a torch. Sweet Candy shot him. Then, a Loma soldier somehow managed to get inside. The crowd watched as the house burned to the ground. When the soldiers later searched the ashes, they only found one heart. They said it must be the Loma soldier's, since Sweet Candy's wife said he magically disappeared.

The Americo-Liberians were patriarchal. They rigidly controlled their wives. My Uncle C.C. used to say, "In Liberia, men rule their wives."

Mr. Greenwood, a West Indian immigrant, had a sugar cane farm near Crozierville. He married a young, light-skinned girl named Salome Wadsworth, who came from a prominent Americo-Liberian family in Crozierville. One day, when she returned from visiting her family, a neighbor girl who was sweet on Greenwood, gave her a note just as he came in the door. She said loudly, "Salome! Hide that note in your bosom! Mr. Greenwood's at the door!" Salome put the note in her dress thinking it was from her.

While Greenwood put away his farm tools, the neighbor girl whispered to him, "Mr. Greenwood, go quickly to your wife. She's hiding a note from her lover in her bosom." Greenwood walked over to Salome and pulled out the note. When he read it, he grabbed the scissors on the table and stabbed her.

The Americo-Liberians constantly exaggerated. They boasted about family connections and Southern ritual. They were always concerned about who was closest to the president — who did what and who got what. They walked with their head in the air to show they were "big" men. They were full of raucous laughter and big talk they never carried through. They had to be right, talking loud and refusing to be interrupted. When someone knocked on their door, they yelled, "Who dat? Who der? When they wanted something, they yelled right away, "Hey! You der, Bubba?"

The Americo-Liberians were isolationists.. Everything was a threat to their own little world. In Monrovia's gossip mill, foreigners were particular targets. My father said about the British, "They dance as though they're sizing up each other." My Uncle C.C. said about the Germans, "They're rough. When they dance, you see their tie way up and they wear suspenders of all colors. They should do like the English and let their tie hang down."

Monrovia Americo-Liberians were a tight-knit community. They feared the upriver Americo-Liberians because of their cruelty. They didn't associate with West Indian immigrants because of their fierce temper. They proclaimed to want more Negroes from America, but too many would pose a threat to their oligarchy. It was as if they said, "This is our territory. You can't have it."

Every newcomer was seen as a visitor from another planet. While they were interested in them, they said privately, "You can't trust them because they don't know Liberian ways."

Insecurity generated an "every man for himself" mentality. The Americo-Liberians lived for self. They cared for nothing that didn't benefit their personal interests. President Tubman focused on his Cape Palmas people, President Tolbert on his family.

Insecurity plus ambition equals ruthless politics. In his drive for power, William V. S. Tubman was the epitome of political cunning. Hailing from far-away Cape Palmas, he was a second-class Americo-Liberian. He initially gained popularity as a poor man's lawyer, trying cases for nothing. When he became a senator, he set an even higher standard of Americo-Liberian ruthlessness.

In Monrovia, Tubman had tea each morning with S. David Coleman, the son of Liberia's thirteenth president. Coleman was not only a prominent lawyer, he was a successful businessman famous for his cane juice from his sugar cane farm in Clay Ashland. During World War II, Negro GI's called it "The Coleman Special." They said, "One drink and it will have you all night." Coleman introduced Senator Tubman to President Edwin Barclay, who appointed Tubman associate justice of the Supreme Court in 1937.

In 1944, when Barclay was about to announce his successor, Tubman warned him that Coleman had been at a meeting with Massaquoi, Tamba, and Grimes — conspirators that Barclay later jailed. Coleman was there but he had told them, "Only cowards go behind people's backs. Go to the man and tell him your complaint. I'm leaving." As a result, Barclay chose Tubman as his successor instead. Coleman knew nothing of Tubman's betrayal. He even loaned him the money for his first presidential campaign. After Tubman was elected president, he appointed Coleman Minister of the Interior. As a fair man, Coleman garnered the allegiance of the natives. Tubman warned, "Don't ever run against me."

During Tubman's presidency, Barclay and Coleman reconciled. Coleman found out what Tubman had done. A group protesting Tubman's re-election told Barclay, "You put Tubman in there and we want him out. We want you to run against him." Barclay agreed to do so if Coleman led the opposition. Even then, Coleman said, "Let me go and talk to him. The object is to change policy. If he agrees, there's no need for opposition."

Tubman refused to meet with Coleman. Instead, he warned against sedition and the overthrow of the government in the newspaper the next day, saying, "I welcome the opposition led by Barclay, Coleman, and Brownell." Coleman became chairman of the Independent Party. When he threatened to publish incriminating evidence about Tubman in the newspaper, Tubman had the printing press destroyed and the editor jailed, along with some members of the Independent Party.

After Tubman's re-election in 1955, a shot rang out at his inaugural ball at the Centennial Pavilion. Everyone panicked — except Tubman. Paul Dunbar was accused of attempting to assassinate Tubman. The gun was said to be Coleman's. Dunbar confessed it was a lie before he was shot for "trying to escape" on his way to Belle Yallah, a notorious government prison in the interior.

Tubman ordered all opposition leaders arrested. Coleman was at his farm in Clay Ashland with Billy Horace consolidating evidence against Tubman, which included burned ballots. In Monrovia, Coleman's wife saw a newspaper headline that said, "Coleman sent Dunbar to Shoot in Pavilion." She and their son John went to Clay Ashland to warn him. He told them, "If I had wanted to kill Tubman, I could have easily shot him from our house as he walked in his roof garden at the mansion. No, I don't want to kill him. I want to disgrace him in court."

When Coleman's wife saw pickup trucks full of Frontier Force soldiers pulling up at their farm she told him, "You should see how many are coming to arrest you."

He said, "I have but one life to give for my country."

The soldiers first drove a pickup under the house on stilts, in order to shoot upwards into the house. But the machine gun mounted in the back, jammed. Billy Horace ran out the front door, yelling, "Let me bring him out peacefully!" As he went back up the porch steps, the soldiers shot him in the back.

One of the soldiers got gas from Coleman's dynamo shed and set the house on fire. The family managed to escape out the back, with Coleman and John running on ahead through the sugar cane fields. After they crossed the St. Paul River and reached the upriver town of Virginia, John tried to buy food. They were discovered and captured.

In Monrovia, Tubman had the men questioned. John asked that the ropes on his father's wrists be loosened and he be given water. Coleman pleaded for his son's life and asked to write a farewell letter to his wife. While John watched, the soldiers hit Coleman in the head with a gun butt and stabbed him in the side with a bayonet. Then they gouged out John's eyes and killed him. Their bodies were dragged through Monrovia behind a pickup truck to the Barclay Training Camp.

Tubman announced, "Anyone who wants to mess with Tubman will have the same thing happen to him." No inquiry or investigation was ever made. When the soldiers cleared out Coleman's house in Monrovia, they destroyed Tubman's IOU's in Coleman's safe.

The destructive cultural mentalities generated by slavery and racism made the Americo-Liberians their own worst enemy. Slavery had made them inferior. Their insecurity kept them that way. They had already "failed" in America and the world was watching. In their fear of failure, "If you don't try, you won't fail." They were unteachable since they couldn't expose their limitations. They couldn't ask questions because it would make them look stupid. They resented being questioned, challenged, or proven wrong. They couldn't receive direction from natives living successfully in the area since the superior cannot learn from the inferior. Throughout Liberia's history, Americo-Liberian government officials resented and rejected any advice or instruction from foreign government advisors.

Their fear of failure guaranteed it. They resented intellectuals and didn't need education. Since they had "brain," they presumed to know. With no ability and no interest, they never attempted to solve any problem. Speaking English aligned them with whites, but they had neither a command of Standard English nor any African languages, except for a few upriver Americo-Liberians who spoke Kpelle.

As the blind leading the blind, most of them had either a poor quality education or none at all. In Monrovia, children were educated in several private rudimentary elementary schools, such as the Wilson School and the Gibson library, a small study area. The two government schools were so poorly managed, they had no supplies and no regimentation, no control of students. With no educational standards, there was no accountability. Many students only went through the fourth grade. Teachers were highly limited, appointed on the basis of "who knows who." Not only was the government perpetually strapped for funds, little was allocated to education. What little was allocated, wasn't necessarily spent. The impetus and support for education came primarily from abroad. It wasn't until the 1960s, that public education was significantly improved with the construction of new government schools.

The few coastal and upriver government schools were so poor that most students remained illiterate. The redeeming factor in these areas were the American Negro missionary schools, such as the Suehn Baptist Mission, considered one of the best of the upriver Negro missionary schools.

The mission had an enrollment of about one hundred students. Since Suehn was in Gola territory, most of the native students were Gola. There were also some Kpelle, Vai, Gbande, Loma, Bassa, Kru, Deh, and Grebo students as well. About five per cent of the students were Americo-Liberian. There were also some native students who had grown up in Monrovia. The Gola students, brought in by the chief for instruction, lived in Suehn. Their attendance varied with rice planting and harvesting. The rest of us lived on campus.

The boys' mud block dorm had a corrugated zinc roof, a concrete floor, and walls plastered with concrete. At one end was a large room for the small boys. It always stunk, even though it was mopped once a week, since the boys did "everything" on the floor. At the other end, were smaller rooms for older boys and the dorm supervisor. We older boys cleaned our rooms and did our own laundry. We used the "bush" for our toilet. Everyone bathed in the creek.

Each morning, we were awakened before dawn by "Devotions! Devotions!" In the dark, we hustled up the hill for prayers at the door of Mrs. Davis, our principal. As the sun rose, we ate breakfast in the student dining room. The girls cooked and heated bath water for Mrs. Davis and the teachers. The boys brought wood, carried water, cut the grass, and cared for the cattle, goats, and chickens.

After morning chores, everyone cleaned up and went to different "palaver" (meeting) huts for classes in Bible, history, English, math, carpentry, and mechanics. The boys spent the afternoons working on campus or in the cassava, potato, and sugar cane fields. Some of them cut palm nuts to make palm oil.

Supper was at 6 p.m. After evening devotions at Mrs. Davis' door, we went back to the dining room for study hall. Before lights out at 8:30 p.m., the boys boiled cassava and yams or they roasted fish over small fires on the concrete slab behind the dorm.

Most of the teachers were American Negro. Some were Americo-Liberians who had been educated in America. We boys liked to tease one of our teachers who said he was from the Congo and bragged about fighting elephants. At Christmas time, we stole collard greens, okra, bitter boils, and eggplant from his garden while the carolers sang, "Weah, weah, Santa Claus Weah," which means, "While we're singing, the others are picking."

Mrs. Davis demanded honesty and strict obedience, telling us, "I have to knock some sense into your heads. I have to teach you to work!" We dared not cross her. When someone did something wrong and she wanted to get to the bottom of it, she had us all line up for reckoning.

Suehn was based on Puritan values. Study hall in the evening was the only time boys and girls could visit with each other. The dining room was lit by two kerosene pump lanterns that hung from the ceiling. Since they were usually turned down low to save kerosene, the tables were dotted with small kerosene lanterns.

Everyone knew that Frederick Nye, a Kru boy, was sweet on Sara Baboo, the daughter of a Portuguese sailor and a native woman. One night during study hall, Frederick and Sara were sitting at a table with their backs to the door. Their eyes were closed and Frederick's hand was up Sara's skirt.

Near the end of study hall, Mrs. Davis quietly walked in and turned up one of the kerosene lanterns. The bright light brought everyone to attention, except

Frederick and Sarah. Mrs. Davis quietly walked up to them and yelled, "Frederick! What are you doing in that girl's skirt!"

All eyes were on Frederick and Sarah. Mrs. Davis stood there glaring. Slowly, Frederick withdrew his hand and began singing in his rich baritone voice, "I can tell Jesus all of my trials..."

Mrs. Davis said, "What trials? The trouble you made for yourself?"

Frederick sang, "All to Jesus I surrender..."

She said, "I'll see you tomorrow, Frederick." She announced, "Study hall is over," and reminded Frederick, "Remember, I want to see you at nine o'clock tomorrow morning."

As we boys crossed the log bridge on the way back to the dorm, Frederick begged us to pray for him. He said, "Satan prowls about like a roaring lion," and sang, "I Surrender All." We all promised to pray.

The next morning, Mrs. Davis told Frederick, "If you ever do that again, you will be expelled. Remember that. YOU WILL BE EXPELLED." Frederick thanked Mrs. Davis and told us that night our prayers had been answered.

The next morning Frederick led the devotions. His opening hymn was "I Must Tell Jesus." His closing hymn was "I Surrender All."

Insecurity stifled any progress in Liberia. Any new idea was seen as a threat. One day, Aaron Brown made a flying machine that flew for a short time. They stopped him from going any further, saying, "That's not in the interest of Liberia. White people have that and if they know we have it, it will create war." I later met up with Aaron and asked him if what I heard was true. He told me, "You can be clever but you just have to do what people want you to do. If you want to do something new, they hate you. They wanted to put me in jail as an enemy of the state if I continued." Aaron learned sculpting in Europe. He carved the two white angels in front of the Centennial Pavilion on Broad Street. But he wasn't allowed to teach sculpting to others.

The Americo-Liberians suffered a double whammy. As rulers and superior "whites," they had a sense of entitlement. Their charm derived from their privilege they took for granted. As parents, they were poor role models. Grandmothers trained the children with the "old man" as disciplinarian. Many times, children knew their grandparents better than their parents.

Family pride kept children from any responsibility, such as chores around the house. Children weren't accountable to their parents. They got what they wanted by playing mother and father off of each other. They had no incentive to learn since they were guaranteed a position in society. Teachers didn't expect them to learn, placing no demands on them. Children enrolled in school hardly attended. Or they attended a month and dropped out. At exam or graduation time, no "successful" teacher dared give them a bad grade or flunk them.

Education in Liberia was "image." Any literacy or Western education whatsoever, equaled being educated. The Americo-Liberians were parvenus with the position, but not the qualifications. They were a rule of incompetence that enforced incompetence. Education made you a "big" man, a gentleman with style and image. It was the symbol of being educated that was important. School children stuck their pencil in their hair to show they could read and write.

The Americo-Liberians were a people of gross ignorance who presumed and pretended to know. One day, I heard Mr. Clark say about a boy he knew, "Oh, he's so clever! He can say his 'ABC's'." I later found out the boy could only say, "ABC," but Clark didn't know the difference.

 Privilege and entitlement plagued the Americo-Liberians throughout Liberia's history. In 1958, when I was a graduate student at Michigan State University, I met up with Vice President William R. Tolbert, Jr. when he attended a Baptist meeting in America. He told me, "A.B. is just a playboy. He's not serious about anything. I'd like to send him to Michigan State to see if it will help him make something of himself."

I said, "Has he been accepted?"

He said, "Oh, no problem about that. He'll be accepted."

When A.B. arrived, Dr. Brookover, the chairman of the education department, told me, "A.B. looks like a very good student. His grades are all A's."

A.B. refused to live in the dorm because people made too much noise. He rented a three-bedroom apartment in Lansing, and invited me to see it. In the living room, there was a large TV and a stereo, with a stack of records beside it. One of the bedrooms had a stash of all kinds of liquor.

Several months later, Gus, a Vai graduate student at MSU, visited A.B. He came right over and told me, "Ben, man, you have to go and talk to that boy right now. You have to get him outta here and send him back to his father. He's gonna spoil the reputation of Liberians. You've got to see for yourself."

As we rang the bell, we heard loud music.

A.B. yelled, "Who der?"

I said, "Ben Dennis."

He said, "What you want?"

I said, "I want to see you. Let me in now."

Gus said, "Tell him he has to go home right now."

The three girls in his apartment were drinking, talking, and laughing. The place was a mess with beer cans and unfinished drinks sitting all over. I said, "A.B., will you turn that music down? I can't talk over this din." When it got quiet, I told him, "You've got exams in all your courses next week. Let's see your lecture notes. Did you go over them like I told you?"

He said, "I was sitting right before the professor. I didn't have to write anything down."

I said, "You've got to stop drinking and study."

He said, "Don't you know what the Bible says, a little for the stomach's sake?"

Gus looked at me and said, "This is a disaster!"

At the end of the first quarter, Dr. Brookover called and said, "A.B. didn't pass a single exam. He scored the lowest any student has ever scored in my class.

I called A.B. and said, "Why don't you try taking one of my courses on Africa next quarter?"

Dr. Brookover said, "You'll see for yourself, Ben."

When A.B. attended class, he was drunk and told me he was tired from staying up all night studying. I couldn't give even him a grade on my first exam because I couldn't understand his half sentences that never addressed the question. Since I graded the exams on a Saturday, I had him retake the test on Sunday. This time, it was worse. I said, "A.B., did you really finish high school?"

He said, "Of course! Why're you askin' a question like that? They wouldn't accept me here if I didn't finish high school!"

I said, "Well, A.B., you're not college material. You're not even high school material. Do you want me to ask your father to take you back home?"

He said, "Oh, no! Don't you know what an American education means? I want to graduate."

I said, "Well, you won't graduate at MSU. I'm going to call Gus."

When Gus came over, he said, "A.B., I'm vexed! I used to take dictation from your father. You people were riding in a big car while I was working my butt off. Now I'm making good grades here. I'm Phi Beta Kappa. You're a big people's son and you're embarrassing us. You came here and we tried to help you, but this isn't Liberia! Even if you pay someone, they won't give you an 'A.' Ben told me you brought him a big bottle of whiskey. You can't bribe him. Your father trusts him."

A.B. said, "Well, I'm doin' my best."

I told him, "I'll write your father. Perhaps he'll send you to another school." When Tolbert withdrew A.B., he was so angry, he left quietly.

Dr. Brookover later asked me, "Say, whatever happened to A.B.? By the way, what's the educational system of Liberia? Here was a guy making A's and he couldn't even make D's here."

I told him, "In Liberia, you don't flunk the son of the vice president."

In 1971, the death of President Tubman brought me back to Liberia for the first time since I had left in 1947. I was impressed by the large government buildings in Monrovia — the Executive Mansion, the Temple of Justice, the Capitol Building, and Monrovia City Hall. My cousin Jimmy hosted me in his lavish home that had walls of glass, hard wood floors, and chandeliers, a grand piano in the foyer and bathroom walls of Italian marble.

And yet, Liberia's modernization was out of sync because it lacked the details. The brand new post office had no mail delivery. The toilets on the ground floor of the Executive Mansion were stopped up and there was no toilet paper. The offices at the Temple of Justice were bare, except for a desk, a chair, and two small file cabinets. Monrovia's streets were paved but you had to dodge the chuckholes in the sidewalks. I heard that the medical equipment at the JFK Hospital had been corroded by sea air. The power went off in Monrovia for hours at a time. When I returned to the states, I had to ship Cadillac auto parts to a friend who couldn't get them in Liberia.

At Jimmy's house, his modern Italian kitchen cabinets remained empty since his Bassa cook got supplies from the market every day. His lawn was "brushed" (cut) with a machete. His clothes were washed by a Bassa laundry man in a galvanized zinc tub in the yard. His house was surrounded by a concrete wall topped with glass shards. There were locks on the doors and rogue bars on the windows. And yet, he had a Kpelle night watchman guard the place.

The Americo-Liberians remained focused on image. The role of the president was to enhance Liberia's image abroad. During his reign, Tubman was worshipped as the zenith of Americo-Liberianism. His visit with President Kennedy during the 1960s was touted in Liberia. During the 1970s, two portraits graced almost every Americo-Liberian home — those of Tubman and Kennedy.

The Americo-Liberians lived a lie. They identified with whites who in no way claimed them or identified with them. White status was based on achievement. Theirs was an assumed status. No matter what they did or didn't do, they never achieved status in the eyes of whites or the West.

The Americo-Liberians glorified America, but that interest was never reciprocated. Today, except for Peace Corps volunteers, Americans know little or nothing about Liberia. And what they know is negative. After the Coup of 1980, America allied itself with Samuel Doe, Liberia's most obvious leader, and threw money at the problem, hoping it would resolve itself. During Liberia's Civil War in the 1990s, as Liberians boarded a helicopter at the U.S. Embassy in Monrovia, they begged America to step in and save Liberia. In the bloodshed during Charles Taylor's overthrow, America responded to world pressure with warships full of Marines sitting off the coast in the Atlantic. They never intervened. In 2006, Ellen Johnson-Sirleaf, Liberia's new president, made her debut in America by addressing a joint session of Congress, although she was not unknown in America. Today, every Liberian wants to come to America for what America can do for them.

Upriver Americo-Liberians lived vicariously through Monrovia Americo-Liberians, but their glory was empty. Monrovia Americo-Liberians lived vicariously through President Tubman, but his glory was empty. He was given respect only as a president, not for any accomplishments. Even that status was moot since

Liberia had no status. Tubman was only respected in the Organization of African Unity as a leader among Negroes, other African nations.

Liberia had the image of Negro freedom and independence. The reality was white control and Negro helplessness. The Americo-Liberians sold out Liberia to foreigners who lived a life in Liberia that natives could only dream of. Foreign investment could never provide an infrastructure for the entire nation. No one could do for Liberia what Liberians had to do for themselves. Today Liberia has nothing but debt and is more dependent on foreigners than ever before, economically and politically.

Liberia was the image of the Negro's hopes and dreams. In reality, it displayed the Negro's limitations on a national and international scale. The Americo-Liberians were like grasshoppers, getting and eating right away. Not a single prominent family made a significant contribution to Liberia or achieved lasting success or wealth.

Sending a degraded people with meager resources to found a new nation in an unknown, challenging environment was a cruel joke and a disaster waiting to happen. And Liberia has paid dearly for it. It's easy to blame the victims and hold them solely responsible — until you remember from whence they came and why, and in what conditions and circumstances.

CHAPTER TWO: THE CYCLE OF RACISM

The Imitation of Supremacy

> We will o'er all prevail,
> With heart and hand our country's cause defending,
> We'll meet the foe with valor unpretending,
> Long live Liberia, happy land,
> A home of glorious liberty by God's command.

—The Liberian National Anthem

In the *cycle of racism*, the Americo-Liberians were victims who became victimizers — displacing their anger and resentment on the natives. The lure of going back to Africa was to be powerful, to be in charge and have power over others. They deserved Liberia, since they were going to civilize an inferior people and transform an inferior society. The Lone Star Republic of freedom and Christianity was their "white" myth of glory. As bearers of truth and light, God was on their side. Cultural superiority gave them the right to control natives and make decisions for them.

Liberia was their chance to rise. It wasn't the "love of liberty" that was the issue. It was who the liberty was for, just as for whites in America. Cultural racism justified dominating and exploiting the natives just as racism justified slavery in America. They were now the "white slave master" as they re-created a Southern society in which both master and slave were Negro.

Natives were condemned before the first ship landed. They had to be subjugated and civilized for their own good. The Americo-Liberians of the superior culture had value and significance. Natives of the inferior culture were nothing. Like Negroes in America, their lives had no value. They were expendable.

During the 1930s and 40s, natives were inferior regardless of tribe. Since the Americo-Liberians had no interest in what had no value, natives remained an unknown quantity, their culture shrouded in secrecy. The Americo-Liberians only interacted with natives on the coast. As they gained control of the interior and ruled it indirectly through the native Frontier Force, they ignored its inhabitants. Their beliefs were reinforced when Frontier Force soldiers told tales of native ruthlessness to enhance their importance. As a teenager, I heard an Americo-Liberian say, "Who will go into those people's country? They can kill people and chop (eat) them!"

The native traditional schools of the Poro and Sande were "evil." Although every man attended Poro, and every woman, Sande, they were called "secret bush." Tribal masked beings that served as authority figures were called "country devils." Natives who set bones and cured diarrhea were "witch doctors." Unwritten tribal dialects were "worthless." Traditional native songs weren't accepted in the church.

In the superficial relationship between the Americo-Liberians and the natives, there was trust only within each group. The Americo-Liberians assumed they knew the natives, ignoring their status or position within the tribe. They derisively called them "country people." Liberia's population was referred to as, "civilized peoples and the other element." Natives were subjects of Liberia, not citizens. Human rights didn't apply to them until they became civilized.

The Americo-Liberians blamed the victim. Natives were "children" — constantly derided for not doing something fast enough. The Americo-Liberians said, "You just gotta give 'em a good whippin'. They don't understand nothin' but brute force." Their classic quotation was, "The tender mercies of the heathen are cruelty." Natives, suspected of evil intent, were easily convicted in Americo-Liberian courts. In contrast, "good" Americo-Liberians were given the benefit of the doubt and exonerated.

In Monrovia, a very light-skinned Americo-Liberian woman went for medical treatment and was seen by a native medical practitioner working under a Haitian doctor. She refused to undress for the examination and told her husband, "He's a raw countryman. Who does he think I am to strip butt naked before him?"

Her husband said, "But you're sick. You have to go back."

She said, "You don't love me anymore. He just wants to look at me when we're by ourselves. He thinks I'm stupid but I'm not gonna do it. The only way I go back is if you go back with me."

The Americo-Liberians focused entirely on Monrovia. As far as they were concerned, the natives didn't exist. They never achieved their lofty goal of civilizing and Christianizing the natives because it required associating with those who had nothing to offer them. The men built a house in Monrovia for their Americo-Liberian mistress. They kept their native mistress on their farm. One of my Dennis uncles divorced his wife when he found out her father was Grebo.

The only natives who had a place in Liberia were those who adopted Americo-Liberian ways. Even when they became Christian and educated, they were never equal. They remained a countryman because they could never completely dissolve their tribal and cultural ties. Since they were never fully accepted, they could never succeed.

There was strong Negro racism across the board until the Tubman regime. Light skin was prized and desired. The Americo-Liberians said of a mulatto, "Oh, he's better than a pure Negro." To marry a light-skinned woman, a dark-skinned man had to have some means of distinction such as a farm.

The Americo-Liberian community was characterized by a relationship of trust/distrust. Monrovia Americo-Liberians treated upriver Americo-Liberians as menials. "Congo" was a disparaging term. They said, "They're Americo-Liberians, but they're drunks. They're lazy."

They manipulated them by saying, "We're all Americo-Liberians." They encouraged their ruthlessness in intimidating the natives. Unfamiliar natives weren't allowed to walk through Careysburg, Bensonville, or Crozierville on Sunday. If caught doing so, they either disappeared or they were arrested and assigned to forced labor on an Americo-Liberian cash crop farm.

Since they were vastly outnumbered, the Americo-Liberians simultaneously united for dominance. Cultural distinction was vital for upriver Americo-Liberians living among natives. Their only claim to fame was "Americo-Liberianism." At their upriver dances, they took pride in their Southern hillbilly music they played on fiddles, harmonicas, guitars, saws, and spoons. It made them bona-fide Americo-Liberians.

These upriver dances fostered Americo-Liberian unity. They were a big thing and very popular. Zach Taylor was quite a star. People said, "Oh, he can sing. He can play." His guitar was so old, it was out of tune. He made up for it with his catchy songs and lively beat good for dancing the quadrille, Liberia's Southern square dancing.

When Taylor played, he tilted his head sideways back and forth to the beat of the music. As he sang with his mouth wide open, he displayed his most signature feature — his top teeth missing on one side of his mouth and his bottom teeth missing on the other.

Taylor's forte was his ability to make up a song on the spot about anything he observed. One night, my Uncle C.C. Dennis rendezvoused with an Americo-Liberian girl named Lottie, in Kakata. That morning, as they were returning to Monrovia in Konyoh's truck named "Kolahun," C.C. sat on the passenger side. Lottie straddled the hump in the middle. Since they were leaving before dawn, she rested a kerosene lantern between her legs. Suddenly, her skirt caught fire. She was rushed to Duside Hospital where she recovered.

Taylor was in Kakata and made up a song about it, that said, "Oh, Lottie, fine, fine Lottie. Kolahun burned your 'nunu.' For the sake of Dennis, C.C. Dennis, Kolahun burned your nunu." The song was so popular that children ran behind Taylor clapping and singing it.

Lottie was mortified. She yelled, "Hey, Zach Taylor! Don't sing that song!" My uncle C.C. told me, "That guy can sing but he can't see anything without making up a song about it. B.G., the girls' hair got all burnt down there. She got hurt and he's singing about that? He's got no right."

Monrovia Americo-Liberians depended upon upriver Americo-Liberians and natives for foodstuffs, which garnered a relationship of familiarity. Upriver Americo-Liberians ingratiated by saying, "Mrs. Gibson, we know you like this palm oil. We have some for you." Americo-Liberian noblesse oblige was reflected in the phrase, "Where's my Saturday?" This expression derived from slavery when the master distributed food supplies at the big house on Saturday. When an upriver Americo-Liberian brought a gift to their family in Monrovia, they said, "Where's my Saturday?"

Upriver Americo-Liberians identified with those in Monrovia. They gave their children to them to be reared as civilized, just like the natives. Their Monrovia family furnished a lawyer if they got into trouble in a court case. If they had a dispute with a native, depending on who they were, the Monrovia Americo-Liberians saw to it that they won. If they killed a native, Monrovia Americo-Liberians defended them, saying it was an accident or self-defense.

The two bedrocks of Americo-Liberian cultural unity were Christianity and Masonry. Christianity was the basis of their goal to Christianize Africa. It bound them together as a civilized people. The church imparted status. Being a Christian was the fashionable thing to do.

Like the American Negro church, faith was primarily an emotional experience. "Receiving the spirit" was a rite of passage. Each year, Providence Baptist Church held a two-week revival with sinners sitting on the mourner's bench. The night began with the song, "Sinner, where were you when my good luck was here? Oh, my good luck has been here, has been here, has been here. Oh, my good luck has been here and blessed my soul and gone."

People leaped, shouted, and fell out. Sometimes they ran into the street shouting, "I got it! I got the spirit!" Everyone said, "Thank you, Lord. That one has religion." Rev. Stubblefield said, "He received God. He received Christ." And everyone clapped.

During the second week, Rev. Stubblefield said, "We still have many sinners who have yet to receive the spirit. Sinner, you're holdin' back. Give yourself to Jesus." Then people would jump up, one by one. Church members said, "We had five people receive the spirit last night."

After the baptisms at the revival, there were always big festivities — banquets and rejoicing. Sometimes the president even came and spoke.

The Prince Hall Lodge in Monrovia was the Negro version of the Masonic Lodge. It was not only a bastion of Americo-Liberian unity, exclusivity, and privilege, it was a major tool of intimidation. The Americo-Liberians were masters of a reign of terror.

As a boy, I watched the Masonic parades down Broad Street. In front, were the men dressed in black woolen tailcoats with sashes over their chests — wearing either a black top hat or a red fez. Following behind, were the women of the Eastern Star in white dresses and white wide-brimmed hats, carrying bouquets of flowers. With pride, they marched in drag-step to the sound of a bugle and a lone drum beat — ta dum...ta dum...ta dum.

As a display of power, these parades generated much excitement. Crowds lined the streets. Children ran around excitedly. The small amount of traffic stopped. Along the parade route, people leaned out of second-floor porches to watch.

Natives in the crowd watched in awe and fear. The torch-lit processions to the Masonic Lodge at night terrified them even more. They "knew" some native would be caught and killed for sacrifice. Wherever the lodges were active, natives reported people missing. Bodies were found with the heart or other internal organs missing. No native dared to walk in front of the Masonic Lodge on Broad Street at night because he would simply "disappear."

The lodge cemented Americo-Liberian identity and status as a culturally superior people. As a fraternal organization, it fostered the camaraderie and shared loyalty necessary for a diverse group to dominate. It "lifted" and supported them in the face of any native threat. Membership was a rite of passage because it was the only way to get a good job or government position. The Prince Hall Lodge in Monrovia was sacrosanct. No native dared enter it. The very few natives allowed to join, did so at great expense.

The Americo-Liberians ruled by "divide and conquer." Natives were always potential rivals since they had the tribe behind them. The Americo-Liberians fed on tribal differences when they said to any native, "What tribe are you?" They preferred and allied with coastal natives, considering them "better off" because of Americo-Liberian influence. They distinguished coastal natives from those in the interior, by saying, "Oh, he's Bassa." Although they included those native individuals who complied with them, they never considered them equal.

The Americo-Liberians ruled through intermediaries. Monrovia Americo-Liberians kept from soiling their honor as a civilized people, by encouraging the ruthlessness of the upriver Americo-Liberians in intimidating the natives. The Americo-Liberians manipulated the native Frontier Force to intimidate and coerce natives in the interior. Barely refined soldiers taking orders from Americo-Liberian officers, ruthlessly enforced the rule of government. Their khaki uniforms, which gave them status, induced them to identify with the Americo-Liberians.

Soldiers had the power of life and death over natives and the authority to arrest Americo-Liberians, but they were hardly a military force. As a teenager, I rode with two soldiers in a canoe on a tributary of the Farmington River. Because of rain the night before, the current was strong. One of the soldiers decided to help the other paddle so he handed me his gun, barrel up. As I rested the gun butt between my legs, my finger brushed the trigger and the gun went off, "POW!" He said, "Now, I'm in big trouble. They only gimme four cartridges. You gotta show 'em at inspection and if you don't, you gotta say why. If it's not a good enough reason, you gotta pay for 'em."

The Americo-Liberians used native tax collectors in the interior, their "salary" coming out of the taxes they charged. Within the Americo-Liberian judicial system, the Americo-Liberians used barely refined native chiefs as judges, which allowed them to control and exploit natives. When I worked as a government medical representative, I was sent to check on the dispensary supplies at the town of Marshall, Firestone's point of entry on the Farmington River. George Williams judged the civilized people in a courtroom on the second floor of the superintendent's office. Kru Chief Nimilah served as judge for the natives, holding court on his front porch.

I became friends with Nimilah when I treated him for gonorrhea. One day, he told me, "You a Kwii (Western) boy. You read and write. Come see my court today."

In the first case, a man said he saw someone take three of his fish traps out of the river and quickly return them. When he later checked those traps, they were empty while the others downriver were full. Nimilah said, "You finish now. You quiet." Turning to the other man, he said, "You! What be your name!"

"My name is Togbah."

"OK, Togbah, you hear this man say you take fish. Is that so?"

"But chief, I never touch any trap."

"Look me for face."

As Togbah looked at him, Nimilah told me, "Ha! Ha! Ha! You see? You see his face?"

He told Togbah, "You guil-i-ty!"

"But chief! I didn't do it!"

"You think you go fool me?"

Nimilah told me, "Look, doctor, he guil-i-ty. Bad look! He think me small boy. I see. I old, old man. I can tell. He guil-i-ty."

Togbah said, "But chief! I have witnesses!"

"No need for witness. Pay four dollar — two dollar for him and two dollar for me. Right now! Hey! You two soldiers, follow him! Bring four dollar before next case." Togbah had to borrow the four dollars.

I said, "Chief, that's not right. Maybe he didn't do it."

Nimilah said, "You too small. You no *sabe* [don't know] nothing. He guil-i-ty."

I later found out this was the rule in his courtroom. Nimilah told me, "They know me. If they not be right, they no come here."

To maintain their cultural distinction, the essence of their superiority, the Americo-Liberians practiced segregation and discrimination. Natives were kept in their place. In Monrovia, they lived in separate tribal enclaves. They sat in a separate place during political meetings, church services, and public gatherings. Servants of prominent Americo-Liberian families lived on the lower level of the house.

Natives in Monrovia were ignored and neglected, especially the market women at Waterside. They had to wait in the yard until the "big" woman invited them onto the porch. When they arrived, they brought a gift and asked if there was anything the family wanted them to do. They had to say, "Yes, Ma'am" or "Yes, Sir." In Lebanese stores, they were constantly watched. Even when they were first in line, they were served last. Americo-Liberian children didn't sleep in the same room with native servant children, even when there was a shortage of space. I heard a man tell his grandson, "What you doin' with those people? Go with you own group!" The Americo-Liberians were so fearful of losing any status, they carefully tested the waters before inviting a refined or educated native to a card game.

No native could marry or even have an affair with an Americo-Liberian woman because that would make him "over" her. Only in extreme cases, did a refined or educated native marry an Americo-Liberian woman.

One of my favorite Dennis aunts married a Sierra Leonean from the Limba tribe, who taught Latin at Liberia College. When he returned to Sierra Leone a short time later, he promised her that when he got settled, he'd send for her.

As a teenager, I teased her, "Auntie, when are you going to your husband? He must want you there."

She said good-naturedly, "Shut up, B.G.! You don't even know the meaning of marriage — what goes on between a man and a woman."

I said, "But you are married to him!"

She said, "You know what, little boy? If he comes back, I'll stay with him but I'm not goin' to that bush or that bush man. Who do you think I am? A bushman?

I said, "Why'd you marry him if you won't go with him?"

She said, "Education, B.G.! I married him because he was educated at Fourah Bay College and makin' good money. But I'm not goin' there. He's from the country."

My Uncle C.C., who was there, said, "I think B.G.'s right. You oughta divorce him and marry someone of your own kind."

Mr. Frederick, an Ashanti from the Gold Coast, owned a popular bar on Camp Johnson Road. One of his daughters fell in love with an educated native who moved easily in Americo-Liberian circles. When the man asked Frederick to marry his daughter, Frederick told him, "Don't ever come round my bar again!"

Frederick found out they continued seeing each other, so he bought a rifle and threatened to kill them both. Everyone in Monrovia, including the police, knew he was out looking for them.

At the upriver dances, Americo-Liberian men could dance with any girl. Native men didn't dare dance with an Americo-Liberian girl, especially an upriver girl, since upriver men were especially protective and jealous of their women. A popular song at these dances was "Razor in the Bottom of My Shoe" which said, "If you're comin' to the dance, be sure to bring your own girl, Cause I gotta razor in the bottom of my shoe. Don't take my girl into the cassava bushes, Cause I gotta razor in the bottom of my shoe."

Natives new to an Americo-Liberian area were usually attached in some way to an Americo-Liberian family. The classic question to any native in an unexpected place, was, "Who boy are you?" A native's value and "status" derived from his Americo-Liberian family's status, just as the personal slave of a prominent slave master in the South had "respect."

The Americo-Liberians played a constant game of manipulation to exploit. They induced natives to work for them on their cash crop farms by promising some small advantage or reward. If they paid any wages, they were extremely minimal. Some Americo-Liberians let the natives living on the land, stay and work for them. Natives considered it a privilege to work for the Americo-Liberians. The Americo-Liberians made them malleable by calling them, "Uncle," which allowed them to feel a part of the family and assume status by association. A few Americo-Liberians gave their workers a small plot of land, about the size of a large garden, to do subsistence farming or raise their own cash crops. At harvest time, the owner transported his workers' produce to market along with his own.

Since there were no racial differences, there was some flexibility. The Americo-Liberians didn't hamper tribal social activities or disturb tribal group relations. They boasted more about where they came from than about what they could do. However, America was far away and their American connection became more remote with each passing generation. They realized they had some limitations in a tropical environment. They saw that natives weren't "inferior" within their own environment and culture. They said, "Only a countryman can do dat. They can do dat." They appreciated African dishes. They went to natives to "make medicine." Upriver Americo-Liberians learned how to make animal traps from the natives.

There was some social integration of natives in Monrovia. Housing was open and mixed. House type indicated status, rather than location. Political meetings and church services were shared social activities. A few select natives were accepted into the lodges. Natives, who became Christian and civilized, shared culture as well as race. In personal relationships, there was some private acceptance of native individuals. Because of sexual needs, taboos against intermarriage weren't rigid. Americo-Liberian men took native mistresses which linked them with their tribe.

Upriver Americo-Liberians were in the minority. Although they carefully maintained their cultural distinction, they wanted and needed the help of local natives. Natives looked up to them as civilized. As long as they were loyal and stayed in their place, there was harmony and respect. Everyone knew everyone. They lived as neighbors, visiting and hunting together. They talked nice to each other. In many cases, they were close. An upriver Americo-Liberian might say as a compliment, "He's a raw countryman who came here long time ago." Local natives were more easily allowed into the less prestigious upriver lodges. At the upriver dances, some refined natives danced with upriver women and even women from Monrovia.

Liberia had the image of a stable, westernized social order. The reality was a rule of raw, absolute power. For the Americo-Liberians, Liberia was their slate to write on, their own little kingdom to do with as they pleased. Impunity made them rulers of the worst sort. Until World War II, Liberia was virtually isolated on the world stage. The Americo-Liberians had no accountability. They were free to do unto the natives as they pleased.

As a small minority, they elected a president to carry out their wishes without the consent or input of the majority population. They made the laws. They set the standard, saying, "We do things different here." While they didn't completely control the interior, they had sanctity. The Prince Hall Lodge was above the law. No member could be convicted of a serious crime. If he was prosecuted, he was given a light sentence.

While Liberia had an elaborate code of law and Monrovia had over a hundred lawyers, the law was used to protect the Americo-Liberians and punish the natives. A native's complaint against an Americo-Liberian wasn't brought to court. If it was, the Americo-Liberian won the case or he was acquitted by a jury of his peers. In a court case between two natives, the native, with ties to the most powerful Americo-Liberian, won.

A small minority of Americo-Liberians had the perks and spoils of a government based on nepotism and cronyism. In contrast, natives in the interior were a disenfranchised majority that paid hut and head taxes. They had no roads or medical clinics — only mission schools. They did all the menial work. Educated natives working as government clerks, never got credit and were barely compensated. Tribal land was taken for the foreign concessions and natives who worked there received minimal wages.

Despite their impunity, the Americo-Liberians were a rule of insecurity, much like the slave master outnumbered on the plantation. In the small area they occupied on the coast, they weren't evenly dispersed. District commissioners in the provinces were considered brave, even with the Frontier Force to protect them. The Americo-Liberians said, "Self-preservation is the first rule of nature."

Although the Americo-Liberians already had power, they used force and excessive cruelty — without shame. Inept Americo-Liberians were a rule of brutality, not competence. Fear and guilt fueled their insecurity. Like the slave master, they did anything to win. They were bold in their barbarity because it carried no consequences. Although they weren't equally cruel, they had a standard of cruelty. To be rough and mean was to be a "helluva man."

They would call a native servant child and beat him for any little thing in front of others, to show they were a "big" man. When a servant child didn't immediately run and yell, "Yes, Sir!" when called, they said, "He walks so slow. He shows no respect."

Cultural racism plus impunity equaled callousness. Natives could be beaten or killed for little or no reason. Nothing was done when an Americo-Liberian killed a native or a native killed another native. In ritual murder, the Americo-Liberians mutilated bodies, taking only the parts needed.

One day in Monrovia, as Mr. Padmore speeded up the hill on Ashmun Street, he hit a native boy crossing the street. He drove on several blocks, dragging the boy's body underneath before he stopped. When the word spread that the boy died, natives in Monrovia were angry. Padmore was briefly arrested and released, saying he didn't see the boy.

As an empty power, the Americo-Liberians ruled by bluff and bravado. They only ruled in their own little world. The only ones they had any control over were natives. Even that control was moot, because they were inept and dependent on them.

Mr. Webster's behavior puzzled me. As an overseer at Firestone, his job at Division 21 was to call the roll of tappers going out that day. Each evening, he was to record the tappers who turned in buckets of latex to keep the payroll from being padded. During the day, he was to be in the field in case there were any problems. Instead, he went home after morning roll call and drank all day.

Although he wore good clothing, he looked disheveled and sloppy since his clothes were too big. His two beautiful daughters told me, "We don't know what to do. He just drinks all the time and he won't eat anything but peanuts. He talks in such a slur, even we can't understand him. We hope he dies soon."

He was so frail, he looked like the wind could blow him over. He took such slow, measured steps, you thought he'd never take the next one. He always spoke in a loud, defensive way, "What's dat? What you doin', Boy? Hey! I'm callin' you!" Then he sucked his teeth in disgust and said, "Come here!" He said to any tapper, "Hey you! Who you tappin' for? Who your headman? Oh, go. Go! I don't want to see you!" He told any native, "Hey! Come right now! Go to the store and get me a bottle of gin. Run! When you come I'll give you some." When the native returned, he'd say, "Bring it. You know our custom. Take the witch out [take a sip]. Not too much! I don't want you to drink it all."

I once asked him, "Mr. Webster, why do you always talk that way?"

He said, "You're too frisky. Stay outta this. That's the way you talk to these people. You don't know these people."

Elite Americo-Liberians displayed that quiet confidence and congeniality that comes from high birth and privilege. Poor Americo-Liberians used bluff, not so much out of hatred per se, as a need to feel superior. Natives new to an Americo-

Liberian area were an easy target. They were convenient whipping boys since they had no recourse and nowhere to go. In any area where there was a random mix of Americo-Liberians and natives, inept Americo-Liberians humiliated and degraded natives, sometimes even chiefs, by saying, "You boy!" or "You bushman!" "You savage!" or "You raw countryman!"

In Monrovia, when a newcomer native in a group of relatives might stare at an Americo-Liberian in curiosity, the Americo-Liberian would say, "Look! Hey! What you lookin' at? Do I look dirty? What you lookin' for? Huh? Boy? You see anything wrong with me?"

Baffled by this diatribe, the native would stare even more. In anger, the Americo-Liberian would hit him with his walking stick. Amongst themselves, the other natives would tell the newcomer, "That's a helluva man!" After natives lived in Monrovia a while, they knew to look away quickly.

On their own turf, the upriver Americo-Liberians used a tongue lashing to establish their authority, power, and control. They took pride in being "bad." With a stern look on their face, they sucked their teeth in disgust and yelled to any unfamiliar native, "Hey you! Come here!" They said, "Boy! Get outta here 'fore dark!"

When natives adopted Western dress and spoke Liberian English, Americo-Liberians had to set themselves apart verbally. The classic expression was, "Do you know who I am? Do you think I'm a small boy?" If they thought the native was too uppity, they shouted in his face, "Do you know who you're talkin' to?" and made the native cower and beg.

Inept Americo-Liberians ridiculed anyone who disagreed with them. If a native asked them a question, they said, "You askin' me? What you askin' me for? Who you think you are? You dare to question me? Ha! Ha! Ha!"

The native would say, "Sorry, Boss Man."

If another Americo-Liberian was there, they said for emphasis, "You hear dat? He questionin' me! You see dat? Askin' me? He has the gall to ask me?"

They resisted any idea offered by a native, saying, "You see what that bushman said to me? You hear that? Ha! Ha! Ha! Look what he's tellin' me! Who are you? Look at him! Ha! Ha! Ha!"

They were masters of ridicule. In the evenings I played a card game called "Whist" with a group of young men at the Cooper House. Three of the other card players were Americo-Liberians — Steve Tolbert, James Hardy, and Morris. Also at the table that night was Peter Bonoh Jallah, the Cooper House boy who was a student at Liberia College.

We were drinking and playing cards when James Hardy stopped and looked deliberately at Peter. After he gave a knowing look at Steve and Morris, he laughed so loud, you could hear him across the street, "Ha! Ha! Ha! Ha!"

I said, "What's wrong, James?"

He said, "Ha! Ha! Ha! Look the way this guy's holdin' his cards! You can see 'em way down the street! Soon you enter the porch, you can see every card he's got in his hand! Jallah, don't you know people will read your cards when they see your hand?"

As Steve and Morris joined in the laughter, James said, "You can sure tell he doesn't know nothin' 'bout this game!"

I said, "But James, everyone's holding their cards the same way."

He said, "B. G., you been away too long. You don't know how crafty we are in Liberia. You can read Jallah's cards the way he's holdin' 'em."

Liberia had the image of a Western democracy with three branches of government. In reality, it was a one man rule, epitomized by President Tubman, who reigned from 1944-1971. Tubman unilaterally made all decisions for Liberia — most notably his Open Door Policy, which ultimately became one man's decision for one man's benefit. Representatives and senators had greater loyalty to Tubman than their constituents. They simply confirmed what Tubman had already decided.

With the government as primary employer, Tubman had the power of appointment for all government and local offices. He was in charge of land appropriation, concession rights, and revenue. The only way to acquire a government job, buy property, receive an overseas scholarship, or secure a business opportunity was to go through him.

Liberia's gross underdevelopment added to his control since the Americo-Liberians believed that whites did his bidding. Any benefit to Liberia from the foreign concessions came in the form of a personal request or favor granted to him. This included paving Monrovia's streets; a hydroelectric plant; a telegraph and later a telephone system; and roads to certain areas including one to his farm in Totota.

Tubman manipulated Americo-Liberians and natives/African-Liberians through the spoils system. The requirement for government appointment was loyalty, not ability. His clannish administration was filled with political intrigue and petty jealousies. He controlled the Americo-Liberians by keeping them in flux. When one family posed a threat, he shifted his favor to a poor family that had no other options.

The world had the image that Liberians loved Tubman. The real key to his power was fear. When the insecure gain power, they become tyrants. As "power corrupts and absolute power corrupts absolutely," Tubman was a megalomaniac. Since the Americo-Liberians admired ruthlessness, they simultaneously feared and admired him. Tubman quashed any opposition by exerting his power so viciously that people thought, "If he can do this to his own elite group, how much more would he do to us?" They called his fear with favor tactics "bite and blow." One edge of his sword was control, the other generosity. He imprisoned an opponent and then rewarded him with a government position. As political opponents became a part of the regime, they shared in the spoils.

In his insecurity, Tubman was a paradox of power and paranoia. He craved adulation. In a cult of personality, he portrayed himself as a successful and triumphant leader playing many roles. And the Americo-Liberians worshipped him as such. In his rule of insecurity, he compulsively maintained his image as a world leader. Any criticism of the president or the government was considered treason. Tubman never trusted anyone he couldn't control. While he displayed a love for people, he kept them at bay.

His mastermind was the "PRO" — Public Relations Officers. PRO's were paid two dollars a week to ferret out and report any disloyalty to the president on any front. The reward for even something insignificant was appointment as a government assistant or a freshly created government job. The PRO gave Tubman access to what people were privately saying. Loyalty to Tubman was paramount. I heard that a wife would report her husband for something he said in the privacy of their home.

Tubman completely controlled the press. The "Liberian Age" and the "Liberian Star" were government owned. During the 1950s, my Uncle C.C.'s privately owned "Daily Listener" dutifully expressed Tubman's views. During elections, there was a conspiracy of silence in the press regarding any opposition views. Libel laws protected Tubman from ordinary criticism.

As a teenager, I admired Mr. Taylor, a West Indian immigrant who published "The Nationalist." His print shop was in the back corner of the Executive Pavilion on Front Street and he lived upstairs. He was a trained journalist. In his independent newspaper, he was outspoken and respected for his integrity.

During World War II, President Tubman's wife died. He chose for his second wife, a woman who had been a favorite of the GIs stationed in Monrovia. She hadn't been the mistress of one GI, she drank and ran around with all of them. Although this was common, Taylor was offended that a prostitute be chosen as First Lady. When he protested this in an editorial, Tubman had him jailed for fifteen years, in which he was not allowed to shave or cut his fingernails.

Since the status of the Americo-Liberians was based on a contrived image, they were rigid. Their society was stagnant. They made the rules and the rules didn't change. If natives were allowed to succeed and compete, it would reveal their weakness. It would shame them and bring about discontent and disrespect from the natives.

It was outsiders, foreign missionaries, who educated the natives. Negro and white missionaries had to encourage the Americo-Liberians to treat their servant children decently and educate them. If an Americo-Liberian trained a native in any way, it was to enable him to serve in some capacity. Educational facilities were initially restricted to Americo-Liberians. Foreign missionaries were required to start schools no more than fifty miles into the interior. The only exceptions to this were the Bolahun Holy Cross Mission, and the Lutheran Training Institute, both located in the Western Province that later became Lofa County. Americo-Liberian authorities watched very carefully those natives who had been servants in elite families in Monrovia, and had graduated from Liberia College. They considered them more of a threat than natives educated in mission schools in the interior.

As a teenager, I was waiting with a group of students assembled outside at Booker T. Washington Institute in Kakata, when Gus Cooper, a prominent Americo-Liberian, arrived in his chauffeur-driven car. Tall and nice-looking, Gus was always well-dressed, with a hat. As he got out of the car, he told the students, "I want to talk to you before you go to eat. It will just take a minute." He greeted the white missionary standing there and then said to the students, "You boys are all Liberians, right?"

They said, "Yeah."

He said, "You know something? I'm a Liberian too."

Everyone laughed since they knew who he was. He went on, "I want to commend you and let you know that I'm one hundred per cent for you. These people should teach you how to work because we need technicians to build Liberia. However, I've got the feeling they're going far beyond that. They're telling you lots of other things that are garbage. They want you to learn the behavior they brought from America and for you to behave like Americans. That's wrong because you can't be like us. You're country boys. You need to learn something to help your people. Our ancestors suffered in America. That's why they came here to make this country for themselves and for you. You should follow us and our advice rather than following these foreigners.

"We're only two groups of people in Liberia — the Americo-Liberians and the countrymen — native Liberians. We can all work together and build our country for our benefit.

"You're countrymen, country boys, and we're Americo-Liberians. Don't ever forget that distinction. These foreign ideas won't work here because they're not in keeping with our Liberian tradition. White people aren't good for us so don't listen to them. They're spoiling your mind. Pretty soon, you'll be so spoiled, you won't listen to your leaders."

By this time, the white missionary's face was red. He told Gus, "Don't ever come back here again."

Gus said, "I'll come here any time I want. This is Liberia."

I later asked Gus, "Why'd you speak like that?"

He said, "B.G., we're having a lot of trouble with these country boys."

World War II brought inevitable social change to Liberia. Under the US lend lease agreement to support the war effort, the US military shipped in jeeps, trucks, tractors, construction and road building equipment, and all kinds of office furniture and supplies.

The United States built an airfield out of the old Firestone landing strip at Marshall, fifteen miles from Monrovia. At the new Robertsfield Airport, they built barracks for the five thousand US GIs. In Monrovia, they built the Barclay Training Camp with the help of Liberians.

The free port of Monrovia was constructed by the Raymond Concrete Pad Company of Texas under the supervision of the US Navy. Monrovia's power plant had two large generators that ran the street lights. Radio was introduced during the war. In 1943, during the Barclay administration, British currency in Liberia was replaced with US currency through an arrangement with the US Treasury. The United States Trust Company opened branches all over.

After the war, the Liberian government didn't want the economy disrupted. If natives had access to all the things the Americans left behind, they wouldn't be content to work at Firestone for ten cents a day. I stood in the crowds at the beach, watching as barges loaded with the new things the Americans had brought, were taken out into the Atlantic Ocean, and dumped. After the war, Tubman's Open Door Policy brought in all kinds of foreign concessions including Bong Mine and the LAMCO Mining Company. When I left Liberia in 1947, the boom in Monrovia was just beginning.

Despite the changes of the war, the Americo-Liberians were united in their belief that they had to stick together. They didn't care so much what natives got, as long as it wasn't power. Their control of inclusion made any native progress "one step forward, two steps back."

Tubman knew social change was inevitable and he was determined to control it. When he came into power, he gradually reversed the fortunes of those few locally educated natives who had risen and been accepted into the Masons. He replaced them with a few select natives of his own choosing. His Unification Policy brought even more control when the provinces became counties in 1964. He brought illiterate native chiefs into the House of Representatives and Senate, who served as "yes men." As they acquired a big house, a car, and a farm, they were more interested in themselves than their people. Tubman's universal suffrage was meaningless. A ballot vote was irrelevant to the vast majority of illiterate natives who made decisions through the oral tradition.

Tubman integrated natives only in a symbolic way. For example, he donned a chief's gown during government festivities. He wined and dined chiefs in the Executive Mansion. He joined Poro. In presidential meetings held in the new counties, he solved a few local problems. While he gave a few select natives some small possibilities, he ensured that the Americo-Liberian elite filled the significant executive, legislative, judicial, and ambassadorial positions.

In Monrovia, a native educated abroad, set up a debate between communism and democracy at Liberia College. Naturally, the students on the side of democracy won. There was talk all over Monrovia and the newspapers reported on it.

My Uncle C.C. told me, "Communism means equality for everyone. Those people are crazy. That means your houseboy is equal with you and has the same rights. We can't have that. How can your houseboy eat with you, use your night chamber pot, and wear your shoes? Who will do all the work?"

During the Cold War of the 1950s and 60s, scholarships to study abroad were plentiful in Liberia. As a result, some scholarships went to African-Liberians educated in mission schools. In 1962, when I was teaching at Michigan State University and working on my doctorate, I became interested in researching the academic success of West African students in America. I discovered from preliminary data at MSU, that other West African students rated higher than the Liberian students. When I divided the Liberian sample into Americo-Liberians and African-Liberians, I found that the higher scores of the African-Liberians had brought up the low scores of the Americo-Liberians.

When I reported this to my colleagues, one of them said, "Ben, Liberia was independent since the 1800s, while other West African countries were under colonial rule. Could this suggest that Africans under colonial subjugation are better off academically and intellectually than Africans under their own rule?"

Another colleague said, "Ben, what you need is two areas of research — the first for all of West Africa and the second, comparing the Americo-Liberians with the indigenous. Let's say the indigenous students scored high because they wanted something better. And the West African students from colonial regimes wanted to please their masters. As a result, both succeeded and did well. You could contrast that with the Americo-Liberians who have everything."

Another colleague said, "Ben, this is a gold mine. People will publish this all over. Don't worry about funding. I'm sure the Phelps-Stockes Foundation or the Ford Foundation will be more than willing to fund this. Talk to the representatives of your country. If they give you the green light, you can do it."

I met with Clarence L. Simpson, the Liberian ambassador in Washington, D.C. Tall and light-skinned, Simpson had served as Tubman's first vice-president. As I walked into his office, he greeted me warmly, saying, "B.G., you're gonna make a contribution! I don't know what it will be but you've got a good head on your shoulders."

I said, "Mr. Ambassador, I've begun research concerning West African students. The results so far indicate that Liberians are at the bottom. When I divided the Liberian students into Americo-Liberians and indigenous, I found that the scores of the indigenous far exceeded those of the Americo-Liberians. These results are only from a small sample at Michigan State. I need your permission to gain access to other university records to see if these early results are valid."

He said, "B.G., this is a high caliber research people do in these universities here. I'm a graduate of Liberia College and I'd never think of doing something like this. None of us would. Since I don't understand it, I'm sure no one at Liberia College will either. You're bringin' a new thing. We need teachers. You should go home."

As David Thomas, the Liberian attaché, walked with me out of Simpson's office, he told me, "Let me talk to him this evening. Maybe I can show him the advantage of this."

The next morning, when the three of us met again, Simpson told me, "B.G., I don't want to be hard on you but you should follow my advice. If you really want to help Liberia, teach! See how that works."

Back at Michigan State, when I told my colleagues what happened, they shook their heads. We even met with President Hannah, but he couldn't risk supporting me. This research would have great ramifications not only for Liberia, but for West African countries striving for independence. Nasser and Nkrumah wanted to unite all of Africa. During the first meeting of the Organization of African Unity held in Monrovia in 1961, they played up to Tubman as the patriarch of Africa. No one wanted to risk bad relations with Liberia.

Americo-Liberian control and rigidity led to hubris. To retain their dominance, the Americo-Liberians had to keep in step. Everyone had to be on the same level and do the same things. Government regulations quashed any outside business effort. Since any questioning was seen as disloyalty, the Americo-Liberians squelched any doubts they had.

Tubman cemented Americo-Liberian privilege. His reward was their only reward — and the rewards were enormous for those select few admitted into the club. Educated African-Liberians succumbed to this as well. A select few became part of the boys, especially those who were young and educated abroad. As they reaped the spoils of government office, they built large homes. Tubman granted them lesser ambassadorships to keep them out of the country.

As a charmed group, the Americo-Liberians were invincible. Even when they identified problems, their *esprit de corps* kept them from acting on them. When the African-Liberians seemed to gain some access to power, the Americo-Liberians assumed their "blessedness" would carry them through.

Despite any social change, the Americo-Liberians were rigid. An educated Loma told me about the rivalry at Cuttington College in Lofa Country during the 1960s. He said, "Although Cuttington was upcountry, there was great discrimination between Americo-Liberian and African students. The African students came from either the Bolahun Holy Cross Mission or the Lutheran Training Institute at Salayea. There were also students from Monrovia who were servant children in the homes of Americo-Liberian government officials. Even though the Americo-Liberians could pay the school fees, they had scholarships with big allowances. They could afford not to eat in the cafeteria. The Americo-Liberian boys were popular with the girls, who were mostly from elite Americo-Liberian families.

"African students couldn't afford the school fees unless they were sponsored by missionaries. If you did well at Bolahun, the missionaries automatically awarded you a scholarship. If you were good at LTI, you had a sponsor. Some Americo-Liberian families in Monrovia took these students to do domestic work and sent them to school.

"The school officials at Cuttington told the African students they should be proud to be in school. They accepted me because I was raised by a wealthy family in Monrovia and I drove a car. They didn't care about my Loma background. They even admonished me, 'Why are you associating with those country boys?'

"When the African students went to eat in the cafeteria and sat at a table with Americo-Liberians, they were ignored. If they said something funny, no one laughed. If they went to get a drink, their food tray was put under the table. If they asked about it when they came back, they were ignored or laughed at. On Sunday, the Americo-Liberian girls dressed certain tables with white linens. They weren't reserving them for anyone special. They just didn't want African boys to sit there.

"If an Americo-Liberian girl fancied an African boy, she kept it a secret. The two of them arranged to meet in the library or wherever. These girls hid the relationship because they didn't want their peers to look down on them. Students called each other by name but the Americo-Liberian girls never attempted to pronounce any name that wasn't from Monrovia. When African students took exams to qualify for overseas scholarships, they used their Americo-Liberian name because they never passed if they used their country name."

During the 1950s, 60s and 70s, as Americo-Liberian students returned home from education abroad, they were given the top government jobs. Educated African-Liberians, as their assistants, actually did the work. A Gbande nephew told me that when he left to study in America in 1968, an Americo-Liberian told him, "You will be our secretaries." Very few African-Liberians educated abroad ever took part in government. Those who did, didn't have access to the top government posts. They took orders from the president like everyone else. Since Tubman frequently changed government posts, they had to remain low key to prevent jealousy or suspicion.

African-Liberian excellence and success didn't change Americo-Liberian perception. Successful African-Liberians were exceptions to the rule that didn't change the rule. "Raw" African-Liberians were still inferior. The African-Liberians could become like the Americo-Liberians, but not quite. As a result, they never gained full acceptance or genuine status in Americo-Liberian society. They remained in bondage while Africans in other countries were declaring their independence.

Inequity persisted. From the 1940s onward, Tubman made the Americo-Liberians into a modern-day class of people. In his Open Door Policy, he cemented his power by sharing the spoils with the Americo-Liberians. New "successful" Americo-Liberians built lavish mansions, which generated a huge gap between the two groups. When I returned to Liberia during the heyday of the 1970s, Americo-Liberian ostentation was in stark contrast to villages in the interior and African-Liberian housing in Monrovia. As short distance from the opulent Executive Mansion, stood slums of bare concrete block housing with zinc roofs. There was no running water, indoor restrooms, or laundry facilities — just a bare light bulb hanging from the ceiling.

I witnessed the same Americo-Liberian practices. If an Americo-Liberian was drunk and hit another car, if the other car was a taxi driven by an African-Liberian, the taxi driver was judged at fault and arrested.

One day, I was on the sidewalk at an intersection when Steve Tolbert, the president's brother, crashed into a car ahead of him that had stopped for a red light. Steve got out of his car and said, "That stupid guy! He saw me coming. Why did he stop?"

I said, "Because the light was red."

Steve said, "I want him arrested!"

A.B., the president's son, walked to the head of any line. Wherever he drove, he created a traffic jam because everyone had to pull aside to let his car through.

In 1973, I was walking by a taxi company on Camp Johnson Road and an African-Liberian friend told me about an incident concerning Tommy Bernard, the owner. I knew Tommy as a boy so I was surprised to hear that he had become successful. Tommy came from a very poor Americo-Liberian family in Monrovia. Although his mother had a big house, the family was destitute. Tommy's older sister was one of my teachers at the Suehn Baptist Mission. She introduced him to us, saying, "This is my little brother. He's so dirty. Look at all the jiggers (burrowing insects) in his toes." From then on, Tommy was known as "Jigger Toes."

My friend told me that Tommy was a notorious speeder. One day, as he drove past his taxi company and approached the intersection at Clay Street, he hit and killed an African-Liberian boy running across the street. He was going at such a speed, the boy was killed instantly. As a crowd of loved ones cried over his body, Tommy jumped out of his car, yelling, "Who's child is this! His blood is sprayed all over my car! Get the parents to come right now and wash it off!"

When Frank Tolbert also hit and killed an African-Liberian child, he complained, "People don't keep their children off the street! I just washed my car.

Now it's all dirty with blood!" He ordered everyone living near his house to keep their children inside when he was in town.

In 1972, I met Ed Cooper, an outside child by a native woman. He had recently been appointed Director of Motor Vehicles. As we crossed Randall Street to use the pay phone, a taxi making a right turn with the light, slowly approached and slowed to a stop.

Ed shouted to the African-Liberian taxi driver, "Do you want to KILL us? What's the matter with you BOY!"

The taxi driver said, "Boss man, the light was for me."

He said, "Light or no light. Look at me. Do you know who I am? Do you know who you're talkin' to? An' you know this man here?"

"Oh, boss man, I beg you."

The traffic was beginning to pile up behind the taxi. I told Ed, "Let the guy go, Ed. Please."

He said to the taxi driver, "Let me see your license. Do you know who I am?"

When the driver showed him his license, Ed grabbed it and said, "I can keep this right now and put you in jail. You'll never drive a taxi again. And you telling me, light, light. No light! When you see me, you stop! You understand that?"

The taxi driver said, "Oh, boss man, yes, Sir."

Ed stood in the middle of the street and yelled at the backed-up traffic, "No one pass! You stay right there! You people all stop!"

He told me, "B.G., I'm gonna teach this countryman something."

For the next ten minutes, Ed made the taxi driver beg for his license back. Then Ed said, "I'm gonna give you your license back but if you do this once more. You see me?"

The taxi driver said, "Yes, Boss man."

"Speak loudly!"

"Yes, Boss Man!"

"Say it like you mean it!"

"YES, BOSS MAN!"

"I'm letting you go now. We're gonna cross the street and if you move one inch before that, I'll put you in jail."

The taxi driver waited. After our phone call, we saw him still holding up traffic. I told Ed, "That wasn't right. You know he had the light. He slowed down. He didn't hit us."

Ed said, "You've been away too long, B.G. I'm tellin' you. These country people — if you give 'em an inch, they'll take a foot. He'll never forget what happened today."

Even after the coup, this disparagement continued. In 1983, Anita sent the boys to Choitrims in Monrovia to buy some tomato paste. As they waited in line, ahead of them was an African-Liberian man dressed in a T-shirt and jean shorts.

Although he needed a haircut, he was neat and clean. As he laid his items on the counter, two light-skinned Americo-Liberian teenage clerks with straightened hair gave each other a knowing look. One of them said to him, "E-i-u-u-u. You ugly. You too ugly. Get outta here." She told the other girl, "Look at him. He ugly."

The other girl laughed loudly, "Ha Ha Ha! Yeah, he ugly!"

As they laughed together, the man turned and walked away.

Instead of a pluralistic or integrated society, there were two Liberias — two social and cultural realms that didn't mesh. Presidential rule was the only thing that integrated Americo-Liberians and natives/African-Liberians. During the 1930s and 40s, when the Americo-Liberians said, "United we stand, divided we fall," they meant their own unity, not national unity. Their insecurity kept them from seeing the national interest as their own best interest.

Their failure was inevitable. They were not only inept, they excluded the vast majority of Liberia's population. In keeping the natives/African-Liberians down, they kept Liberia down. Cultural racism prevented social unity. Unification was a smokescreen. The Americo-Liberians garnered the subservience of the natives/African-Liberians, but not their loyalty.

None of Liberia's inhabitants had any love or loyalty to her. The Americo-Liberians had no identity or pride as Liberians. Their contrived patriotism was an outward show. For example, everyone had to stand at attention when the flag was raised or lowered. Anyone caught walking by was punished. This ended up being the natives/African-Liberians who didn't know what was going on.

Natives/African-Liberians, that were never a legitimate part of anything, had no basis to love Liberia. The Americo-Liberians even elevated Lebanese traders and other foreigners over them.

Liberians had no national consciousness since there was no common history, national hero, or universal motto. Liberia's history, focused solely on the Americo-Liberians, was inaccurate. As a result, Liberians can't be honest and move forward.

Americo-Liberian prominence wasn't based on performance or good governance. They were a burden on Africa rather than Africa being "their burden." Cultural racism made them the opposite of what they presumed to be. On a new continent with freedom and opportunity, they practiced what they had just escaped and professed to hate — domination justified by inferiority. Their quest for freedom and democracy resulted in the denial of liberty and justice for others. Even today, they have never been held accountable. They say, "That's in the past. Let's forget the past."

As Liberia fulfilled Negro stereotype, it substantiated the view that Negroes could do nothing even when they had been enculturated in Western culture and given freedom and opportunity. Liberia is essentially the story of the rise and fall of Americo-Liberianism. A society of oppression can succeed for a time, but it can never ultimately endure. Oppression always carries with it, the seeds of destruction for both oppressor and oppressed.

CHAPTER THREE: IMAGE VS. REALITY

The Imitation of Superiority

> "Immigrants must...come here to make this country like America."
> — Alonzo Hoggard, the founder of Arthington

During the 1930s and 40s, Monrovia and its environs were a microcosm of the antebellum South. Western image was everything. Clothing not only indicated position and status, it symbolized being civilized. The Americo-Liberians were the epitome of "Clothes make the man," dressing well so others would defer to them. Top hat and tails were required at all government affairs and holidays, including Independence Day, Flag Day, Matilda Newport Day, and Pioneer Day. People in Monrovia admired S. David Coleman for his new hat at each special occasion. Some Americo-Liberians, in their identity with the British, wore boots and jodhpurs, called "knee buckles."

Every time my Uncle C.C. saw me, he said, "Let me see how you're dressed."

I said, "How do I look, C.C.?"

"You have to start over."

"I'm not going to take my clothes off!"

"You have to do things properly."

One day, I miss-buttoned the top button of my pull-over shirt. The minute C.C. saw me, he said, "B.G., you can't do that! You look like you've never worn a shirt before. Look at yourself!"

I said, "What's wrong? I was in a hurry."

"You have to dress properly."

One day C.C. advised me, "B.G., you have to put your belt in the loops before you put on your pants. Otherwise, you'll miss a loop and people will think you don't even know how to put a belt on. They won't say anything to you, but they'll say to each other, 'Look at that raw countryman.' Country people just wear twine or a piece of cloth for a belt. You've got to get a good leather belt with a shiny buckle. Girls look at belts too."

One day, I was in C.C.'s bathroom and he needed to come in quickly. When he saw me zipping up my pants, he said, "Wait a minute, B.G. There's a proper way to do that. To save yourself from embarrassment, watch me. First, you pull the zipper up and bend the zipper pull down. Then, as you buckle your belt, you check the zipper pull with your finger. That's the civilized way. People aren't going to tell you your flap is open. Lots of countrymen don't even know their pants are open but they don't have to worry since they wear gowns. You've got to make sure your zipper's up. Any part of your body that's open is a disgrace and tells a whole lot about who you are."

Wearing something to bed at night meant you were civilized. In Monrovia, Americo-Liberian men wore British woolen long underwear, called union jacks or long johns. Those who wore pajamas had them starched.

On my usual walk to Aunt Louise's in the morning, I passed by the house of her next door neighbor, Mr. Stubblefield, the adjutant general to the president.

One day I asked him, "Why are you always sitting on your porch in your pajamas?"

He said, "I tell you, little boy. I believe my grandfather did the same thing and so do my father and brother. It is a blessing to have night clothing and day clothing. Many people go naked. Since I wear my day clothes longer, giving my pajamas a little more wear won't do 'em any harm."

People wore ill-fitting shoes just to be wearing shoes. They said, "The shoe is fine, oh, but the thing is tight, oh." If a woman's high heels didn't click on the pavement, people said, "You mean you got a 'good' shoe and nobody can hear you? What's the good of buyin' shoes? You may as well go barefoot."

Men watching the women arrive at church would say, "You can hear her comin' before you even see her. Look at her walkin'." When the women overheard this, they clicked their high heels even harder.

During World War II, when I saw a prominent Americo-Liberian wearing a zoot suit, I said, "What are you wearing that for?"

He said, "That's the style."

The Americo-Liberians were compulsive in their Southern affectation since it connected them to Western culture. They were the epitome of Southern ritual, formality, and flowery language. They recited Latin phrases. They called each other "Bubbah" and "Billy Bob." When the women danced the Virginia reel, they held up a corner of their skirt as they twirled around.

The Americo-Liberians made the quadrille into an art form. During special holidays, at balls and dances at the Old Executive Mansion, the quadrille sets were called in order of prestige, beginning with the cabinet. At some of the dances my Uncle C.C. called, the first set was the graduates of Liberia College or the College of West Africa; then graduates of American schools; Liberian schools; European schools; and finally graduates of any school. One evening, as I took a lady back to her place in line for the promenade, my cousin Jimmy looked like a strutting rooster as he demonstrated how I should "dance" my way back. He said, "B.G., you have to do it the right way."

Attention to Southern ritual meant you were civilized. One day in Monrovia, I heard a man tell his friend, "I finished drinkin' my Black Horse [whiskey] and got up to go to bed. Look like she never touched it."

His friend said, "What! You mean she didn't turn down the bed? Ha! Ha! Ha! Oh, man, where'd you get that wife from? She must not be civilized. Ha! Ha! Ha! You know better. You should teach her to do it."

The Americo-Liberians were zealous about the smallest details of etiquette. My Uncle C.C. was always teaching me proper manners. One day he told me, "B.G., are you going out? Where's your handkerchief? A gentleman can't go out without a handkerchief."

I said, "I don't need a handkerchief."

He said, "Even when you're not sweating, you must wipe your face with it. It's the proper thing to do."

Another time he told me, "B.G., leave your napkin in your lap and use it each time you take a bite."

When he saw me using a toothpick, he said, "You can't do that, B.G.! You must always cover your mouth when you use a toothpick."

I said, "What for? I wasn't displaying anything."

He said, "You can't do that. It's not proper. Do like me."

He looked ludicrous as he struggled to cover his mouth with one hand while using a toothpick with the other. Figuring it would draw even more attention, I refused.

The social model of the Americo-Liberians was the white slave master, the pinnacle of success in the aristocratic antebellum South. Liberia was their opportunity to redeem themselves. They were determined to outdo whites, just as America's nouveau riche was determined to outdo European nobility. They loved a grand show of ritual and ceremony. The government was full of pomp and formality. Every occasion warranted a parade.

Americo-Liberian hypocrisy derived from its white counterpart in the antebellum South. The Americo-Liberians were the result of American fraud and they became masters of that fraud. Liberia was founded because of white expedience in slavery. Whatever the slave master did was right. The Americo-Liberians replicated white "superiority" in the hypocrisy and immorality displayed to them. They knew that Christianity never kept whites from doing something to their advantage or doing whatever they pleased. Like Southern whites, they saw Christianity as words, not deeds.

They were deeply religious. The first church, Providence Baptist, was organized on the ship before it landed. Founded on Christian principles, Liberia was hailed as a bastion of Christianity in Africa. There was a blending of church and state.

Because the Americo-Liberians were Christian, they could do no wrong. Since they were in power and they were right, they had no shame. Christianity never kept them from dominating and exploiting the natives just as it never kept whites from slavery. Cultural racism superseded Christianity just as racism did.

Uncivilized natives deserved whatever happened to them. Like the antebellum South, the Americo-Liberian society was at odds with itself. The Americo-Liberians acted the opposite of their stated morality and goals. They advocated justice, but practiced abuse. They came to spread civilization, but acted barbarically.

In each *cycle of racism*, evil is ratcheted up. The South's society of hypocrisy became Liberia's national standard. Hypocrisy granted "status" since a utilitarian view of morality was the way to succeed and be superior like whites. The Americo-Liberians did what needed to be done to get what they wanted. They succeeded through nepotism, corruption, bribery, falsified elections, and ruthless control. Even when they saw the need for change, they couldn't abandon self-serving practices.

Like the master with the slaves, the Americo-Liberians were "those who know" carrying truth to the natives. Although Christianity was the greatest thing they had to offer, hypocrisy canceled out their witness. While the church included civilized natives, the Americo-Liberians had little interest in evangelism. They instead used Christianity as a tool of exclusivity to keep uncivilized natives in their place. Only Christians were a part of the church, a significant social organization. As a result, the Americo-Liberians ended up coming to Liberia to practice their Christianity freely, rather than bringing it to Africa. Foreign missionaries evangelized the natives.

Morality is meaningless in any society unless it is practiced. The Americo-Liberians had no true standard, no true integrity to any standard. Their Christianity was a cultural practice, a social standard, not a personal commitment. Since they were illiterate and inept, their religion was reduced to ritual. They fanatically copied the American Negro church. Church attendance required "Sunday best." Devotions were held on Sunday morning before church.

Christianity was outward show, a symbol of Liberia's religiosity. The Americo-Liberian image was based on surface values. The church functioned primarily as a social organization, an avenue to status. Christianity was a way to gain advantage, theology a way to advance oneself. Church attendance was habit. As a social club, the church gave exposure to "big" men or women who went to great lengths when they wanted something done. Church leaders and ministers of the gospel exhibited brutality, viciousness, and ruthless womanizing.

Annual church conventions were a big affair. Members of the denomination, living in the upriver and coastal settlements, were all invited. Everyone attended no matter how far away they lived. Donations at these conventions granted status. A big man would make a speech and donate twenty-five dollars, a lot of money at that time. President Tubman, as a gesture of good will, would donate fifty dollars to defray expenses. When he really wanted to show off, he offered free housing or free "everything."

American Negro missionaries displayed the same hypocrisy. Every missionary in Liberia, white or Negro, had status. The Americo-Liberians and natives deferred to them. Missionaries lived on a pedestal. Nothing could touch them. They were never questioned. Negro missionaries allied themselves with the Americo-Liberians. They never protested the vicious treatment of the natives.

At the Suehn Baptist Mission, Mrs. Davis' four-bedroom house stood alone at the top of a hill. On the other side of the hill were the teachers' quarters. Student housing was at the bottom near the creek. Mrs. Davis and the teachers never ate with the students. Each morning, native boys carried water up the hill to fill the metal drums beside Mrs. Davis' house. Native girls heated water and filled her bathtub.

One day, she complained that a handkerchief was missing from her clothesline. Determined to find the culprit, she lined us up for reckoning. We watched as a Gola man heated a machete in a small fire until it was red-hot. She said each of us had to lick the machete. If we were innocent, nothing would happen.

The boys were lined up by height so I was first and Joe second. When she ordered me to lick the machete, I said, "Mrs. Davis, why don't you have the medicine man lick it first to demonstrate how it works?"

She said, "We're not here to test the medicine man! He didn't do it. Now, lick the machete!"

I said, "Why would I steal your hankie? My father can buy me a thousand hankies! A cow probably pulled it off the clothesline."

Furious, she pushed us back, saying, "Step aside! I'll deal with the two of you later!"

The next in line was Albert Nebo, a Kru boy. I told him, "Albert! Don't do it!" But he cowered and licked it. He fainted and fell backward — the top of his tongue stuck to the machete.

Everyone scattered. Albert was taken to the school nurse but all she could do was rinse his mouth with salt water. Two days later, his tongue was horribly swollen, his mouth full of maggots. He died a week later.

When the word got to Monrovia, some of us were taken there for a government inquisition. I was the only one in the courtroom who told the truth. Everyone else said, "I didn't see. I don't know what happened." Nothing was ever done.

Christianity in Liberia was diluted by syncretism — the tendency to combine or reconcile differing beliefs. The Americo-Liberians, in their "whatever works" mentality, were religiously eclectic. African superstition and Muslim elements were incorporated into Christianity. As the Americo-Liberians accepted whatever brought the desired result, Christianity in Liberia was "form without function."

Most Americo-Liberians believed in witchcraft and were as deeply super-stitious as the natives. They feared African "juju" and used bush remedies. The government recognized "trial by ordeal." Every event in Liberia was interpreted through the lens of superstition.

On New Year's Eve, a popular song was, "Happy New Year! Me no die, oh! (I lived to see this year)." Young people went from house to house loudly sing-ing this, including the Kru people in Kru Town. It echoed their hope that they wouldn't die in the coming year.

The Americo-Liberians, in their lip service to Christianity, readily adopted Muslim customs. At Easter, "Beating Judas" was similar to the Muslim ritual of stoning of the devil. Effigies of Judas, a scarecrow in old clothes and a hat, were hung from posts in common areas in Monrovia and the upriver towns. At the scarecrow's feet lay cut switches. Everyone participated in this to garner some favor with God, not just Christians. Natives used their own rattan switches.

From Good Friday to Easter, people picked up a switch and beat Judas for betraying Christ. Their faces were somber as if they were beating a real person. They said, "Judas! You're a bad man! You did bad! You betrayed Jesus!" Through-out the weekend, people asked each other, "Have you beaten Judas yet?"

The reply was, "Man, I lashed Judas. I struck him so hard!" Or they said, "No, but I'm gonna!" On Easter morning, old people and women heading for church lined up at the effigies.

Like the natives, the Americo-Liberians relied on charms, magic, and talis-mans for supernatural power, regardless of Christian belief or Western values. Every Americo-Liberian participated in this from the president on down to the illiterate farmer. Talismans were used to ward off calamity, manipulate others, or protect from disease. Men used them to get a girl to fall in love with them or to convince her parents to agree to the marriage.

Every request was accompanied by some form of talisman. An imam would write the appropriate words of the Koran on a piece of parchment and then fold it and put it in a little cloth. This cloth was put into a little leather pouch that was hung around the neck; tied on the arm; fastened around the waist; or at-tached to the handle of a walking stick. As the request was made, the talisman was squeezed.

If the request was made by phone, the imam wrote the words of the Koran on a wooden slate and washed them into a bowl of water. The person making the request first rinsed his mouth with the water. If the request was made by letter, the imam wrote the words of the Koran on a piece of paper, prayed over it, and burned it in a small earthenware pot. Then he spread the ashes lightly over the letter so they wouldn't be detected. These ashes were also put into talcum powder and rubbed on the face. When the person made the request, they looked directly into the other person's face.

As a Methodist preacher, President Tubman looked on missionaries with favor. But he never fostered their success. He frequently invited Muslims to the Executive Mansion and had his own imam. In his paranoia, he continuously consulted with soothsayers and fortune tellers. He carried talismans in his pockets.

The Americo-Liberians practiced ritual killing, much like the native Leopard society. Taking someone's heart ensured power, wealth, popularity, long life, and good luck. Tubman had a private room in the Executive Mansion that only he could enter. It supposedly held a freezer full of sacrificed bodies and hearts that gave him power.

Liberia not only represents the worst of Negroes, it represents the worst of whites taken to its obvious conclusion. When the Free Negroes and freed slaves went to Liberia in 1822, slavery and racism were at their zenith. The Americo-Liberians not only displayed the circumstantial inferiority of slavery, they had a flawed white social model. As victims, they displayed the degradation of an oppressed people. As victimizers, they displayed the evils of white rule.

Americo-Liberian decadence stemmed from Southern decadence. The white man's number one asset was his power and sanctity. Negroes wanted the power of whites. Although the Americo-Liberians weren't equally decadent, Liberia's cultural standard of "excellence" was a pathetic replica of Southern evil. Those who came to impart civilization instead transplanted the evils of the culture that had enslaved them. In a double whammy, they displayed the destructive cultural mentalities of both Negroes and whites.

The upriver Americo-Liberians associated agriculture with slavery. Liberia was their chance to escape drudgery now that they were free and civilized. As Old Man Dennis said, "You could sleep till noon if you wanted to." The majority of them had never been in charge of their own lives, much less a nation. Since nothing in Liberia was guaranteed, in their fatalism, they lived for the moment. They focused on the "now."

A life of leisure was a symbol of white superiority. The slave master arranged for work to be done. Free Negroes in Monrovia, focused on trade and borrowed capital to the neglect of industry or agriculture. Trade was a refined type of work that didn't require hard labor. The early successful merchant class in the 1870s, functioned as middlemen selling native farm products or natural resources to foreign markets.

During the 1930s and 40s, the Americo-Liberians were absentee owners of cash crop farms. In their entitlement, they consumed or sold what they didn't produce. A derisive comment was, "You're just a laborer." Laziness and inactivity led to obesity. A big stomach was admired as a sign of prosperity. Jacob Brown was famous for being able to eat a small goat in one sitting. Smoking had status. People said, "Oh, look how that man smokes."

Every Americo-Liberian aspired to a life of leisure and comfort, being served by others. People in elite families threw their things all around the house, with native servants scampering to clean up after them. Servants did the miniscule. They brought the master a glass of water, took off his shoes, and trimmed his corns. Natives said, "The only thing the Americo-Liberians had to do for themselves was wipe their butt. If they could have had someone do that, they would have." During afternoon card parties, men sometimes used the night chamber pot instead of going to the outhouse. Then they ordered the servant to come and clean it.

The Americo-Liberians always quoted, "Consider the ant, thou sluggard, and be wise." The truth is they were all sluggards. There was no work ethic. Everyone wanted to be a government official in order to avoid work. The purpose of education was to work for the government. The Cooper business school in Monrovia was very successful because everyone wanted to learn typing and shorthand to get a civilized desk job. Native clerks did the work in the government offices of the "big" men. During rainy season, big men said, "Oh, man, it's rainin' too much today. Time to stay in bed and let your woman warm your feet." Most of the time, the Americo-Liberians went into the office at 11 a.m. and "knocked off" at 2 p.m.

They displayed frivolity and shallow pursuits. Any plans they made were grandiose and unachievable. They focused on play. Afternoons were spent talking, boozing, and playing cards. Evenings were spent at parties. As masters of the party, they were quintessential party animals. They dressed well and danced well. No one partied like they did or did it better.

Their rascality stemmed from slavery. Slaves were forced to do anything to survive. They had to please the master despite what they thought was right. During the 1930s and 40s, since the Americo-Liberians were inept, they could only succeed by illegitimate means. In Liberia's isolation, they lacked moral restraint. Even when there were charges, government officials cloaked their activities with a show of innocence. The Americo-Liberians never admitted wrong doing. They simply called it by another name.

In Liberia's frontier society, people took things into their own hands. In Monrovia, when someone yelled, "Rogue! Rogue!" everyone got into the chase. People beat rogues so mercilessly, they were relieved to be arrested by the police. Some rogues escaped by blending into the crowd and yelling "Rogue! Rogue!" themselves.

As a boy, I watched people chase a rogue for stealing fifty cents. He became so frightened, he jumped into the Du River at Waterside. People watching him flail in the water, said, "Who he thinks he's foolin'?" When the water got calm, they said, "He's gone, man." When others came to see, they pointed and said, "That's where he got away." The next day they realized he had drowned when they saw his body floating in the water.

Rascality was admired as cleverness. If someone could dupe or manipulate others, talk fast, or be "rascal," people said, "Oh, he's clever,"

As a boy, one of my Americo-Liberian friends told me he was a medicine man. Johnny said if I gave him fifty cents, he would call his grandfather out of the grave. He was so convincing, I paid him and followed him to the graveyard to see if he could do it, even though it was pouring rain.

As we stood over the grave, he kept saying, "He's comin'! He's comin'! He'll soon come!" A half hour later, he said, "B.G., do you have your eyes open? You were supposed to keep them closed!"

I said, "But how can I see your grandfather if my eyes are closed?"

He said, "Oh, man, you spoiled the whole thing."

In Monrovia, a story circulated about Dr. Sejue, a Haitian doctor who served as Liberia's chief medical officer. In his medical practice in Monrovia, he treated a pretty young Americo-Liberian woman who couldn't get pregnant. She told her husband that the doctor had to give her an injection each week. As time went by with no results, her husband asked her to explain these injections.

She said, "Well, he puts medicine on his thing and goes to bed with me. He says it's a very powerful medicine and it's the only way it can be applied."

Her husband discussed this with one of his friends who told him, "I don't have a medical degree. But I can certainly treat your wife the same way and I bet she'll have a child for you."

Americo-Liberian success was based on exploitation. The Americo-Liberians were only interested in Liberia for what they could get out of it. Their whole purpose in dominating was to exploit. They were consumers, not producers. They used their raw power to get whatever they wanted from natives who existed to serve their purpose. They were always scrambling to get anything they could, any way they could, except by working for it.

In the name of official government business, the Americo-Liberians acquired land, foodstuffs, porterage, and farm labor from natives through confiscation, extortion, or government fines. Or they simply demanded whatever they wanted. Cultural racism justified an economic purpose in Liberia just as racism did in America.

The government defined land ownership as private and individual, laying the groundwork for the Americo-Liberians to take land in the coastal and upriver areas for their cash crop farms. If they paid for the land, they were in essence, paying themselves since the money went to the government.

There was an even bigger land grab after Tubman was elected. In the Open Door Policy, the Americo-Liberians exploited Liberia's natural resources for their own profit. Since whites couldn't own land, foreigners had to collaborate with the government. The acquisition of land for the rubber plantations at Mount Barclay and Harbel were arranged by Americo-Liberian "big men" without the consent of the Bassa and Kpelle tribes living there.

Forced labor was the government's mainstay for porterage; road and bridge building; and the construction of government buildings in the interior. When the district commissioner commandeered labor for government projects, chiefs were fined for not supplying a full quota of men. In road and bridge building, natives not only provided their own food and tools, they had to supply their Americo-Liberian overseers with rice and palm oil. District commissioners routinely commandeered labor, not only for their own cash crop farms, but for the farms of their benefactors as well. This forced labor continued on a lesser scale into the 1970s.

The district commissioner's official role was to enforce the law in the provinces — to impose and collect taxes, settle disputes, and conscript labor for government projects. His informal role was to exploit. Since he was only accountable to the president, he had a free hand. Some commissioners were ruthless petty despots. Since they were poorly paid, they rewarded themselves by extorting goods and services throughout their district. It was the paramount chief's duty to provide supplies for government officials. Under this guise, district commissioners regularly confiscated cows, goats, sheep, and chickens in large numbers. An Americo-Liberian uncle, who served as district commissioner, told me the Americo-Liberians in Monrovia continually asked him to get things for them.

The Americo-Liberians exploited native domestic labor through a system of paternalism. Every leading family in Monrovia and in the coastal and upriver settlements had native servant children, a large number of them granting status. However, relatively speaking, these children were few in number. As informal house slaves, their reward was to "learn book" and "the fashion of the white man." Most of the time, their expectations, and that of their parents, were fulfilled to the bare minimum. They were menial servants. I saw servant children literally dressed in rags going down to Waterside in the pouring rain to get firewood. The only "education" they received was to be taken to church regularly. Some were educated and given other advantages. A few in elite families were well educated and superficially included in the family which made them feel good.

Americo-Liberian success was based on manipulation. After the reserve of President Edwin Barclay, Tubman was the man for the times. Open and friendly with everyone, he not only hosted parties in his home in Monrovia, he always livened things up as he made the rounds of parties. As a consummate politician, he gained power by catering to Americo-Liberian tastes. To get everyone drunk, he continually proposed toasts, while merely sniffing his own glass. When he left for the next party, his glass remained half-empty, as before. People said, "Wow! That guy can never get drunk!"

Tubman won the love of the people, saying, "I don't know politics. I only know Bible." At any public affair, whether it was Americo-Liberian or native, he joined in the dance and took a few steps. After his first election, he garnered support by freeing Barclay's enemies from jail.

Americo-Liberian success was based on corruption and graft. Since the Americo-Liberians were above the law, they rewarded themselves through corruption. Presidential rule superseded the law, which made the president a law unto himself. Throughout Liberia's history, the Americo-Liberians paid lip service to all kinds of reforms they never acted upon. No one could ever be prosecuted for corruption since they were all guilty. Commissions appointed to study corruption did nothing.

Since corruption was Liberia's bedrock, her leaders were her greatest enemy — the higher their position, the greater their capacity to exploit. Any conflict of interest was ignored. Taxes weren't paid due to intimidation or bribery. The wages of government employees were docked for party dues or the president's birthday. While the slogan of the True Whig Party was "Deeds, not words," the Americo-Liberians were all talk and no action. Because business opportunities compensated low government salaries, every government official was expected to participate. Everyone wanted to emulate those in power to get their own piece of the action.

Americo-Liberian promiscuity stemmed from slavery. What was an element of Southern society became Liberia's cultural standard. The Americo-Liberians had a formal norm of Christianity and marriage. Their informal norm was womanizing. It was expected of every leading Americo-Liberian in Monrovia and even more pervasive amongst the upriver Americo-Liberians. Multiple sex partners were a way of life. In trying to outdo the slave master, Americo-Liberian men had a sexual appetite that was unquenchable. They didn't care how or with whom it was satisfied.

It was fashionable and civilized for married men to have a girlfriend. Men routinely had affairs with single Americo-Liberian women and built houses for them. Those who could afford to do this were envied by the others. Many times, single women ended up having three or four children fathered by different men. Missionaries in Liberia completely failed in dissuading the Americo-Liberians from this.

Church conventions were full of hanky panky. One day, my Uncle C.C. told me, "That church convention was a wild one!"

I said, "How was that?"

He said, "A guy was almost caught by his wife. She wasn't supposed to go, but she suddenly showed up the third day just before the evening banquet. If she'd arrived any later, she'd have caught 'em red-handed."

Because of racial similarities, outside children, as a rule, were more accepted than mulattos in America. Children by an Americo-Liberian woman had more status than those by a native woman. Their fathers supported them. Some were placed in good government positions and they attained a high status because of their father's status.

Married women had their own affairs. Every Americo-Liberian woman, single or married, wanted to be the girlfriend of a government official. Older women liked young men. They called their secret Americo-Liberian lover, "my son" and supported him.

I admired my Aunt Louise. Widowed in her twenties, she was short and shapely. Always smartly dressed, she wore a small hat on the right side of her center part.

At her shop on Benson Street, people sat on the little front porch drinking cane juice and talking. Her most regular visitor was Mr. Trinity, a very prominent Americo-Liberian. He worked as a typesetter for government documents at the Old Executive Mansion on Ashmun Street and was known to spend more time at work than most government employees. Trinity was Methodist and very prominent in the Masonic Lodge.

Aunt Louise was Baptist, a staunch supporter and kingpin of Providence Baptist Church. She served as the head of every church social event, community project, or charitable effort. Mrs. Clement, the pianist, was her assistant. Whenever anything was proposed, someone said, "Talk to Louise." If she wasn't busy preparing for church retreats or picnics in Clay Ashland or White Plains, she was raising money for food, clothing, and medical care for poor Americo-Liberians. No one could turn her down when she collected, whether they were Americo-Liberian or a foreigner.

Everyone in Monrovia knew that Trinity was Aunt Louise's lover and that Trinity's wife was having her own affair with an American Negro preacher at the Jehovah's Witness church.

One day I asked her, "Why does Mr. Trinity come here every day?"

She said, "He's my lover. Don't you know? Everybody knows that."

I said, "But he's married and you're going to church and working hard for the church. Isn't that a contradiction?"

She said, "Benjamin! You're a Liberian! This is Liberia. You ought to understand."

Since I looked puzzled, she continued, "Well, I guess you'd have to be a real Liberian to understand it. We're not doin' it in secret so it's not cheatin'. Everyone knows about us. You'll learn when you live here long enough and grow up. I bet you'll accept it too."

The next day, I said to Mr. Trinity, "Does your wife know about your relationship with my Aunt Louise?"

He said, "Ha! Ha! Ha! Of course, she knows! I'm here every day and on Saturdays, I'm buyin' things for her and the store. We're hidin' nothin'. She knows everything."

Just as the slave master had easy access to slave women, Americo-Liberian men saw native women as sex objects and had clandestine affairs with them. Cash crop farms not only granted prestige, they served as sexual playgrounds. Every notable Americo-Liberian with means had a farm upriver or in the coastal areas. Elite Americo-Liberians in the upriver towns had a farm three or four miles away. Americo-Liberian men had their social and legal wife in Monrovia, who kept their household and bore them legitimate offspring — and their native "economic wife" on their farm, who bore them outside children. District commissioners routinely took native women to their cash crop farms, many of them permanently.

Native mistresses and their children were an accepted and integral part of Americo-Liberian society. Men regularly spent their weekends on the farm with their other family. Their wives in Monrovia knew what was going on. They occasionally visited the farm. They had no option to protest or get a divorce, since fathers were granted custody of the children according to Liberian law. Men always had a sexual alternative unless both "wives" were pregnant at the same time.

Men educated native girls and women educated native boys with the expectation that they would be their lover in the future. They supported them by sending a bag of rice to the mission school or providing them medicine. When they traveled to America, they brought back clothing from Good Will and let their future lover select whatever he or she wanted.

Outside native children, raised by their mothers, had a similar advantage to servant children. Although they weren't brought up in Monrovia, they carried their father's name. Their fathers provided for them to some extent and looked out for them. Some fathers had their children educated or they blessed them with a small gift.

Even so, these children were socially and culturally marginal since they didn't belong in either culture. Those who didn't receive any favors from their father were truly marginal. Natives rejected them as part Americo-Liberian. Although these children gravitated to Americo-Liberian society, they weren't accepted. Many became alcoholics, fast talkers, and crooks who went from one tavern and town to another in the upriver settlements. Outside Lebanese children shared the same fate.

The Americo-Liberians couldn't lead effectively because they set new lows of degradation. In their impunity, they were no curbs on their behavior. Although they conducted their sexual affairs in private, they were common knowledge in Monrovia's rumor mill. Government leaders, with unlimited power and influence, womanized on a grand scale and they had plenty of time for it. In essence, they were sexual predators of young girls.

As director of the youth program, Aunt Louise counseled many girls. One day I was at her house, when a young girl from church walked in. Aretha was a slim, attractive upriver Americo-Liberian girl, who was very popular in church. She walked in so troubled, she completely ignored I was there and blurted out, "Miss Louise, I got a problem and I need your help. Otherwise I'm gonna run away from home."

Aunt Louise said, "I don't know how much I can help, but let's hear the problem."

Aretha said, "If I don't go to bed with Mr. Wilson, my father won't get that position in government."

I knew Mr. Wilson. I played checkers with him. Tall and nice-looking, he was a married man in his forties with lots of money.

Aretha went on, "My father's forcin' me to go to bed with him cause he's close to Tubman. He told my father he could get him any job if only I'll 'love' him. Miss Louise, I tried three times but it hurts. I'm not gonna do it anymore. When I told my father, he said, 'You're a woman. You gotta help me get this job.' Will you talk to my father? Please? Otherwise I'm gonna run away from home even though I don't know where to go."

Aunt Louise said, "That's not right. I'll do what I can." A few weeks later, Aretha moved in with her.

President Tubman, a Methodist minister, was a master womanizer. It was common knowledge that he went to bed with all the wives of his cabinet ministers and other government appointees, as well as many others. This included sisters and a grandmother, mother, and daughter from the same family. His forte was demonstrating his power by taking a man's wife. When he traveled in Liberia, he would take a pretty sixteen or seventeen-year-old girl, telling her father, "I'd like her to go with us to get some experience." The father gratefully agreed knowing he'd be rewarded with some government position.

When Tubman traveled outside of Liberia, he selected a pretty young married woman as his personal secretary. He'd ask her, "Who's your husband?" and turn to an aide and say, "Have him brought here."

When the husband arrived, Tubman said, "I have a trip coming up and I'd like to take your wife along. Would that be all right with you?"

The man would bow and say, "This is an honor you're bestowing on me, Mr. President. I'll tell her. Thank you, thank you, Mr. President."

If the man didn't already work for government, Tubman told him, "I'm going to appoint you to one of our bureaus. I'll call the head right now. When would you like to start?

"Today, sir!"

"Go there. We'll call them."

The only avenues for competition and status were sex, alcoholism, and rascality. Men took great pride in their sexual prowess and how much liquor they could hold. As they sat around playing cards and drinking, someone would brag,

"Last night I went wild with three different girls." They said, "So many women and I'm only one man." Or they said, "We need more eunuchs around here. These men are goin' wild." If they didn't brag about sex, they boasted about rascality, saying, "He's a helluva man. He can do that cause he's so clever."

The only activity that a family or group of young men competed in was drinking. People said, "He's a man-pekin' [man-child]. Drink somethin' like that? That's a man-pekin." They bragged, "That man can drink! He got so drunk he peed right in the street." Or they said, "Oh, man, who's that? He can't even drink."

Alcoholism, as a way of life, provided an escape from idleness, boredom, and anxiety. The Americo-Liberians were afraid of failure. They were equally afraid of natives and their possible success. During World War II, every other storefront in Monrovia was a bar. Elite Americo-Liberians drank imported liquor. For everyone else, there was a two or five-cent shot of cane juice served by shopkeepers. Imported schnapps from Holland cost ten or fifteen cents a shot. Alcoholism was worse in the upriver settlements because many upriver Americo-Liberians made their own cane juice.

Drinking signified success. It was the mark of a true gentleman. When you respected someone, you gave him a bottle of whiskey, saying, "Here's the cold water."

Every social occasion was based on boozing. It was routine for someone to say, "Where's the bottle, man?" Alcohol was served at every dinner party. Guest rooms were supplied with whiskey. People brought their own bottle to dances. They carried beer to soccer games. After a game, the ground under the bleachers was littered with empty bottles. The only time people stayed away from alcohol was on Sunday when they had to go to church.

The custom at every card party or social event was to "kill the bottle." Everyone knew the rules. When there was only one drink left, someone said, "Let James kill the bottle!" James would pour the last drop into his glass and produce a new bottle. After people played cards and drank for a while, they started looking around at each other to see who hadn't killed the bottle recently. Then someone jumped up and said, "Let me kill that bottle!"

"Hey, man, kill it!"

"We been drinkin' Scotch. Man, you should send for some Johnny Walker."

Men sitting on a porch would call out to a passerby, "We wanna play cards. Come On! You wanna kill the bottle?"

The man would say, "I'll come. I'll be back!"

The names of a number of early prominent Americo-Liberian families were lost when whole families died out from alcoholism. These were not poor people. They had good homes with wood plank floors and corrugated zinc roofs. But they sat around all day staying drunk all the time. Their eyes were red and bulging, their face and hands puffy. There were sores at the corner of their mouth. The final stage of alcoholism was called, "dropsy." A person was not far from the end, if the dent remained when you pressed your finger into their leg or foot.

Over the years, regardless of any outside influence or social change, the Americo-Liberians remained compulsive about their image. My cousin Jimmy, who dressed impeccably, was the epitome of this.

In 1956, he came to live with me in St. Louis, Missouri, when I was at Washington University working on my doctorate. He had so few clothes when he arrived, that every night he carefully washed and pressed his shirt and pants and shined his one pair of shoes. This got on my nerves so I bought him some more shirts. Of course, he wanted French cuffs that "showed." When I got him three sets of cufflinks, he said, "Oh, B.G., this is good!"

Jimmy knew all the styles, including what kind of hat, shoes, and tie went with a suit. Each time he stepped out of my house, he looked like a groom going to pick up his bride. He never wore a pair of shoes that had a speck of dirt on them. He even had his pants starched so the crease stayed when he sat down. One day, while he was pressing a tie, he said, "B.G., how does this look?"

I said, "It looks fine, but I'm not going to wear a tie once and clean and press it like that."

He said, "B.G., we're Liberians. We Dennises have a family history."

"Take me out of that history. I'm not going through all that."

"But B.G., you have to do it. People will talk about us, about our family. You know, appearance means everything. That's what people talk about."

"Let 'em talk!"

After a while, I helped Jimmy buy a used Pontiac. Every day thereafter, he was out cleaning that car. On Saturdays, he did a more thorough job, scrubbing the wheels with a wire brush. After polishing and buffing that car all day till it shined, he'd say, "B.G., want me to do yours for you?"

I said, "No, you just shine yours. I'm afraid someone's going to steal your car — shining like that and parked on the street."

He said, "Oh no, my friend Dugan won't let that happen. No one'll steal my car."

When he cleaned his car, Jimmy wore white pants and polished shoes. Although he stepped back as he used the sponge and buffer, invariably he said when he finished, "Well, my clothes got a little soiled. I'll go change before someone sees me. Then I'll go and pick up Doris."

I said, "Just put your clothes in my laundry bunch."

"Thanks B.G."

Whenever the clean laundry arrived, Jimmy inspected every item, especially the cuffs. Once he once found a small spot inside a pants cuff and told me, "B.G., she didn't do too good a job here."

I said, "Don't bother her about that. No one sees the inside of a pants cuff."

He said, "Well, I'll wear them tonight when it's dark."

The Americo-Liberians remained frozen in time. To maintain their cultural superiority, they preserved a Southern way of life long abandoned in America.

When I returned to Liberia in 1971, it was easy to see why Liberians called Liberia "little America." In Monrovia, local radio stations played popular songs in America. On TV, American programs advertised Western products. Movie theatres showed current films. Bars and restaurants served American food. The police wore the summer uniforms of the New York City Police department. At the Independence Celebrations on July 26th, the Liberian military band played the "Tennessee Waltz." Monrovia was still "party land." A black woman married to an Americo-Liberian told me she stayed slim in Liberia because they went to parties every night and danced till dawn.

In 1973, when my family and I stayed with an Americo-Liberian family in Monrovia, it was like stepping back into the Old South. The front parlor, reserved for guests, had portraits of 19th Century ancestors hanging high on the walls. Lace doilies covered chair armrests.

Each morning, African-Liberian servant children straightened the Southern quilts on the beds. They emptied and washed the night chamber pot. To prepare for supper, they walked to an outdoor market to buy fresh greens. On Saturdays, they cleaned the house; washed clothes in a large black tub in the back yard; did the weekly ironing; and polished the shoes for church.

On Sunday morning, the mistress led family devotions in the parlor, the servant children sitting on the floor. They rarely attended church since they had to prepare the Sunday dinner. After the family ate at the dining room table, the servants ate the leftovers standing in the kitchen or sitting on the back porch.

Each afternoon, the master came home from his government office barking orders, "Gwey! Bring me water! Nora! Fetch my paper!" The girls burst through the swinging door from the kitchen, rushing to comply.

As the master read the paper, he said, "Ophelia, where are my white gloves? Have you washed them?"

As she returned from the bedroom, he chided, "You're so slow. You know I need those gloves for the party meeting tonight."

In a Southern slave ritual, he said, "What do you think I should wear?"

Ophelia led him into his bedroom where they looked over his vast array of suits in the closet. After narrowing the selection to three, Ophelia laid them on the bed, each with coordinating shirt and tie. The master pointed to one and said, "How about this one?"

She said, "Oh, I think your white suit would look much better."

"What's wrong with this one?"

"Oh, they're all fine but the white one goes better for the occasion and you know how good you look in white."

"Are you sure, Ophelia?

"Oh, I'm sure. I just can't describe it but you just look so fine in that suit. I'm telling you the truth, oh."

He said, "Alright." And she hurried to press the suit.

The mistress, arriving an hour later, went straight into the kitchen to see how supper was coming along. That morning, she had screamed at Nora for wetting her bed again. "I'm sending you back! You're not going to school until you wash these sheets!" As Nora washed the sheets, tears ran down her cheeks. The other girls gave her a sympathetic look but could do nothing.

Just as slave loyalty salved the master's conscience, the loyalty and gratitude of servant children vindicated the Americo-Liberians. Several years later, we met up with our hostess. When we asked about the children, she told us, "I had to send Nora back to her village. I'm especially disappointed in Ophelia, although some say she's done well. Instead of finishing high school, she took up with a man in government and has two children by him. I never see or hear from her. I don't even know exactly where she's living. I just don't understand it. I did my best for Ophelia and she just left. Gwey's gone too, now that she's grown. That's what these kids do to you after all you've done for them. I've given up on all of them, although Daniel did well. He put himself through college and graduated from the University of Liberia."

Southern affectation never abated since it symbolized Americo-Liberian superiority. Without the trappings of Americo-Liberianism, there was no elegance, no glory, no fun. In 1972, when I and my family stayed with my cousin Jimmy, his luxurious house in Monrovia was exquisitely furnished and immaculate. His laundry man came every day, even if there wasn't much to wash. As I noticed his well kept grounds, he said, "This grass is imported. It won't grow high so it won't need mowing."

One day, as we were going somewhere, I opened the car door and got in. He called me over and said quietly, "B.G., let me talk to you a little bit. You shouldn't have done that."

I said, "I'm not a magician. I can't get in a car without opening the door."

He said, "That's what we have the chauffeur for. I pay him good money to open the car door and check the seat first to make sure it's clean. After you get in, he closes the door. That's what he does with me and Doris. Then he gets in and drives. When we get home this afternoon, exercise a little patience. Let the chauffeur get out and open the door and let you out. Wait for him to close your door and then let the other people out. That's how he's supposed to serve the passengers. If you bring anything home, he's supposed to carry it into the house. If it's raining this afternoon when we get back, he's supposed to hold the umbrella over the door and escort us to the door one by one. Then he parks the car. Please, for my sake, B. G."

I said, "Jimmy, I'm not sick. If it's not raining hard, I'll just run to the door. It's not that far. Why should I make the chauffeur get out in the rain? It doesn't make sense."

He said, "That's what he's paid for and he's happy to do it. All the chauffeurs do it, not just him. B.G., you've been away too long."

The summer of 1976, when I stayed with my Uncle C.C., he told me, "B.G., remember tomorrow is Sunday. Put your clothes out for pressing or call the girls to look through your things and prepare everything. Are your shoes polished?"

"No."

"Look what you're doin' to me! Shoe polish can't be that expensive."

"I don't polish my shoes every Saturday."

"This isn't America. This is Liberia. We're goin' to church. You have to look good. I'll have Jimmy polish your shoes."

"Jimmy has his own shoes to polish."

"You're a Dennis. You mean you never learned to polish your shoes?"

"I polish my shoes."

"They don't look polished."

"When they get dirty, I polish them."

"B.G., you never go to church without shinin' your shoes, dirty or not. You're goin' to church and there'll be a lotta people there. What will people say of us? What're you gonna wear? Let me check your suit and shirt. You have to look good."

Liberia's formalism and love of show never abated. During the 1960s, government pomp included an entourage of black government vehicles. Tubman, more than anyone, understood the importance of image, using it to please the Americo-Liberians. In 1961, during Queen Elizabeth's visit, he "pulled out all the stops" in a grand display.

Opulence was a signature of Americo-Liberian style that showed they were a civilized people. During slavery, a house was an elusive symbol of success for Negroes. During Liberia's heyday of foreign trade and investment in the 1960s and 70s, the Americo-Liberians put their newfound spoils into lavish material possessions to bolster their image. As masters of conspicuous consumption, they displayed the pinnacle of Americo-Liberian style.

The Executive Mansion was Liberia's crown jewel, along with the new Masonic lodge. It was the seat of power since everything began and ended with the president. Built by the Israeli's in 1964, Tubman spared no expense. As his personal triumph, it displayed the apex of Americo-Liberianism — wealth concentrated in the hands of a few.

An imposing seven-story white building, it stood in stark contrast to the rest of Liberia. As it faced the Atlantic Ocean, it was surrounded by an expansive, well-kept lawn. Inside, there were Italian marble floors and mahogany doors and wall panels. Furnishings included ornate and upholstered European furniture, oil paintings, crystal chandeliers, and brocade draperies.

President Tolbert, who ruled Liberia from 1971-1980, won the support of the masses in his rhetoric of "Higher Heights" and "Mat to Mattress." In 1979, when the Organization of African Unity met in Monrovia, he had an elaborate OAU "village" constructed as a demonstration of what Liberia could do.

In 1973, when I chaperoned fourteen college students during a Summer Study Abroad Trip to Liberia, President Tolbert invited us to meet with him in the mansion. In a tour afterwards, the guide took us to the formal state dining room that had a mirror ceiling and wall of glass facing the ocean. He told us to imagine a formal state dinner with a thousand guests — men in tuxedos and women in African gowns. He described butlers serving large silver platters of shrimp and fish over rice to people seated at tables covered with white linens, fine china, and large floral bouquets.

The presidential trophy room showcased gifts from all over the world, as well as ivory and wood carvings. While we had been waiting to see the president that morning, we saw men carry in two five-foot-high carved ivory tusks as a gift to the president.

Tolbert called Liberia's youth his "precious jewels." Although he was a Baptist minister, he was said to specialize in virgins — a new one every night from Ricks Institute, a Baptist School he sponsored.

Corruption remained the only way to succeed. During the 1970s, people said, "Come on, man. You mean he's been in government four years and hasn't built a house?" Our Americo-Liberian hostess complained about the high prices in the Lebanese stores, saying, "You have to come back, B.G. and help us. Our own people are killin' us. All these foreigners, the Lebanese, the Indians, even the Nigerians and Ghanaians, and all the white people as well, are paying bribes to stay in business. The government's gettin' money for nothin'. You know Abijoudi? He's payin'. The only ones who aren't payin' are the country people — the market women and people sellin' tie-dye. You can't stay in business here without bribing."

African-Liberian government clerks lived on bribes since their salaries were abysmally low. To get anything done, you had to grease someone's palm. Otherwise it was "Go, come." You could wait in a government office all day only to be told that the minister didn't have time to see you.

In 1973, Anita and I wanted to ship some African artifacts and country cloth back to Michigan. Everywhere we went, we met frustration. Here we needed a stamp. There we needed a letter or a form filled out. It was always, "Go, come." When I mentioned this to an African-Liberian friend, he said, "Doc, you gotta dash [bribe]. Have you forgotten?"

That afternoon, as we went back to each office, everything changed the minute I slipped some money into the clerk's hand. It was now, "Yes, Sir!" We got done in an hour.

In 1985, I became reacquainted with J. Cooper. We were close in age and had known each other as teenagers. J.'s father had been in charge of paving Broad Street. He later served as ambassador to the Netherlands, where he died of a heart attack. J.'s mother ran a successful business school in Monrovia and was a scion of Americo-Liberian society. When J. called me from Lansing, Michigan, and visited me in Flint, he displayed that typical Americo-Liberian charm, calling me "Bubba."

He told me how he had fled Liberia with his mother, his young, educated African-Liberian wife, and their two small children. During that first visit, as he shared his struggles and dilemma, it got late. I suggested he spend the night. As a gesture of kindness, I offered him a drink from my newly opened bottle of Johnny Walker Red that Anita gave me each Christmas. The next morning, I was shocked to see it empty.

I helped J. get a teaching job at a small business college that had just opened in Flint, so they moved to Flint. However, J. was lost without his privileged status. Nothing seemed to work out for him. He lost his job after the first semester. The administrators said his performance wasn't adequate. After that, he got a job in Zaire, and I lost touch with him.

A year later, I heard he was back in Lansing, staying with his daughter who was a student at Michigan State. His wife had left him when he became HIV positive in Zaire. Because of mounting medical bills, he returned to Liberia. His mother told me that when he died at Duside Hospital, he only weighed sixty pounds.

In 1995, I visited my cousin Jimmy who was living in Georgia. Once again, he had a luxurious home that he was he was working hard to pay for and maintain.

I said, "Jimmy! What a place you have!"

He said, "Well, B.G., you know I lost everything. But I can't live like an ordinary man."

Liberia was doomed from the start. The sins of the master were inevitably passed on to the slave. Since it implied status, the Americo-Liberians blindly followed the worst of whites. Hypocrisy made them what they imputed to the natives. While they rejected the best of African culture, they could only display the trappings of Western culture. Image was all important. But that's all it was — image. With only a "taste" of Western culture, they imagined the white way without truly understanding it, which made Liberia a caricature of Southern society.

The expression, "All dressed up and no place to go" aptly describes them. Just because they dressed the part, didn't mean they fit the part. They could only imagine themselves superior by comparing themselves to natives even more naïve. Their success and economic growth were empty because they weren't based on productivity. Government bureaucracy was a façade because it was based on nepotism and corruption.

A society and nation of self-delusion cannot stand because it's not based on reality. Instead of combining and incorporating the positive elements of both cultures, the Americo-Liberians rejected the best of African culture and retained the worst of American culture. They emulated a society that had enslaved them — that made them wear rags, eat left-overs, and live in slave huts like pigs.

CHAPTER FOUR: IDENTITY

The Superiority/Inferiority Complex

> Your hair grows so fast, you look like a bushman!
> You've got to part it.
> — My sister Angie during the 1930s

Although I didn't grow up in the village, I am a Mende and Gbande at heart. As the "older" twin I was named after my father, I was a favored child, and I remain a hereditary chief. The two most influential men in my childhood, besides my father, were my maternal grandfather, Morlu, and my maternal uncle, Komah, who were always trying to make a good Gbande out of me.

During the 1930s and 40s, Liberia's sixteen tribes were self-sufficient in-groups that were distinct and divided. Because of colonial arbitrary boundaries, tribes have connections across the border — the Mende, Gola, Kissi, and Vai in Sierra Leone; the Kru and Mano in Ivory Coast; and the Loma, Kpelle, Mandingo, Mano, and Gio in Guinea.

My Mende and Gbande tribes are representative of traditional native values. They were face-to-face, communal societies, where everyone had a place in his family and society based upon a complex kinship system. Family was everything. Everyone wanted a large family so they could have the largest rice farm. Families practiced their religion and solved their problems together.

The tribe's mainstay was equity and sharing. Prestige was based on how much you gave away, not on how much you accumulated. A chief had little more in material goods than the rest of the village. His status derived from his large number of wives and children.

Since tribes were self-sufficient, natives were interdependent. A native never saw himself apart from his tribe or its interests. His goal was to see his family and tribe succeed. While he was a "slave" to his tribe, his tribe was equally a slave to him. Anyone's crisis or problem was everyone's. Natives were irrevocably linked to their tribe and supported by it, whether or not they succeeded.

When I was six, my grandfather Morlu told me the story of the hero buried beneath the rock we were sitting on. During Morlu's childhood, there had been a deadly plague the Gbande called, "kpley–kpley."

People were dying so rapidly, villages could scarcely bury their dead. Everyone was in mourning. The elders said, "We've done something very bad to make

'Ngawongola' (the Gbande word for God) angry with us. A person must be sacrificed to beg Him to forgive and help us. It must be a man of means who willingly offers himself — and he must suffer greatly."

When Harley volunteered, he asked to first visit every Gbande village to assure everyone that his sacrifice was voluntary. His head was shaved and a wreath of leaves placed on it. Everywhere he went, people came out to greet him. At Somalahun, the place of sacrifice, people came to spend the last three days with him. On the third day, his grave was dug and his machete, hunting clothes, and bow and arrow placed inside. A meal of chicken and rice was prepared as well for his journey to the ancestor spirits.

The next morning, Harley said he was ready to go. The people first asked Ngawongola to accept the sacrifice. Harley was shot with four arrows, one for each division of Gbandeland. His eyes were plucked out. Lying on his back in the grave, he said, "Put the dirt in now." His groaning stopped as the grave was filled in. The people gradually stopped dying. From then on, the people of Somalahun paid the taxes for Harley's family and future generations. They fulfilled the government's forced labor in their place.

In traditional society, children were taught the exact skills they needed in adulthood. Boys hunted and fished with their fathers. Girls grew up caring for younger children. By the age of twelve, a girl could cook for the whole family. At every social event and town meeting, children were expected to observe and listen carefully. Afterwards, fathers asked, "What happened at the town meeting today?" Those who answered with insight and understanding were praised.

My Uncle Komah was the best and most fearless hunter in the area. You could smell him coming when he wore his hunting clothes, since he smeared them with animal blood for good luck. When I was eight, he took me with him at dawn to check his traps.

We reached a clearing where the grass was all shredded and the bark torn from the tree trunks. I was at one end looking for clues, when suddenly, from behind the trees, a large bush cow with a torn trap around its neck, snorted and focused on me. I ran to Uncle Komah as fast as I could, the cow right behind. In a split second, he chopped the cow's nose in two with his machete. As it turned to get away, he chopped the hamstrings of its front legs. Its front knees buckled. As blood gushed from its nose, it snorted and struggled to breathe. I knew then why the Gbande say, "If you don't kill a bush cow outright, it will kill you."

Elders passed on the knowledge of the past through the oral tradition. Each of the four clans of Gbandeland had a "great" storyteller respected for his ability to perform, as well as a "grand" storyteller over the entire tribe. On nights of the full moon, teenagers stayed up all night telling stories, boys in one circle and girls in another. Each circle had a few elders who observed and gave advice. The younger children learned by listening.

Storytelling aided memorization, vital to the oral tradition. Each story had to be told in exact detail with the correct voice and gestures. If the storyteller missed a single detail, someone jumped up to correct them. The new storyteller started at the beginning until he made a mistake and someone else jumped up.

Riddles were challenging. One of the older boys said, "One man said to another, 'I'm faster than you are.' The other said, 'Oh, no. I'm faster.' They were walking along when they came to a log bridge. As the first man started across, he slipped but took off all of his clothes before hitting the water. The other man behind him caught his clothes before they hit the water. Tell me, who was faster?" Since the old people knew the answers, they liked to tease the teenagers.

Some riddles were accompanied by a man playing a stringed instrument. When someone was close to guessing the answer, he played fast. If not, he played slow. An elder began by giving a clue to the story. Someone would guess, "It's about a woman...," pling,...pling... "It's about a mother,"...pling, pling, pling! "It's about a head wife," pling.....pling.... "the second wife,"....pling, pling, pling! This went on until the guessing was exhausted. Then another clue was given until the story was complete or the riddle solved.

Each story, legend, or riddle had a moral lesson. My favorites were about Spider, who was always getting into trouble. Spider lived in a village that didn't have enough food. When he heard that the next village had lots of food and the people were sympathetic, he decided to go there. First, he stopped and took out one of his eyes and hid it in a leaf.

Everyone felt sorry for Spider and gave him food. This went on for three days, until a little boy got curious and secretly followed Spider home and saw him put his eye back in. The next day, the boy hid and watched as Spider took out his eye. After Spider left, the boy soaked his eye in hot pepper juice and put it back in the leaf.

When Spider came back and put in his eye, he yelled, "Oh! Oh! What happened to my eye? Isn't this the way it goes?" While Spider yelled in pain, the boy quickly called the villagers. They said, "Spider! Is that what you were doing?" As we laughed, the elders said, "It's not good to cheat."

There were two sessions of formal training — the Poro Society for boys and the Sande Society for girls. Boys were sequestered in the forest for four years. During the first year, they were supplied with food. After they harvested their first rice farm, they were self-sufficient. During that time, they memorized the genealogy of their lineage, clan, and tribe. They were taught common medicines, the laws and regulations of the tribe, and how to meet and treat strangers. They learned which animals, reptiles, insects, and birds were useful and which were dangerous. They memorized everything about trees and grasses and their uses. They honed their hunting and fishing skills. Boys with a certain aptitude were trained by a specialist in that skill.

Learning sessions were determined by teacher availability. Each class began by reciting yesterday's lesson. The final testing in a category took an entire day — the teacher announcing the general topic and the boys reciting everything they knew about it. These tests were accompanied by a musician who rewarded right answers by playing fast. Boys competed to do well in order to bring praise to their village. When students graduated, they had all the rights and privileges of men. They were ready to marry.

Traditional society was couched within a world of superstition where good and bad spirits inhabited anything and everything. The Mende and Gbande lived their religion. The people in Somalahun said the birds sang in the morning to give praise to their Creator. When you asked people how they were, they said, "I thank God I'm well." If they made any plans, they said, "God willing." As people were born, lived, and died, they revolved between the natural and the spirit world. Death was a journey to another community of family members. There, as ancestor spirits, they interceded with the supreme creator of everything.

Families sacrificed to their ancestor spirits to intercede for them. In times of great trouble, the elders and "zoes" (doctors) from each village met for a joint sacrifice. The last person to speak was the oldest who told the ancestor spirits, "We haven't had good crops. Too many of our young women are dying in child-birth. Our children are dying young. We are your children. We must have done something wrong but we don't know what it is. We have prepared this food for you. It is the best we can do. Please beg the great 'Ngawoh' [the Mende word for God] to forgive and spare us."

Zoes specialized in bone setting, diarrhea, lung diseases, sexually transmitted diseases, eye problems, snake bites, bleeding, and injuries from falls. Since the blacksmith was considered powerful in working with iron, he had certain medical knowledge and skills as well.

Death was caused by witches and witchcraft. When I was a boy, an uncle in Somalahun carried in a big log from the forest and the next day, he died. People said the log witched him. When I got malaria, the zoe in Vahun ran around inside the hut as if he was trying to catch something. He told me he caught the sickness and put it in his gown. When I asked him to show it to me, he refused. Later, he took me to the creek to cool me off.

There was a perpetual aura of suspicion. The Mende and Gbande were afraid of being punished by God for their evil deeds, being harmed by evil spirits, and being witched by witches — people controlled by evil spirits. People could unknowingly be witched or lured into witchcraft. They could be cursed with a witch by someone who had a witch. They could be witched by coming into contact with something witched. This aura of fear created a paradox of distrust in a community of trust where everyone relied on family. Group-oriented natives had no concept or need for individual privacy. Anyone who insisted on solitude became suspect since a family member could be witched.

Childbirth was "war." Women gave birth in a sacred place away from the village, attended by older women. Those who died in childbirth were warriors who had given their lives for their people. They were buried privately. No mourning was allowed. The women vented their fury and frustration by rushing though the village beating the thatched roofs with pestles they used for beating rice.

Death brought great wailing in the village. After the body was washed and laid on a burial mat, the family asked if the dead relative owed anyone. Someone might address the dead person by saying, "You know you owe me. I want to be paid back." Or they excused the debt by saying, "You don't have to repay me because you're my relative." Graves interspersed throughout the village reminded the people that their ancestors remained a part of the community.

Every individual was respected and given his say. Although the men generally dominated the town meetings, the women had their say. Leadership was based on age and heredity. In the oral tradition, the elders held the societal values. They were closer to the ancestor spirits who acted as intercessors to God.

Rigid mores and high conformity were necessary to maintain trust. Moral authority resided in masked beings who "punished" those who did wrong. The Poro and Sande schools instilled a fear and respect for these beings. The position of the masked being was hereditary. No one, except the elders and a few zoes, knew who was inside the costume.

Benii is the highest ranking masked being of the Mende. Of the Gbande, it is Landai. As the highest moral authority, they provided a balance of power. When they exposed or rebuked a chief for open or secret wrongdoing, he was helpless, despite his power and influence.

Since trust was vital, chiefs were the epitome of integrity. As a student at the Suehn Baptist Mission, I witnessed this in a Gola chief. We had just gathered for devotions at Mrs. Davis' door, when Chief Panagova arrived with his son and three other men. The minute Mrs. Davis opened the door, he said, "Ma, I fit for see you now. Oh, big, big woman palaver [a man having an affair with another's man's wife]. The man asks plenty money. I want you to help me."

Mrs. Davis said, "Woman palaver? Chief, you have many wives. You're too old for that!"

He said, "You right, Ma. It be me pay the money but it not be me go for the woman. It be my son. I no fit do nothing." He fumbled with his gown and said, "Oh, Ma, I tell you the truth. Let me show you."

She said, "No, no, no, chief! Don't do that!"

"No, Ma. You no believe me. I show you the thing."

"Please, Chief! I'll give you the money!"

As we started giggling, Mrs. Davis yelled, "You all shut up! You don't listen to this! If I hear any more noise, I'm coming over there!" We clamped our lips shut, but our bodies still shook from laughter.

She ran inside the door and came out quickly, saying, "Just go and pay the money."

He said, "Oh Ma, you too good to me, oh. It not be me. It be my son. I want send him for mission to learn something, but he just go for palm wine and women."

From then on, whenever it was time for chores on campus, someone would ask, "Whose turn is it?" and someone would say, "It not be me! It be my son!"

The Mende and Gbande were societies of high agreement and conformity. Although there were few laws, the rigid moral code was strictly enforced.

Lying was a very serious crime. Because it generated distrust, it had the potential to destroy the society from within. Everything in the town meetings was confirmed in the presence of everyone.

As a boy in Vahun, I saw a group of men use "jepe gutio" (short talk). Several of the men had seen a young man do something wrong and he refused to admit it. They wrapped his wrists with a woven cord of palm fiber. A stick was placed between his wrists. As the stick was twisted, the cord tightened. The Mende believe a man can bear pain if he's innocent. If he's guilty, the pain makes him confess. The young man winced with pain and cried out, "Yes! I did it! I did it!" As soon as he confessed, the cord was loosened — but not removed. After he explained why he didn't admit what he had done, and promised to tell the truth, the matter was settled. The men walked away and nothing was ever said about it again. There can be no lingering blame in a society where everyone is interrelated and lives his entire life in one village.

Theft was a serious crime. One day, I was playing with the boys in Vahun when we heard a commotion and ran to see what was going on. We found everyone gathered at the town square. In the center sat two young men from another village. Next to them were two rattan carriers of food.

When the chief arrived, he asked the young men, "Did you eat of the things on the farm until you were satisfied?"

They said, "Yes."

He said, "Then why did you take this food to carry with you? Put them in jail."

Each young man had a three foot log attached to one of his ankles, secured by an iron loop. A small rope tied to each end of the log allowed them to lift the log and hobble around. They stayed in the town hall. Each day, they were brought food and allowed to leave only to go to the bathroom, bathe, or do community work. Their first assignment was to clean the grass from around the town hall. As people passed by, they made a face at them and sucked their teeth.

The following summer, as soon as I got to Vahun, I asked, "What happened to the rogues?"

A man told me, "They live here now. They've built a fine house. When they come in from their rice farm, you can talk to them."

As soon as I saw them, I said excitedly, "Are you the rogues?" They laughed and hugged me. My uncle said, "Don't call them rogues anymore. They're a part of Guma now."

The most serious crime was rape, with the severest penalty. In Somalahun, as an eight-year-old, I was scratching Morlu's back when we saw some boys playing with some girls, which was unusual. When the boys got rough with the girls, Morlu scolded them.

After they left, he paused, putting his fingers together, and said solemnly, "Gongoli, don't ever play with a girl like that. You can't understand now but a man can love and hate a woman at the same time. He can force her to do something bad she doesn't want. I'll show you a place where this act of love and hate was punished."

At a small clearing near the village, he told me, "A young woman named Korpoh was washing clothes by herself in the women's area of the creek. When the sun was directly above, a young man grabbed her and took her into the bush and did something very bad to her. She ran into the village, naked and screaming, her arms up in terror. As the women ran to her, she wept and said, 'Kwaoifi did this to me.' The men blew the village horn and beat the drums summoning everyone. Kwaoifi was quickly caught. When Korpoh pointed to him and said, 'He did it,' his father got so angry he had to be restrained. The people said, 'Let Kwaoifi talk.' Kwaoifi said, 'I did it, but I'm so very sorry. I want it finished. I don't want to live out this day.'

"The punishment was being burned alive. We are standing where the men piled up the firewood first brought by Kwaoifi's family. The men soaked the wood pile with palm oil. After Kwaoifi lay on it, they poured palm oil over his naked body. They quickly built a frame of sticks over him. Kwaoifi's parents walked up and lit the wood with a small torch."

In varying degrees over time, natives were gradually impacted by the Americo-Liberians as well as Negro and white foreigners. Their wide range of response depended on the level of contact and control. Natives weren't slaves but neither were they free.

Tribes in the upriver and coastal areas were in closer contact with Monrovia, the Americo-Liberian seat of power. Cultural racism had a greater initial impact on them since they were directly controlled and manipulated by the Americo-Liberians. By becoming civilized, they had some limited access to Americo-Liberian culture. The Bassa served as cooks and laundrymen for the Americo-Liberians. Before the Freeport was constructed, the Kru served as dock workers, bringing in the ship's cargo in their canoes. The few natives from the Western Province that were deeply affected at that time were servant children and Frontier Force soldiers.

Americo-Liberians and natives were essentially separate groups — geographically and socially. Regardless of contact, they lived separate lives, each with greater loyalty to their own cultural group. While upriver and coastal natives were in close contact with the Americo-Liberians, they knew manipulative benevolence didn't mean acceptance. Although they lived amongst the Americo-Liberians and adopted the new culture, they kept their traditional ways and remained a strong language group.

Natives in the interior had the greatest resistance. The least affected were the isolationist tribes in central and eastern Liberia that lived in enclaves in the mountainous forest. Belle territory in central Liberia included the headquarters of the Frontier Force with its notorious Belle Yallah prison. However, the Belle were so secretive, there were no paths to their villages. They walked in the creeks.

Americo-Liberian influence was moot in the interior since tribes were a vast majority with a strong culture. Tribal identity and values were intact. Natives looked to each other for economic support and social comfort. Tribal culture was more appealing. Monrovia was a curiosity more than anything else. The Americo-Liberians lived in shacks with leaky zinc roofs. Streets were unpaved. People drank rain water.

Every native was claimed by his tribe, regardless of his refinement or education. I was a "Mende" among Mendes, a "Gbande" among Gbandes. Because of my advantages and education, I was regarded as "wingee" (civilized), but I was simply called "Gongoli."

Since natives in the interior posed no significant threat, they were exposed to minimal change. Those in the Western Province hardly knew what "government" meant, except that they had to pay taxes two or three times a year. When a district commissioner made a rare visit to a Gbande village, the people were curious and surprised to see he wasn't white.

The Mende and Gbande heard about the Americo-Liberians through rumors of Frontier Force soldiers who came back to live among their people. Because of their exposure, these soldiers were considered successful. To cement their status, they talked about Monrovia as if it was a far away country. They said natives there disappeared and were never found because the Americo-Liberians ate them or used them for medicine. When a native from the Western Province happened to see an upriver Americo-Liberian, he looked for what he had heard about — stained, rotten teeth and patched clothing.

The Mende and Gbande felt sorry for the Americo-Liberians because they didn't know how to live. When a soldier said they only bathed once a week, a Mende woman said, "Don't they have any water?"

The soldier said, "Oh, they have lots of water, but that's the way they are."

She said, "Maybe since they live near the coast, salt gets in the water and they can't bathe."

Natives distrusted the Americo-Liberians in a mixture of indifference, curiosity, negative ideas, and fear. They had no respect for "foreign rulers" who treated them harshly, made them pay taxes, and gave them no reward for their labor. They were secretive of their culture, as if to say, "You will know us but not completely. We will have access to your experience but you'll never have access to ours."

Soldiers left the Frontier Force. Servant children were in a constant state of flux. The majority of them were primarily oriented to their tribe, regardless of how far away or how often they visited home. Their goal was to return home and do something for their people. Only a very small percentage of these children stayed in one household throughout their childhood or remained in Monrovia when they grew up.

While natives in the Western Province admired the different culture and wanted to acquire it, there was nothing about the Americo-Liberians they wanted to emulate. Although the Americo-Liberians had a new way of doing things, they couldn't perform. They were inept and lazy. They were serious flaws in their appearance and behavior. Natives had no respect for those who didn't work. The inadequacy of the Americo-Liberians was confirmed by the fact that natives did all the work.

Amongst themselves, natives said, "The Americo-Liberians are evil, stupid, and cruel. They're not civilized as they appear to be. They can't be trusted." In the intimacy of the master/servant relationship, servant children were well aware of Americo-Liberian inconsistencies. They knew the Americo-Liberians better than the Americo-Liberians knew them.

Natives distinguished between the Americo-Liberians. They particularly rejected the upriver Americo-Liberians since they were so poor. They said, "Those Congo people are wearing rags! Clothes like that must have lots of lice." They said, "They can't do anything and they're lazy. They look so hungry, the wind could blow them over. They're dirty. Even birds bathe once a day. They should 'take bath' twice a day like we do."

Because of the brutality of the Americo-Liberians, natives in Americo-Liberian areas were afraid to be out after dark. They were constantly intimidated and disparaged, ridiculed for anything and everything. They had genuine respect only for those Americo-Liberians who treated them nicely. The others, they respected only out of fear. They lived in terror of the Congos, saying amongst themselves,

"That man is a pure Congo man. He's bad." They warned each other, "That's a cruel man. Don't go near his yard at night 'cause he always has a knife or gun. He's too bad. The way he looks and the way he talks! I fear him plenty, oh."

They said, "White people must have made them demons. They don't behave like human beings. They don't reciprocate our kindness." Natives had a saying, "No matter how bright the chicken's eye is shining, he's going to be killed just the same," which meant, "No matter how good a native looked, Americo-Liberians would treat him just as bad."

Natives outwardly complied, coping as best they could. They wore a mask of deception when they said, "Yes, Ma'am" or "Yes, sir." Because of their tribal integrity, they were frustrated that they could never respond truthfully or sincerely.

As a teenager, I traveled on the Cooper boat with a Mende man named Alieu. At the dock at White Plains, we were sitting in the back of the boat when Mr. Mars got on and sat in front. As a leading Americo-Liberian from Congo Town, Mars was always dressed in a black woolen suit with a white shirt and suspenders.

When he took of his suit coat, everyone saw his underwear sticking out of the split seam in the back of his pants. People stared and whispered, but no one said anything. I started to get up to say something when Alieu put his hand on my thigh, and whispered, "You're just a little boy. Let the others tell him." He watched me carefully until the boat landed at Waterside and Mars put his suit coat back on.

When we visited Brima Manju in Monrovia, Alieu told everyone there, "Mars' trousers were completely torn in the back. This boy's been in that white people's country so long, he doesn't have common sense. Everything comes out of his mouth. The whole way into Monrovia I was nervous because his eyes were fixed on Mars' butt. Thank God, I stopped him from saying anything."

I said, "I was just going to whisper in his ear."

Another Mende lectured me, "Don't tell a big person anything. Let it go."

Americo-Liberian dominance gradually made natives dependent. Those living in Americo-Liberian areas were forced to ally themselves with an Americo-Liberian family, who called them, "My boy," or "My girl." They were only valued for what family they belonged to and what they could do for them.

For those natives directly affected, cultural racism had the same impact as racism. Before World War II, the Americo-Liberians ruled in a closed society. Monrovia's population of twenty thousand was stable with only a small native in-migration. It included Vai Town, Kru Town, and Bassa Town with two to three thousand natives each.

Americo-Liberian policies and behavior affected the pride natives had in themselves. Natives who were secure in their traditional culture were gradually made socially and culturally insecure. Since the Americo-Liberians had all the power and authority, natives were helpless to change things. Despite individual differences, the Americo-Liberians were uniform in their cultural racism. Although natives knew the Americo-Liberians were self-deluded, it didn't dissipate the effect of their negative treatment. They came to see themselves through the eyes of the Americo-Liberians.

As a boy, I was at a party at the Cooper house, when over the din of talk and laughter, we heard the Frontier Force band marching down the street. Everyone rushed onto the second floor porch.

The band was coming from the barracks on the outskirts of town and was headed for Broad Street. Ten men marched, wearing khaki shorts, a short-sleeved khaki shirt, and an army overseas cap. A few wore shoes. As they played trumpets, flutes, drums, a tuba, and a baritone, a long line of children followed behind, marching, singing, and clapping.

As they played, they leaned forward and then back, to the right and to the left, to the beat of the music. People clapped at intervals as they sang their signature tune, "Oh Yah, Oh Yah,... Baboo Jon Soljah,... Baboo Jon Soljah,.... Now Baboo Jon Soljah....He too 'wauh wauh.' (Baboon is happy to join soldier, but sad, he too ugly.) "Oh yah," is a Liberian expression of joy or sorrow. In this song, it's both. Although the song was sung in jest, as a classic example of self-hatred it had a ring of truth.

In Americo-Liberian areas, natives conformed so the "superior" would like them and approve of them. In a love/hate relationship, despite their treatment, they looked up to the Americo-Liberians. In resignation, they acquiesced. In subservience, they ingratiated. Whenever they sought to talk with an Americo-Liberian, they brought a gift of chicken or rice. Hat-in-hand, they begged, "Please take my child to learn your ways."

Westernized natives ranged from the barely refined who spoke a raw Liberian English, to the refined who were literate and spoke Liberian English, and finally, to the educated with an eighth grade or high school education. A rare few had a college education. They served as middlemen — their allegiance evenly divided between the Americo-Liberians and their tribal people. Since they more culturally resembled the Americo-Liberians, they were somewhat accepted by them. Their opinion had weight because of their ties to their tribal people. The Americo-Liberians depended on them to garner the cooperation of natives in the interior.

If a servant child gave a good report to his people back home, this encouraged other parents in the village to send their children. Servants already working in the household, praised the new recruits to the host family. They told the new recruits, "Never sit down. Learn fast."

On cash crop farms, if a native who wanted to see the "big man," he had to come through those the big man already knew. Workers commended a new prospect, saying, "That boy's a good worker. He's nice and puts his whole mind into his work."

Natives seeking employment at Firestone went to a fellow tribesman working there. He took them to the headman, who in turn, took them to the overseer who hired them.

As natives envied Americo-Liberian status and aspired to it, they came to identify with their role models. They adopted Americo-Liberian ways to prove themselves worthy in their eyes. They thought and behaved like them to be accepted and have self-esteem and respectability within their culture. They assumed status by association, saying, "I'm Kwii" (Western) or "I'm Congo."

A Bassa man named Sam Gibson had a truck route between Monrovia and Kakata. As the truck was loaded, he ushered two or three Americo-Liberians to sit in the cab with him. He directed natives to sit on benches in back. Natives had to pay up front. The Americo-Liberians paid when they got off.

Long term servant children closely observed and rigidly imitated the Americo-Liberians in order to succeed. They did well in school and were more grateful and dutiful than the Americo-Liberian children in the family. They took the family name and stopped speaking their tribal language. Sometimes it was years before they visited home. They passed for "Americo-Liberian."

I knew a Kpelle boy named Yakpawulo King, who was brought up by President C.D.B. King and his family on their farm. When they sent him to Booker T. Washington Institute in Kakata, they told the missionaries he was "their boy." Since BWI was near the King farm, Mrs. King had the driver walk to the campus from the road to bring Yakpawulo back so he could get the things they brought him.

One day I asked him, "Do you ever visit your people?"

He said, "I have no people now. My people gave me to President and Mrs. King. They reared me and brought me to this school. All the missionaries know how they care for me."

At the Suehn Baptist Mission, the Negro missionaries chose native students to be their personal attendants. Moima was a long time student who became Mrs. Davis' head attendant. She instructed the other servant girls and they looked up to her. One day, Moima's Loma mother arrived on campus with the usual gift to the mission, two chickens and a small bag of rice. She looked tired. We all knew she had been up at dawn working on the rice farm and had walked a long way.

One of the students went and got Moima. When she arrived, she took one look at her mother and said in English, "I don't know this woman. She's not my mother." As Moima glared, her mother looked confused. When one of the Loma boys translated what Moima said, the mother stood there, tears running down her cheeks.

Western influence, in a white and Americo-Liberian context, made natives culturally marginal. While they doubted the Western culture, they knew it had status in a broader context. As they acculturated to Americo-Liberian and Western ways, they came to doubt themselves and their culture. In order to fit into the new culture and be accepted by the Americo-Liberians, they had to become something they weren't. Even then, their "inferiority" remained, just as in race, because only in very rare cases, can a person leave his people and culture completely behind.

During and after World War II, with the construction of the Freeport, there was a much larger migration of natives into Monrovia. Although tribal values were reinforced in the tribal enclaves, they were out of place in a Western, urban area. Natives living in Monrovia served as entry points. As relatives moved in with them, tribal rights and obligations worked against their success as individuals in a modern economy. They compensated for this by exploiting rural relatives, demanding bags of rice and other foodstuffs. As middlemen, they now allied themselves with whichever group suited their purpose at the time. They leaned more towards the Americo-Liberians, who "accepted" them since they served their purposes. They alienated tribal relatives back home, who loved them unconditionally.

From the 1950s onward, modernization led to urbanization as natives migrated as well to the foreign concessions and other towns. Villages were gradually decimated, leaving only the two most dependent groups — the old and the very young. With the loss of manpower in the rural areas, rice production decreased. Traditional skills that fostered self-reliance were lost.

The influence of Westernization gradually altered every aspect of traditional society. Social control was no longer rigid. The arrival of Western education in mission schools in the Western Province meant that young people had more options. Westernized and Christianized natives "lost" their tribal names and thus their identity. The young no longer depended on the old as the source of everything they needed to know. Since the West focused on the future, the tribe's retention of the past became moot. Islam and Christianity challenged traditional animism.

According to census reports, from the 1970s to the 1980s, Liberia's rural population went from 71 to 63 percent — her urban population from 29 to 39 percent. With such social change, Westernization came to affect every African-Liberian in some way or another — whether they lived in Monrovia, the foreign concessions, or in their village upcountry.

Westernized African-Liberians lived in two worlds that could never be reconciled. Western values were at odds with tribal values. Modern materialism inevitably generated inequity which clashed with the material equity of village life. There's a difference in emphasis between developed and underdeveloped peoples.

Westerners prefer things over people. Traditional peoples, as a rule, prefer people over things. Tribes were group-oriented. The individual succeeded to benefit the group. In contrast, the modern Western world is based on rugged individualism. Individuals compete to acquire personal wealth.

Literacy challenged the memorization of the oral tradition. Instead of continuity in training, Western education shows us how to think and find resources. It's analytical, encouraging us to explore and challenge accepted ideas.

Western educated African-Liberians became more oriented to the Americo-Liberians than their tribal people. An educated Loma, who was reared by a wealthy Americo-Liberian family in Monrovia during the 1950s, told me, "They didn't treat me any different. The mistress changed her car every two years and gave me her old one. I was well educated. Other servants did the house work. Now she relies on me more than she relies on her own children."

During the 1950s, 60s, and 70s, educated African-Liberians became socially marginal. Because of Americo-Liberian rigidity, their inclusion into Americo-Liberian society was superficial and restricted. At the same time, their success as individuals, which included urban living and good housing, meant they were no longer content with village life. They were marginal men — outsiders in both traditional and modern culture. In addition to traditional tribalism, there emerged a *modern tribalism* based on the distinction and disparity between Westernized and traditional African-Liberians.

Despite their educational success, educated African-Liberians were insecure in their loss of self and their social and cultural marginality. They were classic examples of the insecure personality. My friend, Gus, a Vai graduate student at Michigan State, had worked in the Executive Mansion as a secretary. Due to his ties to the Americo-Liberian circle of power, he was awarded an overseas scholarship. While Gus was successful academically, he was insecure and deeply sensitive. Although he wanted to succeed and be accepted in every setting, his point of reference was the Americo-Liberians.

I co-signed for a car for Gus. One morning when it was sleeting in Lansing, he called me and said, "Ben, I'm in trouble." When I got there, I found him standing by his car by the side of Kalamazoo Street, his nose running from the cold.

I said, "Gus, what happened? Did someone hit you or push you off the road?"

He said, "I was going slow when a little girl passed me like I was standing still — like I was a small boy! When I speeded up to get a good look at her, I found myself in this mess."

Gus could be incredibly charming in the right social situation. However, most of the time, he mimicked Americo-Liberian bravado, even while he ridiculed it. Gus liked to pick on Nigerian students. He described a dynamic Nigerian doctoral student by saying, "He's ugly like ape but he has good mind."

Gus' particular target was Sumo, a Loma graduate student. One day, he told Sumo, "Look at your pointed head! You look like 'Yangbai!'[a masked being] Why don't you go home and make palm wine? If you fall, your head will stick in the branches and hold you up until someone comes to help."

I said, "Gus, leave Sumo alone. He has a paper due in two days and I'm going to help him."

Gus said, "You're wasting your time, Ben. Sumo says the mole on his head is soft and he can't think. He can't take it, Ben! If you help him, you're gonna kill him because his brain will bust! When that happens, I'll tell everyone it was your fault. You gave him too much book and he couldn't take it."

Sumo said, "This half-Vai, half-Bassa has too much mouth!"

Gus said, "I may be half and half but look at my grades. If it wasn't for Ben, you'd be buried because you're academically dead! Ben's only prolonging your agony."

Everywhere he was, Gus created a stir with his endless criticism and raucous laughter as he pointed out inconsistencies in others. He didn't even spare white graduate students. One day, Gus and I were eating with Clint, a sociology graduate student from South Dakota. Clint said, "When you live in a farm area, you see all kinds of things. Our neighbor's goat always came and nibbled the flowers in our yard and the vegetables in our garden. When the goat had two kids, the problem got worse. My father told the neighbor, 'If your goats do this anymore, I'm gonna kill 'em.'

"The neighbor said, 'You'll have to deal with me before you do that.'

"My father said, 'I'll deal with you right now!' and he slugged him. He beat him soft! You can bet those goats never came back in our yard!"

Gus said, "Ha! Ha! Ha! You mean your father beat someone up about a goat eating leaves? Was your father an educated man? Ha! Ha! Ha! Your parents must be barbarians! Our goats in Africa eat our cassava leaves. The chickens do too. But we don't fight about that! You live in South Dakota? I don't wanna go there! Ha! Ha! Ha!"

By this time, everyone in the lounge was staring at us. Gus was oblivious. He went on, "You know, Clint? We've got a parable in Africa, 'A leopard never changes its spots.' Even when you get your degree, I bet you'll be just like your father — beating someone up because his goat ate your leaves! Ha! Ha! Ha!"

I said, "Gus, that's enough, please. Maybe the neighbor thought Clint's father was a small boy like they do in Liberia. It's the same thing."

Gus said, "Ben, you like to dress things up. Let's call it like it is."

I said, "That's the way it is, Gus."

Clint sat there watching us, his face beet red. From then on, he avoided Gus. Even then, whenever Gus came across him on campus, he told those with him,

"Here comes Clint! His father slugged a man because a goat ate his leaves! You gotta watch him. He may be the same way! Ha! Ha! Ha!"

Gus and I were waiting in front of Burke Hall, when a group of students dressed in overalls came walking by carrying some containers. Gus was curious so he said, "Are you going to class dressed like that? What are you carrying?"

One of them said, "These packages are part of our agricultural project."

Gus said, "What are you getting your degree in?"

The student said, "Packaging."

Gus said, "What do you mean by that?"

The student said, "There's a technique in cutting and packaging meat that preserves it. We're learning how to package meat in such a way that it keeps fresh even when it's shipped from one end of the country to the other — even to Canada or Central or South America."

Gus said, "Let me get this straight. You're getting a degree to learn how to cut and pack meat?"

He shook his head slowly and said to me, "Ben, this is a strange university. The people in my village are one hundred per cent illiterate. And they've been cutting up and butchering elephants before my great grandfather was born. And they're still doing it! I grew up on that meat."

He told the graduate students, "You're getting a degree to cut and package meat? Ha! Ha! Ha! Can you believe that, Ben? This is a s-t-r-a-n-g-e country, Ben, I tell you. That's a lotta money to get an academic degree just to cut and pack meat! If I didn't have just a year and a half to go, I wouldn't even get a degree from this university! If I told anyone in Liberia that people in America can get a college degree from my school to cut and pack meat, they'd send me to Piso Island where they keep the crazy people!"

The students, at first puzzled by Gus' diatribe, were now red-faced. Gus went on to demonstrate, saying, "Watch me. For a chicken, we just hold the head and swing. After that, we put it in hot water and take the feathers off and cut it up and eat it."

I said, "Gus, please. Leave them alone."

Gus said, "But that's the truth, Ben! None of us would come here to get a degree to cut and pack meat! Except these people. Something must be wrong with them! If our lives depended on getting such a degree, we'd all be dead!"

During the 1960s and 70s, as tribal values were lost, African-Liberians in Monrovia became more culturally marginal. Tribal languages that had no value in the broader society were forgotten. Today, urban Kpelle can no longer speak "deep" Kpelle. I can no longer understand or speak "deep" Mende.

In 1972, I returned to Vahun after twenty-five years away. I had with me Anita and our two-year-old son, Ben. From Monrovia, we took a pickup truck to the end of the motor road in Yanduhun in Lofa County. As we walked through the high forest over the Cambui Mountain, Anita was carried in a hammock. Ben Jr. was carried on a man's shoulders just as I had been as a boy.

Word had gone ahead that I was returning. As we approached Vahun, I heard the same gunfire and shouting I had heard when my father returned. Much had changed, yet much remained the same. Vahun was a small village of about fifty huts, only now it was teeming with Mende relatives from Sierra Leone.

As we entered the outskirts, we were swept up in the momentum of the crowd to the center of town. The grave "house" of Chief Ngombu Tejjeh was a half-walled concrete structure with a zinc roof. As I stepped inside, I was painfully aware that my parents and my brother Joe were no longer living. After so many years away, I was unprepared for my role of elder. I struggled to keep my composure as my older brother Patrick guided me in pouring whiskey over my grandfather's grave as a sign of respect. When I looked up and saw the crowd watching in reverent silence, I broke down and wept.

Relatives who thought I had died rejoiced to see me. The old women, my "wives," surrounded me in toothless laughter, hugging me. The men played the drums. The women played their "sassas" (gourds covered with a stringed net of buttons). They paraded in matching lappa skirts and bubba blouses.

The Mende say, "You don't talk to a stranger on an empty stomach." A cow was slaughtered for the festivities. Anita and I were shown to a mud block house at the other end of town.

The next morning began three days of Mende custom. In a town meeting the first day, the people shared the news since I had left. My brothers kept saying, "You forgot something. Let me explain," which started a long discussion. I heard about every relative who had died and who brought what gift to his funeral. Each report was confirmed in the presence of everyone as my brother Patrick prompted, "Is this true?"

On the second day, Anita was accepted into the tribe. The Mende say, "We don't look at the color of a person's skin, but at their heart." She was renamed "Baindu," which means, "Gracious one." As a sign of acceptance, she was given her own handmade stool that women use in the hut.

On the third day, Benii came out to honor me. The village fell silent at the sound of drums in the forest, the women and children sequestered in the huts. An acrobatic attendant announced Benii's arrival by first dancing around each hut.

Benii was surrounded by attendants waving scarves. As he moved in his characteristic way, his raffia dress brushed the ground. He went to the grave house to pay honor to Chief Ngombu Tejjeh. When he came out and bowed before me, I was overwhelmed by the same honor given my father. I was home. This was my village. These were my people.

Social harmony was vital since the tribe was self-sufficient. Mediation was available to every member of every family and clan. The pressure to reconcile was tremendous. People could be ostracized for refusing to reconcile, although I never saw it done.

In the summer in 1976, I traveled with a companion through Mende territory in Sierra Leone. As soon as we arrived in Kailahun, I could sense the tension. Someone told us there was a great conflict between the two oldest sons of the paramount chief. The chief's oldest son had taken over his father's responsibilities since he was quite old. The younger son, educated in Freetown as a doctor, hadn't shown his older brother the proper respect. It was a serious rift. The younger son had arrived that day.

The next morning, the town was abuzz. People gathered at the village meeting house. Sitting before them was the older brother in a large, traditional chair befitting a paramount chief. The night before, the younger brother arrived in a shirt and tie. Now he was barefoot and wearing a traditional Mende shirt, as he slowly walked to the meeting house.

It was midday and hot. Even the children were quiet. The younger brother walked over and lay prostrate before his older brother, his face to the ground. Putting his hands on his brother's feet, he said, "I beg you." The older brother never looked at him. Instead, he scanned the faces of the crowd that was counting on him.

After a long pause of silence, he tapped his younger brother's shoulder as a sign to get up. The younger brother slowly rose to his knees and looked up. For the first time, the two brothers looked into each other's face. Everyone was frozen in silence. After a moment that seemed like an eternity, the older brother tapped his younger brother's shoulder again, pulled him up, and the two embraced weeping.

The village exploded in relief and rejoicing. Everyone hurried to prepare a feast. The men played the drums. The women sang.

In 1983–84, when I spent my sabbatical in Vahun, my greatest joy was when Ben, now sixteen years old, asked to join the last three weeks of the Poro in session. My mind went back to when "Kosipoi" had kidnapped me in Somalahun when I was twelve.

I knew Poro would take him into the heart and soul of Mende life. It was more than training. It was the essence of male identity, bonding, and shared responsibility so well developed in Mende and Gbande culture. Poro men of the same class were blood brothers. They would do anything for each other. When I told my brothers, Patrick and Brima, about Ben, they hugged me and beat on my back in joy. Patrick volunteered to be his sponsor.

At Ben's graduation in Gbongoma, I went with the elders to hear the teachers report on the session. Addressing the graduates, I said, "You are now men accountable for your actions. You know your responsibilities. The tribe is counting on you."

Landai, the masked being of Poro, "swallows" the boys as they enter training and "excretes" them when they graduate. As a result, boys come out with a pattern of scars on their back representing Landai's teeth marks. Their covering of white chalk represents his feces.

As Landai approached, the village was quiet. Women and children were sequestered in the huts with the wooden shutters closed. As Landai marched around the village, his raffia skirt brushing the ground and his machete sticking out in front, the graduates followed behind.

The men rushed to greet him. The women and children watched from afar. Landai sat down in the village square so the parents and elders could redeem their sons with gifts of rice, goats, country cloth, and money. Through an interpreter, Landai said, "Here are your children. They have been reborn." My brothers and I looked on in pride as Ben was honored by being allowed to sit on Landai's raffia dress.

At the reception at our home in Vahun, the women sang, "Father you did well to let your son go to Poro. It made us all feel good. He's a real Ngombu Tejjeh. Nothing of his people must be hidden from him. He's a real Poro man."

Today, racism has come full circle in the Liberian Diaspora in America. Educated African-Liberians no longer belong in Liberia nor do they belong in America. An educated Loma told me, "A white Episcopal priest talked to me on the phone the other day. He spoke such good Loma. It's been twenty-four years since he served in Liberia. My own kids can't even speak Loma. They call themselves 'Liberian' to distinguish themselves from blacks, but they know nothing about Liberia."

For African-Liberians, the Liberian community is their only community. They aren't accepted by whites nor do they feel comfortable with lower-class blacks. They don't feel as though they belong in black churches, nor are they welcomed or included in white churches. Since they can't count on their children, they worry about getting old. Their perpetual dream is to go home, where they assume they'll have prestige and honor and play a leadership role among their people.

Westernized African-Liberians never fulfilled their longing for status — just like the Americo-Liberians. They have no genuine status except among their peers, their Western cultural group. Whites see them as blacks. The Americo-Liberians see them through the lens of cultural racism. Educated African-Liberians are exceptions to the rule that still applies to traditional African-Liberians.

Educated African-Liberians remain a paradox of confidence and insecurity. As students in America and Europe during the 1960s and 70s, they never achieved genuine status as Africans and blacks. They were seen as a novelty. Although their new skills and capabilities made them confident, they remained powerless under Americo-Liberian domination and rigidity. Now free of such domination, they remain insecure in Liberia's economic plight and their social and cultural marginality. They are in as much limbo as the Americo-Liberians were. They no longer belong with their traditional people. Nor are they accepted by whites or fully accepted by Americo-Liberians.

Social change affected traditional African-Liberians for the worse. Their way of life has been weakened by modernization and destroyed by warfare. In addition to tribalism, they are rejected in *modern tribalism*. They have genuine status only in their own little world — their longing for status fulfilled only amongst themselves.

Imitation of Supremacy

> The war was too bad. We were running, running. We would hear gunfire ... pu pu pu pu pu. Then we'd run. Then we'd hear gunfire again ...pu pu pu pu...and run again. When soldiers come to the house, they look for young girls, so I hid my youngest daughter under the bed. If they found only one or two girls, five men raped one girl.
>
> — A Loma woman talking about Liberia's Civil War

During the 1930s and early 40s, tribes in the Western Province didn't know much about tribes on the coast and vice versa. Tribes in the Western Province resented the Bassa on the coast for their subservience to the Americo-Liberians. Coastal tribes equally resented tribes in the interior as uncivilized warring peoples. If a Bassa on the coast saw a Loma from the Western Province wearing shoes, he said, "Zamba na mae," which means, "Chief Zamba is dead." If Zamba were alive, a Loma man would never be down on the coast where he could get shoes.

The isolationist tribes of central and eastern Liberia, were the most suspicious of foreign missionary education. As a result, they lagged behind tribes in the Western Province. There were many rumors about their area including tales of unusual animal skulls being found there.

Tribes distrusted and looked down on each other. Although natives of different tribes cooked the same kinds of foods, they called their dishes by different names and ridiculed each other's cooking. The Mende and Gbande said the Krahn were cannibalistic. They called the Loma "hard skin" (rough) because so many of them served in the Frontier Force. Although the Belle were an adjacent tribe, the Gbande considered them mysterious because they were secretive. While the Belle spoke perfect Gbande and Loma, the Gbande never learned Belle.

When I was eight, Uncle Komah took me on a far hunting trip. We left at 3 a.m. By dawn, I was tired. We arrived at a Belle village just as the people were leaving for their rice farms. I was thirsty so I asked a young girl walking by for a drink. She handed me a drinking gourd of water from her bucket. As I reached for it, Uncle Komah walked over, grabbed the gourd, put it back in the bucket, and ordered the girl to leave. He told me, "It's better to drink running water from a creek we'll soon reach. These are a dirty people. Even their water is dirty."

I said, "The water was clean! I saw it."

He said, "They're spoiling you in that other country. You don't have any sense because you don't know our ways."

As a common formidable enemy, the Americo-Liberians diffused tribalism. No single tribe dominated. Tribes shared traditional values. The Gbande, Mende, Belle, Vai, Loma, and Kissi all had Poro and Sande schools.

In the Western Province, tribes that shared boundaries spoke each other's languages. A powerful chief of one tribe married women from an adjacent tribe, which was the case in my family. Adjacent tribes competed in a cooperative way as they maintained paths and built bridges in shared areas. The Mende came to the Kissi for help in planting rice since they were skilled in it. The Kissi bought country cloth from the Mende and Gbande because of their designs.

As a boy, I admired Yekeh, a Gbande soldier from Somalahun. The people loved him so much. Yekeh was tall and handsome. He looked distinguished in his uniform. Since he had lived in Monrovia, he was somewhat sophisticated.

Whenever he visited Somalahun, there was a feast. He always brought a hamper of chickens and a few goats he had commandeered from another tribe. As he arrived, he called out, "You all come! Let the boys kill and clean these chickens! Tell the women to make goat soup! Bring palm wine. Let's drink together."

I once asked him, "Where'd you get all this from?"

He said, "The Belle people. There are so few of them, they've got more chickens than they can eat. You people in Somalahun are many. You need these chickens."

I said, "Maybe they ran away when they saw you coming."

He said, "Little wingee (civilized person), you like to talk complicated things. How do you know about the Belle people? They don't even have trails to their villages because they don't want people to know where they are."

The Frontier Force was a classic example of Americo-Liberian conditioning. Barely refined soldiers were easily manipulated to do the dirty work. They completely submitted to Americo-Liberian authority, assuming they were superior and thus right. Their eagerness for status made them vulnerable. Those who followed orders well were rewarded with a higher rank. Their compliance allowed soldiers to assume status by association with the Americo-Liberians.

They were the ideal soldier. They followed orders unquestioningly. Despite risk or danger, they never hesitated. They would have marched into hell itself if ordered to do so. Their determination to carry out any order was expressed in the classic phrase, "Order be order."

When they arrested a native, they grabbed him harshly, saying, "Let's go right now!" If it was an Americo-Liberian, they pointed their rifles and said, "Excuse, Boss. Boss man, I come for you. It be government send me, so let's go."

If the man said, "I have to do something first before I go," they grabbed him by the necktie and said, "Who you talkin' to? Let's go. You no go talk, Boss man. Order be order. We go now."

They were notorious for their brutality and lack of discipline. There was never any disciplinary action or court martial. In their raw power, soldiers were ruthless. They spared no punches. Even the upriver Americo-Liberians were afraid of them.

In the *cycle of racism*, the soldiers replicated the cruelty of their Americo-Liberian masters. At times, they treated natives of other tribes even worse than the Americo-Liberians. In the Western Province, natives were so terrified of the Frontier Force, they ran for their lives whenever they saw someone in khaki.

When soldiers entered the village of another tribe, they said, "Bring palm wine! Bring chickens! Bring rice!" Sometimes they demanded their laundry done, the guest house swept, or girls to sleep with. If natives knew soldiers were approaching, the village was deserted when they arrived. Only when the soldiers were their tribesmen, did people come out. The headman took the brunt of the soldiers' brutality. Many times, as he approached the soldiers saying, "What can we do for you?" they beat him as they made their demands.

As a boy, I saw a Gbande headman knocked down, kicked, and hit many times because there was no cooked food ready for the soldiers. Although he was a large man fully capable of defending himself, he refrained to avoid calling down the wrath of the Frontier Force upon his village, and to keep the district commissioner from imposing a large fine.

Refined natives appointed to collect taxes in the interior, were in a "no man's land." Although they served the Americo-Liberians, they weren't accepted by them. Nor were they content to be "native." They got their pay by overcharging taxes. Some were ruthless and exacting. The Gbande nicknamed one of them, "hard skin." Every time he came to town, those who couldn't pay fled to their farms. Although he kept coming back, he gave up in some cases, assuming the family moved to another village. Conscientious tax collectors were caught between conflicting loyalties.

Yekeh became a tax collector for the Kissi and Gbande. The Gbande praised him for refusing to collect from those who were suffering. He deeply resented Commissioner Carter because he ruthlessly confiscated cattle, sheep, and goats for his ranch in Arthington.

While Yekeh was conscientious in collecting taxes, he didn't always turn in all the money. More than once, he gave some of the money back to the people, saying, "We're not going to give them all this money. Carter's stealing, making our people suffer for nothing." He gave twelve shillings of tax money to his mother that he intended to repay.

Carter wondered why the tax collection was low so he sent spies to check on Yekeh. One of them blabbed to Yekeh's friend who told Yekeh, "Carter's sending soldiers to either kill you or take you to Belle Yallah from which you'll never return."

In Somalahun, Yekeh called everyone to the town hall. He said, "Goodbye to you all. I've done my best for you. You know I'm not a liar and I didn't steal one single cent. They'll never take me alive. I'd rather die than keep on stealing from you to give to Carter. Don't move the gun so they know I killed myself." With that, he shot himself in the head. The women stood in the rain wailing and weeping. His mother had to be restrained.

Yekeh was so well-loved, everyone in Gbandeland was stunned to hear of his death. Carter demanded proof. As the men carried Yekeh's body to Kolahun on a stretcher, they took his body to the town hall of each village they passed through. The women wept and wailed, "Yekeh's gone! He was so good to our people. Why did he do this?"

Before World War II, the small number of natives in Monrovia, who weren't servant children or soldiers, scrambled to survive. Many worked as "woloco" at Waterside carrying firewood and produce for Americo-Liberian shoppers.

Tribal unity was maintained in the tribal enclaves. Language identified any native outside of his tribal area, linking him with his tribe. Those of the same tribe shared camaraderie. They trusted each other. In the uncertainty of the urban setting and social change, refined and educated natives knew they needed their tribe. Knowledge didn't necessarily lead to a feeling of superiority.

Tribal values were retained. Whenever someone did something bad, natives in the tribal enclaves said, "What tribe is he from? What town or village? Who are his family?" The success of one meant the success of all. Natives respected native government leaders. They bragged, "Look at his house. It's better than those Kwii people. He's doing better than they are."

World War II brought significant social change. It was a turning point. Liberia couldn't remain isolated forever. The war especially brought an influx of new ideas with the arrival of five thousand American GIs, a thousand of them, Negro.

The military barracks at the new Robertsfield Airport were segregated. There with two dormitories — one for whites, one for Negroes. There were two mess halls for whites, one for officers and one for enlisted men, and one mess hall for Negro officers and enlisted men.

Negro GIs were great change agents. The war exposed them to Africa and exposed Liberians to them. When they discovered that whites couldn't own property or become citizens in Liberia, they acted as if they owned the place. They increasingly identified with Africa and wanted to be a part of Liberia. They said, "This is home for me. This is power! This is what freedom is all about and you have it all here. Nobody never told us this before. I'll come back."

They brought into Monrovia in their jeeps, canned meat, sugar, salt, cigarettes, candy, and chewing gum from the PX. In and around Monrovia, they distributed this in wheelbarrows, calling out, "Do you have any meat? Meat here! Canned meat here! Canned food here!" Although the army destroyed everything before they left, Negro GIs still gave out a lot of typewriters and office supplies to refined natives in Monrovia — despite the threat of a court martial. They gave away so many uniforms to refined natives, the Liberian rule against wearing khaki became unenforceable.

Every other building lining Broad Street was a bar. Streets were full of jeeps carrying GIs and their girlfriends for the night. One morning, Monrovia was swarming with white MPs. There were roadblocks. They were looking for Big John, a large, muscular Negro GI, who was very popular and well loved.

In the street gossip, I heard that he had missed curfew a few nights earlier. He and some white GIs arrived late in separate jeeps. The white officers let the white GIs go. They made an example of Big John, severely punishing and humiliating him. He waited until dinnertime, the next evening. As the white officers talked and laughed at the tables, he walked into their mess hall and opened fire with a machine gun.

The MPs never found Big John in Monrovia. They later discovered his body lying in a pool of blood, in the tall grass behind the white officers' mess hall. He had shot himself in the head. The white officers were buried in caskets at Firestone. Big John's body was thrown into an open pit.

Relations between the white and Negro GIs had never been good. After that, they got so bad, the army ruled that every GI had to disarm before going into Monrovia. In the bars and dance halls, Negro GIs constantly picked fights with white GIs and beat them up. Until the end of the war, white GIs were restricted to two or three bars.

I heard that one night at Yango Bar, when a white GI tried to pick up an attractive Liberian girl, a Negro GI walked over to the table and shoved him, picking a fight. The white GI got up and the two went at it. Finally, the Negro GI threw the white GI out on the street, saying, "These are our girls! I couldn't do this in Mississippi or Georgia cause you'd lynch me!" The other Negro GIs came out and watched with arms crossed as the white GI's buddies got him up and into a jeep.

One day, I heard a white sergeant call a Negro private "Nigger." The Negro private lifted him up off the ground with one arm. As the sergeant's legs dangled, the Negro private said, "What did you just call me? Apologize right now or I'll bust your belly out!"

The sergeant said, "I'm sorry."

With that, the Negro GI dropped him on the ground. When I later saw the Negro GI at Aunt Louise's shop, I said, "Why'd you do that to that white man?"

He laughed and said in his deep voice, "You never know what those guys'll do. They'll kill you in a minute without feeling. You got to show 'em."

I said, "He's not a German. He's an American like you."

He said, "He'd rather kill me than a German and I'd rather kill him than a German."

The war was a real eye-opener for refined and educated natives in Monrovia. As Negro GIs drank and socialized with them, they talked openly and freely. They said, "Those Americo-Liberians came here long ago. Have they learned the ways of Africa? Can they speak any of the African languages? If I was here, I'd learn a whole lot about the culture." They said, "In America, we're considered no account. We're deprived. We've got no rights. We can be killed and no one will say anything about it. We're fighting as soldiers to change this."

Natives began saying amongst themselves, "These Americo-Liberians think they're somebody. They've been mistreating us all this time — and they were really nothing!" They no longer worshipped them as before.

The war increased native aspirations. America's intention was to turn the Frontier Force into real fighting men. The army built the Barclay Training Camp, with the help of Liberians, to train Liberian soldiers, and especially officers, to serve as part of America's effort in the North African campaign. Soldiers had to first take a qualifying exam. Most of them flunked since they were illiterate. The army then recruited anyone to join, saying they would train them. Native graduates of mission schools now had the opportunity to become officers and many of them did. They remained as officers after the war.

The free living and free spending of the GIs planted seeds of discontent. Natives were no longer willing to blindly accept a life of poverty. After the war, they became more openly dissatisfied with the Americo-Liberians and the government.

In 1947, a group of Frontier Force soldiers protested at the Barclay Training Camp against the mistreatment of some native boys. The light-skinned Americo-Liberian captain told them, "If any of you country people come any closer, I'm gonna shoot. Move outta here or I'm gonna shoot!"

One of the soldiers walked up to him, took his gun, and said, "I'm not gonna hit you cause you're older. This Americo-Liberian business has gone too far. We're human beings too. In fact, we're better than you." He emptied the gun cartridge, threw the gun at the captain's feet, and turned to the crowd, saying, "Come on, man. Let's go."

The war weakened social segregation in Monrovia. At GI dances, native high school students at the College of West Africa danced the quadrille with Americo-Liberian girls. As more natives became refined and educated, some were accepted into the lower level lodges. Since traditional natives fit stereotype, they weren't seen as a threat.

Natives accepted with reluctance those Americo-Liberian individuals who treated them nicely in private day-to-day relationships. Natives, as a whole, believed in Tubman. When he shook their hand at the mansion and gave them a dollar, they said, "He shook my hand! He gave me a dollar!"

The war weakened sexual restrictions. Kru Town was located on a sandy beach on the Atlantic Ocean. The Kru were expert fishermen. At night, they propped their canoes upside down on sticks on the beach. In the morning, they turned them upright, pushed them out into the water, and jumped inside. On moonlit nights, people walked the beach at Kru Town. Uptown boys and men went there to have sex with a Kru girl. Since they wanted to avoid gonorrhea, they preferred Kru girls who kept the same boyfriend, for the most part.

When a boy followed close behind a Kru girl, she said, "Hey! Why you walk close to me for? What's matter with you? You can't see?"

If he kept following, she turned around and said, "What you followin' me for?"

He'd smile and say with all the charm he could muster, "I wanna to talk to you, girl."

She'd suck her teeth and say, "I don't know you. What you wanna talk to me for?

If she liked him, she continued the banter.

If she didn't like him, she said, "What you wanna talk to me for? You better go."

"Oh, you fine, plenty. You too fine."

"Go away! I no be fine for you!"

"I no feel for go away. You too fine, oh."

While this was going on, the girl would stop snapping her bubble gum and quietly take some hot peppers from her lappa skirt. Chewing them, she said, "You come. I feel for see your face."

As the boy drew close, she spit hot pepper juice in his eyes. As he yelled in pain, she ran away. Kru people on the beach said, "That girl peppered him! You go hear him crying, 'Oh! Oh! Oh!' "

After the war, Tubman's Open Door Policy was another major change agent. The influx of foreign concessions economically opened up Liberia to the world. Foreign entrepreneurs worked with the government to develop Liberia to facilitate their businesses. Roads to the concessions opened up the interior, to some extent. As more natives migrated to the foreign concessions, they were exposed to white Western influence.

After the war, in the large wave of migration into Monrovia, young people left the village for the "good life." Because of increased possibilities, urban living presented new opportunities. As urban dwellers, natives desired and relied upon imported Western goods. Everyone in a Gbande village could name a relative living in Monrovia. Natives in Monrovia had more exposure to other groups. Enrollment at the College of West Africa was mixed. Natives gained confidence working at Duside Hospital, since they were highly trained.

Urbanization weakened tribalism. As different tribes lived side by side in the tribal enclaves, they acquired a new understanding of each other. White Western influence weakened tribalism. As different tribes lived together at Firestone, they spoke a common language — Liberian English. They worked together; shopped at the company store together; and entertained themselves together. As they observed each other, they realized the negative rumors they'd heard about each other weren't true.

Racism at Firestone not only diffused tribalism, it weakened cultural racism. Whites saw every native as a Negro, regardless of tribe. They saw the Americo-Liberians no differently. For the first time, natives, in a "we-they" attitude, said, "We're Liberians," in addition to tribal affiliation. It wasn't a true unity with the Americo-Liberians, but it was a new awareness.

Modern tribalism emerged. Western influence made barely refined, refined, and educated natives doubt their intelligence and ability. They began to question and find fault with their tribal way of life in comparison with the "superiority" of Western culture. Racism and cultural racism made traditional natives ashamed they weren't civilized. As they came to see each other as whites and Americo-Liberians saw them, they called each other "savage."

The standard of native superiority was now the level of Western sophistication. Natives in the Western Province looked down on natives reared by the upriver Americo-Liberians, especially those in the more remote towns. They said, "You go there and they're so raw."

Barely refined and refined natives in Monrovia were glad they were better than a raw native. In order to "rise," they disparaged new arrivals, saying, "Look at that guy walkin' with high steps. He must be a Loma man just comin' from the bush. He thinks he's still walking through high grass instead of a smooth street." They said, "Look how he eats. Must be a lotta hot peppers in there." With equal resentment, traditional natives described barely refined and refined natives by saying, "He thinks he's something acting like those Congos. He even tries to talk like them."

During the 1950s, 60s and 70s, African-Liberians educated overseas, who were rejected by Americo-Liberians and whites, in turn, rejected traditional relatives. Because of urban possibilities, they identified more with Americo-Liberian culture. They now had "status," a feeling of superiority. They were "too good" to go back to the village. They were no longer content to live there without the amenities of modern life. If they built a home there, it was an urban house type and they came and went. In their sophistication, they were not only better than the Americo-Liberians, they were "too big" and "too way up" to help their people. Those who failed in their overseas education were also lost to the tribal community since shame kept them from returning.

A relatively small number of African-Liberians from different tribes were successful in education abroad. When they returned home with masters and doctorate degrees, they were talented, sophisticated people who mixed well. Employment on the foreign concessions validated their skills. They worked in the same managerial posts as whites, with the same rights and privileges. They had better salaries than Liberians working for government.

Although they resented racism and cultural racism, they wanted to be Western and modern in order to succeed and attain status. The rigidly imitated the West, since it had status. Being educated meant modern dress and housing, speaking Standard English. It entailed Western foods, eating practices, and entertainment.

African-Liberians from the most rural areas had the most to prove. They conformed the most rigidly to prove themselves to both groups — the Americo-Liberians and their family and tribe. Cuttington College was located upcountry in Lofa County. Students there worked hard academically and did well.

Westernization diffused tribalism. Educated African-Liberians from different tribes shared Western values — a common, modern outlook based on Western education, the English language, and Christianity. Those who studied abroad were lonely without their African support system. They developed bonds with Liberian college students from other tribes. They intermarried on the basis of educational compatibility and Western romantic love. As Christians, they shared the mission school experience.

As they worked together in Monrovia and on the foreign concessions, they formed a "village" of camaraderie within the urban community. In their sophistication, they had more in common with each other than inept Americo-Liberians. They could speak freely amongst themselves in contrast to guarded exchanges with Americo-Liberians. Liberia's military became united across tribal lines as soldiers lived and worked together and spoke a common Liberian English.

Western forces, Americo-Liberian oppression, and cultural racism simultaneously generated divisiveness. Westernization promoted individualism. African-Liberians succeeded in Western education as individuals. They were only accepted by the Americo-Liberians as individual exceptions to the rule. Since only a select few were allowed to succeed, they competed as individuals for the scarce spoils available — all of which combined to generate an "every man for himself" mentality.

Despite their academic success, they were perpetually insecure as a Western cultural group because of Americo-Liberian domination and rigidity, cultural racism, racism, and their own social and cultural marginality. Their overseas experience led them to assume influence with whites. They became more "Americo-Liberian" than the Americo-Liberians in replicating their ruthlessness. When they were accepted into the Masonic Lodge, they fought to keep out other educated African-Liberians. They rejected and cut off contact with rural relatives. They extorted their own people.

Tribal rights and obligations were distorted in a Western economy. New arrivals had the right to food and housing. They had the obligation to provide household help. Urban relatives had the right to household help. They had the obligation to provide food and housing.

The problem was, it wasn't an even exchange in the urban setting. The traditional system of reciprocity was based on barter. Everything in the modern economy required money. African-Liberians inevitably became leeches on each other. As urban relatives became drained in providing for new arrivals, they offset it by extorting food supplies from their people back home. Despite the extortion, their people continued to revere them. There was no gratitude expressed on either side since these were fulfilled obligations.

In the *cycle of racism, modern tribalism* was fueled by the insecurity of self-hatred and social and cultural marginality. Modernity increased the cultural disparity between: Western vs. traditional values; urban vs. rural; educated vs. illiterate; and Western Christianity vs. animism and Islam. It increased the economic disparity between urban have's and rural have not's. There emerged a distinction between African-Liberians educated locally and those educated abroad. Those educated abroad were "superior" because of their higher level of sophistication.

Americo-Liberian rigidity generated African-Liberian radicalism. Cultural racism became diffused by classism as a small number of educated African-Liberians became more prosperous. In their wealth and higher standard of living, they had more prestige. As they built large homes and married Americo-Liberian women, it was hard to distinguish them from the Americo-Liberians. However, they couldn't make a contribution since they couldn't apply what they had learned. Their government posts weren't related to their training. Nor could they bring about change.

While Tubman's Unification Policy eased restrictions on intermarriage, it was still frowned upon. An educated Mandigo told me, "Doc, You know how it is back home. I would never dare court or marry an Americo-Liberian woman."

His educated Kpelle wife added, "If an educated man dared to date an Americo-Liberian woman, her parents gave him the third degree. They invited him to dinner and said, 'And where do you come from? Who's your family? What's your background? Your education? What's your degree in?' In the end, you know they'd never willingly give their permission for him to marry their daughter."

An educated Vai who married an Americo-Liberian woman during the 1960s told me her family opposed it. The Americo-Liberians told her, "And you're married to a countryman?"

As more educated African-Liberians became qualified without genuine inclusion, their unity of opposition grew more intense. The few who participated in the spoils of government didn't enjoy the same level of power and success, since they weren't really a part of it. Educated African-Liberians considered themselves worthy of more.

I met Togba Nah Tipoteh as Rudy Roberts during the 1960s, when I was teaching at Ohio University. He visited me on campus when he was a student at Purdue University. In my apartment, he told me, "Dr. Dennis, my eyes are opened. You, me, all of us, we have to serve Liberia."

I said, "How?"

He said, "Not only through education. We have to change the government. Those running the government are blind men. They can't go up or down, right or left. If we don't change the government, nothing will change in Liberia. Do you know our people are getting masters and doctorates in all kinds of fields? Why should we let these Americo-Liberians keep running the government? Their minds are archaic. They don't know the first thing. They're ugly, stupid people who met us there. Now we've shown them and the world that we've got brains by virtue of our degrees. I'll soon be through and I'm going home. There are others who feel like I do. There's a community of Liberians in Maryland and some in the Washington D.C. area who are working on a project to take things over. You know Baccus Matthews? He's in school in Washington D.C."

When I returned in 1971, Liberia was a different place. The population of Monrovia had exploded to over two hundred thousand. When Vice President William R. Tolbert Jr. came onto the stage after President Tubman's death in 1971, Liberia was hailed for its peaceful transition of power. I reconnected with Tolbert at the funeral. At his home in Bensonville that evening, he said, "Our country is still very divisive. Our people are still being short-changed. I want all Liberians to feel like Liberians. I want to find a way for all Liberians to be paid for what they do. I want them to have equal access to me as their president, their servant."

I said, "I've been away for a long time but I want to do something for my Mende and Gbande people. The problem is, there's no road to my father's village because of the Cambui Mountain Range. I've heard my people are faithful in paying taxes and doing government work but they're virtually cut off from Liberia."

He said, "You're really needed in Liberia. Is there any possibility you'll return home?"

I said, "Well, I have a family and I'm teaching at the University of Michigan-Flint right now. I'll have to think about it. I won't rule it out though. I'd like to keep in touch."

He said, "About that road to your village, we'll talk about it when the time comes."

In 1972, just before I returned to America, I met with Tolbert in the Executive Mansion. We spoke freely as friends. Having just witnessed the plight of my people, I pleaded for a road to Vahun.

He said, "I'd like to visit Vahun and see the problem for myself. Will you join me? If you come with me, I'll visit and perhaps build the road. I'll let you know when the arrangements have been made."

I said, "Mr. President, I will do so by the help of God."

He kept his promise. The following Christmas, I received a call from mansion. I turned my final exams over to a colleague and took the soonest flight. On the way to Vahun, we stopped at his farm in Bellefani and spent the whole night talking in our pajamas. He said, "Tomorrow, we'll drive to Foya Kamara and take a small plane to Vahun. I'll be going in on the first trip. I want you to bring up the rear."

By the time I arrived, the festivities were well under way. As I got out of the plane, I heard music and saw people dancing. I found out two cows had already been slaughtered for the feast. Someone said, "Come on over here, Doctor. The president's over here." As I walked into a new palaver hut, Tolbert stood and gave me a hug. Everyone clapped. He told me he had already toured the village and said, "You're quite right. The people of Vahun are so nice. They're loyal Liberians."

I asked someone in the crowd to show me the money they used. He handed me a Sierra Leonean coin. I showed it to the president and said, "They're not even using Liberian currency."

The next morning, the national anthem was played as the flag was raised. When he saw the children laughing and dancing, he said, "You're right. They've never even heard our national anthem. I'll do my very best to include these people in Liberia. The road will be built. It's a worthwhile thing to do."

As a Baptist minister, Tolbert shared my interest in Christianity. He told me, "We want more Christianity in Liberia. Let your church people come in." From then on, my loyalty to him was forged by gratitude.

The first crack in the wall that led to the Coup of 1980, was a weakening of Americo-Liberian unity. As the prosperity of the Tubman era was waning, poor Americo-Liberians resented rich Americo-Liberians. Tolbert stepped on Americo-Liberian toes. As a businessman who valued efficiency and productivity, he held the Americo-Liberians accountable for the first time. He streamlined the government. He insisted on a full day's work and fired those who weren't in their offices at 8 a.m. When he spoke to government appointees, he expected them to know what was going on in their offices.

Tolbert wanted to make Unification a reality. His "Mat to Mattress" and "Higher Heights" were focused on African-Liberians. He increased support for higher education. He appointed a number of African-Liberians to offices previously held by Americo-Liberians, such as, Minister of Finance, County Superintendent, Director of Immigration, Minister of Education, Postmaster General, etc. Old-time Americo-Liberian government officials said, "Take my job away? Bob Willie, you gotta be outta your mind! Let the country boy work and tell me what to do? How can you have a countryman tell a Congo man what to do? Those country boys, they can't be like me!"

Tolbert established a new standard of justice. For the first time in Liberia's history, he dared to hang Harmon, the son of a prominent Americo-Liberian family, found guilty of murdering an African-Liberian.

The new rules didn't have the old spoils system to soften them. To cut costs, Tolbert dismissed the PRO spies. He didn't dole out gifts like Tubman did. The Americo-Liberians said, "Tubman picked the fruit off the tree, and shook it for others to gather. Tolbert picks the fruit, shakes the tree, and puts the last fruit into his pocket."

Americo-Liberian hardliners said, "Tolbert's goin' too far. He's makin' those boys too frisky." They didn't identify with him as they had with Tubman. When Tolbert spoke Kpelle at his inaugural, they said, "What's Liberia comin' to? No Americo-Liberian should disgrace himself on such an occasion." They questioned his legitimacy since he was never elected to public office. They were not only angry that he left their children out, they resented his initiatives for African-Liberians. With less spoils, why give the country boys anything? I overheard an Americo-Liberian say, "Who's that Dr. Dennis he does so much for? Vahun? Where's that?"

Tolbert initiated too much change. By holding everyone to the same standard, he put Americo-Liberians on the same level with African-Liberians. The Americo-Liberians not only resented their loss of influence and rewards, they resented the new standards since they applied to everyone except Tolbert's family. While Tolbert condemned cronyism, he couldn't reign in his brothers — Steve's greed or Frank's ruthlessness. Steve's Mesurado Group of Companies had a monopoly on fishing, housing, food distribution, transport, and catering. Each member of the Tolbert family had his own estate in Bentol (formerly Bensonville,) along with a zoo and artificial lake.

Tolbert could never change things radically enough for the African-Liberians. Since success seemed almost within reach, educated African-Liberians increasingly resented their exclusion from the government power structure, even though Tolbert appointed more of them to government posts than ever before. Their increased exposure and some access to positions of influence generated even greater expectations. Since Tolbert was controlled by the Americo-Liberians, his policies could never bring about sufficient change.

Their cause became greater than opportunity for a few educated African-Liberians. It was justice and equity for all African-Liberians. While African-Liberians had more rights, no change was sufficient after years of injustice and gross economic disparity. Educated African-Liberians were angry that the vast majority of African-Liberians lived in abject poverty. They not only believed they deserved a piece of the pie, they wanted to use their broad knowledge and new ideas to improve Liberia. They said, "We can do it better for our people."

In 1972, I met up with Tipoteh, who was a professor of economics at the University of Liberia. At lunch at Rosalie's, he told me, "Dr. Dennis, you were teaching at a Southern university with all white professors. If you could run a department of white professors in a conservative university like that, you can certainly help run a government of old men with no brains."

I said, "If they have no brains, that would make it very difficult."

He summoned the waitress for more beer and said, "Don't you see my point? This is your country too. Look at this place. Tomorrow, I'll take you to visit some government offices so you can see for yourself. Then you'll really believe me."

After we visited several key government offices, he said, "Did you see that the heads of these offices were Americo-Liberians and their assistants were our people? There's no logical reason for this. We've got to take things over. Dr. Dennis, you wouldn't make the money you're making over there, but together we could make things better for Liberia. If we accomplish that, it'll be worth more than pay. Mark my words. We're going to take over. They call us country people. Yes, we're country people — the country belongs to us. The reason I dress like a Kru man is because I don't even want to look like them. It's only the beginning of my protest."

I said, "Be sure to analyze everything and have a blueprint for how this is going to work. You must build Liberia rather than simply instigating destruction based on hate. If that happens, we'll have nothing."

Gross economic disparity was the defining point of African-Liberian hostility. According to the Northwestern University Economic Survey Team, in 1962, Liberia was an extreme case of "growth without development." The jobs most Liberians held were working for the government, which made it top heavy. During the 1970s, foreign investment was reduced due to a drop in world prices for rubber and iron ore. In the Tolbert regime, four percent of the population owned more than sixty percent of the wealth.

Tolbert's "Higher Heights" and "Matt to Mattress" accomplished nothing. Liberia imported rice during the Tolbert regime, just as it had in the Tubman era. Only sixty percent of African-Liberians practiced "slash and burn" subsistence farming. The rest were wage employees on the foreign concessions. When Tolbert ended the government controls that kept the price of rice low, the rice riots during the spring of 1979, sparked a powder keg of pent-up hatred and frustration. Two thousand students and citizens participated. As the police panicked and shot into the crowds, soldiers joined civilians and students in the rioting and looting. Tolbert had to call in troops from Guinea to restore order.

The coup was an overthrow of the government by the most dissatisfied in both camps — lower level Americo-Liberians and upper level African-Liberians.

The African-Liberians that pulled off the coup were barely refined "upcountry boys" in the armed forces and police. Discontent forged a new alliance in Monrovia, between barely refined and refined African-Liberians with radical educated African-Liberians. African-Liberians in Monrovia talked the same language, "We do all the work and they get all the pay. They're lazy but they get the credit for everything. These people think they're 'big men.' Our children are doing better than theirs but their children still get all the big jobs and all these things. We're tired of these people." Radical educated African-Liberians recruited barely refined African-Liberians in the Armed Forces of Liberia to take over the government for them. Tipoteh declared after the coup, "Doe was a good soldier for us."

Tolbert displayed a paradox of hubris and paranoia. He initially welcomed suggestions and criticism. In his drive for legacy, he wanted his progressive actions to garner him status not only in Liberia, but worldwide. His fear of shame drove him to excessive measures. The rice riots not only devastated Liberia, they lessened his image and status in Africa and the world community. He intimidated opponents by making accusations of treason and alleged plots. He used violence as a first resort.

Hubris blinded him to rising dissent. He responded to the rice riots with empty rhetoric — symbolic changes that weren't sufficient. While he wanted to move forward, he was steeped in the past. He wanted a government based on bureaucracy, while favoring his family. He included some educated African-Liberians, but maintained Americo-Liberian privilege and advantage.

He lost any base of support by alienating Americo-Liberians without really gaining the loyalty of African-Liberians. In his attempt to liberalize Liberia, he elevated African-Liberians as personal bodyguards. His son, A.B., said during the coup, "I told my father he gave them too much power. I told him not to do this."

Liberia is a classic example of the successive stages in the *cycle of racism*. The purpose of the coup was to destroy the Americo-Liberians, rule Liberia, and be free and self-sufficient. April 12, 1980, was called "Independence Day." Only pure force gave the African-Liberians the upper hand. As African-Liberians became oppressors themselves, they displayed an even greater ruthlessness. Throughout Liberia's history, natives associated power with decadence. Soldiers replicated the Americo-Liberian culture of power. Now in charge, they were above the law. As they used the means used on them, they were a tyrannical rule of the worst sort.

The coup was revenge. The purpose of the coup was to humiliate, not just punish. President Tolbert's body was thrown into an open pit. Government officials were stripped to the waist before they were tied to electric poles erected on the beach. My uncle, C.C. Dennis, was dragged to death from the back of a pickup truck. Soldiers machine-gunned the presidential oil portraits in the waiting room of the Executive Mansion. They raided the Masonic Lodge. When I saw it in 1983, ragged drapes hung out of open windows. It was filled with squatters.

Barely refined soldiers had never been part of Americo-Liberian society. In a euphoria of power, they destroyed Liberia as if to say, "If we can't have it, no one can." As they roamed Monrovia and its environs, they ransacked the homes of Americo-Liberian "honorables," stripping them bare. They burned a home after looting it. They shot a field of hogs.

Soldiers saw this as real power. They had never fully trusted the educated African-Liberians who instigated the coup. Now that they were in power, the Americo-Liberians had nothing to offer them. They relied instead on individuals of their choosing from both camps.

The coup made Liberia more divisive than ever before. To survive, the Americo-Liberians said, "We're all the same." They wanted to be a part of the power structure but they didn't know which African-Liberians they could trust. They were ambivalent among themselves, as if to say, "What will they think if I cooperate with those boys?" Amongst themselves, they criticized the African-Liberians, "They're not even doin' what we did. Those country people don't know anything about runnin' a government."

The African-Liberians had been divisive as an oppressed group. Now they were even more divisive as they vied for power and the spoils of the coup. There was a split between the "Old Monrovians," those on the coast favored early on, and those from the interior who had come into their own during the 1960s and 70s, and were predominant in Liberia's military.

The coup wasn't a revolution. The African-Liberians didn't want a new form of rule. They wanted to be rulers. Their rigid imitation of Americo-Liberian rule made them their own worst enemies. They couldn't see what was in their best interest. They couldn't imagine any alternatives.

When I spent a year in Liberia in 1983-84, the change in Monrovia was striking. Black mold crept up the walls of government buildings. The front lawn of the Executive Mansion was ragged.

To allay any suspicion, I decided to meet with Doe before going up to Vahun. As Anita and I arrived at the mansion, things were tense. In the early 1970s, security guards joked and called visitors, "Boss man." Now they were guarded, gruff and matter of fact. There was a subdued spirit in government that reflected its lack of legitimacy. At the same time, things seemed the same since one-man rule had only changed hands.

The lavish European furnishings in the mansion were gone. Drapes flapped out of open windows. The exit door of the presidential office was covered with a spray of bullet holes. This building held so many memories for me. I was reluctant to have anything to do with Doe, but felt I must make the best of it.

As we walked in, Doe stood from behind his desk and reached out his hand. My arm was like lead. I couldn't move it. I couldn't shake the hand of the man responsible for the death of my friend. In the embarrassing silence, Anita reached out her hand and Doe shook it. It allowed me enough composure to do the same. The next day, we left for Vahun.

As society creates its leaders, Liberia created Samuel Doe. Of the seventeen privates and non-commissioned officers who stormed the mansion, none had a high school degree. Doe was a rule of insecurity. There was constant fear after the coup. In the need for order, Doe politicized the Liberian military and catered to them. Liberia became a police state, with Marshal Law replacing civil law. Civilian courts were put under a military tribunal. Guns were carried in public places. There were shakedowns by soldiers.

Doe was paranoid. I heard that he never slept two nights in the same place. He considered the Executive Mansion a trap. If you weren't with Doe, you were "anti-Doe." His Decree 2A in 1982, forbid the spreading of lies, untruths, and unproven claims.

He kept things in flux, parting ways with radical educated African-Liberians and putting in members of the True Whig Party. He marginalized coastal African-Liberians and manipulated Liberia's most disenfranchised tribes — the Krahn, Gio, and Mano, from Liberia's least developed counties of Sinoe and Grand Gedeh. The People's Redemption Council was originally composed primarily of Krahn, with a sprinkling of Kru, Gio, Grebo and Loma. Doe only trusted those more inept. He elevated the Krahn despite their lack of qualification.

Doe was a leader of only those Liberians who saw things his way. The "educated" became his enemies — African-Liberians educated abroad. He favored those educated in Liberia. During his presidential campaign in 1985, he established a special criteria for political parties to register. There was a ban on politics. Anyone running for president had to resign from government office, except for him. To guarantee his leadership, he stalled on the new 1984 constitution.

The existence of multi-parties was cosmetic. Doe's National Democratic Party of Liberia was in reality, the military. Opposing parties formed along tribal lines. For the Krahn, it was Doe's NDPL (National Democratic Party of Liberia); for the Gio, Jackson Doe's LAP (Liberian Action Party); for the Loma, Kesselly's UP (Unity Party); and for the Kissi, Kpolleh's LUP (Liberia Unification Party). Despite the fact that it was widely acclaimed that Doe lost the election, he proclaimed himself president and was inaugurated in January, 1986.

He manipulated the legislature and senate. An educated Gbande nephew told me, "Uncle, we were supposed to represent the people, but we were rubber stamps. It was useless to speak out for our people because we didn't have the support of the other members of the house. I told my colleagues, 'We have to prioritize. The people have no water, no roads, no communication.' We were supposed to be telling the president, but we were followers. Provided we had the right man, we could have forged a new direction, but when you have a president who's a robber and criminal, what do you tell him?

"Doe wanted an amendment in the constitution to let him stay in office as long as the people wanted him. I was supposed to sign the amendment so it could go into referendum. I said it would only create more chaos and problems for Liberia because it would perpetuate the president for life. Who would stand before the president and say, 'We're tired of you.'

"The Lofa County caucus speaker said, 'Any reason you refuse to sign?' I told him, 'Let's leave it as it is. Let him go one or two terms, no more.'

"He threatened me, 'If you know what I know, you'll sign it.'

"So I signed under protest. I told them, 'This will make the American government talk against us.' Sure enough, the news got to the embassy. When Charles Taylor was coming, the U.S. wouldn't intervene because we weren't following the rule of law. We ourselves contributed a whole lot to this."

The players had changed, but the game was the same. Doe was a reign of terror. He openly executed more people than any Americo-Liberian president — including his sixteen cohorts who made up the People's Redemption Council. His Krahn SATU (Special Anti-Terrorist Unit) was especially ruthless. In August of 1984, they pillaged campus of the University of Liberia because of a student protest over the arrest of Dean Amos Sawyer, for "plotting to overthrow the government."

We had come into Monrovia from Vahun and were staying at the mission house behind the campus until we left for America. That afternoon, two Americo-Liberian girls ran to our door, sobbing. They told us, "We hid in a closet, but they found us anyway. They said, 'You act like you're different from our Krahn women.' Then they raped us."

Doe's political machinations evolved a Krahn/non-Krahn divide. After a failed Gio coup attempt, he enacted a brutal campaign against the Gio and Mano in Nimba County. Five hundred to a thousand people were executed, castrated and dismembered.

All of this set the stage for Charles Taylor to invade Liberia from Cote de Ivoire in December, 1989, with an army of Mano and Gio rebels bent on getting revenge. They were joined by others fed up with Doe. Rebel groups included: Prince Yormie Johnson's INPL (Independent National Patriotic Front of Liberia); and the two factions of the Muslim ULIMO (United Liberation Movement of Liberia for Democracy) — Alhadji Kromah's ULIMO-K and Roosevelt Johnson's ULIMO-J.

As anarchy accelerated ruthlessness, Liberia descended into utter depravity. In 1990, Doe's AFL (Armed Forces of Liberia) slaughtered six hundred people of other tribes, mostly women and children, who had taken refuge under the auspices of the Red Cross at St. Peter's Lutheran Church in Monrovia. In 1992, Taylor's NPFL's assault on Monrovia left over three thousand dead. In 1993, Kromah's ULIMO-K murdered and tortured hundreds in Lofa County — many with ears and hands cut off and hearts removed.

Somalahun wasn't spared. A Gbande nephew wrote me, "Doc, my younger brother was among more than a dozen people killed in Manjotahun by Charles Taylor's rebels. They killed a number of our people in Somalahun and Ndambu as well, falsely accusing them of supporting Kromah's rebels. They barricaded people in their huts and set them on fire."

In 1996, my son Ben called and said, "Dad, get a copy of the *New York Times*. There's an article and picture of refugees in Vahun on the front page. Vahun has become a refugee camp of fifty thousand people." In 2002, when my son Peter did a law internship in the Sierra Leone refugee camps, he brought back a cassette tape of my Mende people recounting what happened in Vahun. As I heard about all those killed, I wept for my people.

Liberia's civil war wasn't simply tribes fighting each other. It was groups of disenfranchised rebels from different tribes fighting each other to gain control of Liberia to reap its spoils. In this free-for-all, the victims were Liberian civilians of every group. The war was the implosion of a nation in which every citizen was socially and culturally marginal.

The coup had failed to live up to its promise. Doe's favor of his Krahn tribe destroyed the former unity of all African-Liberians against all Americo-Liberians, inevitably opening the door for the disenfranchised of all tribes to compete. The war was based on *modern tribalism* as well as tribalism. It was fueled by inequity. Disenfranchised cutthroats competed for what was left of Liberia's resources. Soldiers normally fight to save their country. Rebels in Liberia fought to destroy theirs.

Warlord Charles Gankay Taylor was a native outside child of an upriver Americo-Liberian father and a Gola mother. Although he received a college education, he was disenfranchised as a Congo. He used elements of tribal loyalty to manipulate barely refined rebels for his own power and success. His focus was on Liberia's diamonds which he sold in Belgium; timber which he sold in France and Malaysia; and rubber, gold, and iron ore sold to other European countries. From the profits, he reportedly purchased weapons in Europe and had them shipped through Burkina Faso and Cote d'Ivoire.

Soldiers normally die with honor as they give their lives for the state. Taylor sacrificed Liberia's youth for "nothing." Boy soldiers, pumped full of drugs and given machine guns, had only the empty power to destroy. During the war, an educated Mende nephew told me, "Doc, everybody wants something. Taylor's giving a little bit, here and there. He's giving those boys guns to kill anyone they want. They think they have power because they're doing horrible things with impunity. It makes them think they're somebody. Somalahun, Yanduhun, and Vahun are all deserted."

Barely refined rebels were the "lost" of the lost. They had nothing to lose. In the *cycle of racism*, in their rage of helplessness and hopelessness, they displaced their anger and frustration on the only ones they could — traditional Africans even more helpless.

Rebels didn't belong anywhere. The discipline of a pseudo military provided an escape from their untenable existence. Rebel fraternity satisfied their craving for identity and belonging. Wearing uniforms gave them "status." Rebel leaders bolstered their status with empty rhetoric. When Prince Johnson's ULIMO-J splinter group killed Doe in 1990, Johnson declared himself a "humanitarian" as he orchestrated Doe's slow death by mutilation.

Rebels derived status from raw power and violence. They wanted the same power as Doe, as if to say, "If a raw Krahn man can have all that power, what about me?" To get supernatural power, they practiced juju. When Doe was killed, rebels feared his voodoo. He was left to die with his arms tied so his spirit couldn't get free and gain control of anyone.

Liberia's "civil war" was mass murder. Instead of rebel bands fighting each other, they looted, murdered, and raped an unarmed population with impunity. They treated helpless civilians as if they were armed soldiers. The government normally protects its citizens. In the free-for-all, people fled government troops and police as much as rebels. An educated Mende told me, "Streets in Monrovia used to be crowded with people laughing and going to bars to drink cane juice. Now people are hiding. They don't want to come out."

Power evokes fear even in those who wield it. Rebels joined in the destruction to protect themselves, generating even more fear. In war, enemies are normally considered "less than human." The rebels, in their self-hatred, saw civilians that way. In callousness, they used atrocities to instill fear. When they commandeered young men to join them, they forced them to kill their parents in front of villagers. They ripped open pregnant women "to see the baby." They raped to intimidate.

The purpose of war was to humiliate, not just punish. As Doe was interrogated, a soldier rubbed his head as if he was a small boy. He was forced to plead for his life. A video tape of his death was played over and over in bars in Monrovia. Soldiers singled out someone and said, "Are you Congo? What dialect you speak?" If the person couldn't speak an authentic tribal language, they blew his head off. Rebels taunted and toyed with their victims before torturing and killing them.

Everyone in Liberia at that time has a "war story." In 2000, we sat at the dinner table of a Liberian home in Ft. Myers, Florida, and listened as the guest, a dean at the University of Liberia, give this account, "It was only the Lord who brought me through the war. I believe it was for a purpose. I must remain in Liberia and do what I can for my country.

"One Sunday, as I came from church, a soldier said, 'Arrest him! He was Doe's teacher!' I was taken to the home of an Americo-Liberian who was murdered and his body dumped in the well behind the house. I was locked in a bathroom with three or four others. I prayed and tried to give them courage.

"One was one of Doe's policemen. His elbows were tied so tight behind his back, he was delirious with pain. With my hand cuffs, I managed to give him a cup of clean water from the toilet tank. After he drank it, he cocked his head and threw himself headfirst into the tub to break his neck. When it didn't work, he yelled, "Kill me now! I can't stand anymore!" A rebel came in and took him out. We heard gun shots and it was quiet.

"The next day, someone looked at me and said, 'Why'd you arrest him? He's a big man! Let him go!' I was lifted up and unshackled — taken to the bathhouse to wash and given food. In the course of twenty-four hours, I went from impending death to respect and honor. I can never forget the horror or my rescue.

"The losses of the war have been staggering. All the microscopes in the science labs are gone. The natural history museum is gone. The university records are gone. Everything's gone. There's nothing left."

After failed peace agreements from 1991-1994, as well as a failed interim government, Taylor entered Monrovia in 1995, to cheering crowds. Until then, nothing had been relevant, including Doe's death, since Taylor hadn't achieved control.

Taylor destroyed Liberia in order to have it. When the war ended, over two hundred thousand people had been killed, mostly civilians. More than seven hundred thousand were in refugee camps in Cote de Ivoire, Guinea, Sierra Leone, Ghana, Gambia, and Mali. The coup ravaged Monrovia and its environs. The war decimated and destroyed the entire country.

When Taylor was elected president in 1997, he was a rule of insecurity. Despite his power, he was a loser who looked only to himself. Despite his college education, he was intimidated by educated African-Liberians. He succeeded by playing both sides. While he aspired to be an upper class Americo-Liberian, he wore an African gown and carried a scepter. When deposed in 2003, he insisted on a grand exit.

In his paranoia, I heard that he traveled in a thirty-five car motorcade supervised by the police chief. No one knew which car he was in. Sometimes he wasn't in any of them. When he traveled, all cars had to stop. He shut down Star Radio, an independent radio station, because of negative news reports about him. He had those who sang "Suffering" beaten and harassed because he didn't like the phrase, "We don't know where the money goes."

If he had one girlfriend a night, he made sure his cronies had two. Once a month, he sent his girlfriends to Cote de Ivoire for an AIDS test. He used them as spies to report anyone who complained he wasn't doing a good job.

Taylor controlled all revenue. An educated Loma told me, "Anyone in Taylor's government who got even an outside check made out to him, had to endorse it over to Taylor in order to survive in government." He refused offers from other countries if he couldn't have complete control. Mohammar Khadafi offered low cost housing. Korea, Japan, and China offered to work at the JFK hospital. Taylor closed it. I was told an American company offered to re-electrify Monrovia with their own funding — provided it was on their own terms. Taylor refused. He said all funding had to go through the government.

Taylor took every Americo-Liberian vice to the zenith. As a master of charm, he manipulated loser African-Liberians to follow him. Even the Americo-Liberians supported him at first. An educated Loma told me, "Charles Taylor could convince anyone of anything. He convinced people whose children were killed to support him. During his election for president, the chant in Monrovia was, 'He killed my brother, I'll vote for him. He killed my mother, I'll vote for him.' And there was an element of truth in it. Corruption notwithstanding, Taylor received a sizable support that can't simply be attributed to, 'He wrecked the place. Let him put it back together.' Taylor could charm anyone. Doc, if you spent fifteen minutes with him, you'd support him too."

His ruthlessness was legendary. After the war, he killed off his rivals. His ATU (Anti-terrorist Units) executed people summarily. After a student protest, the leader would turn up missing. Government soldiers executed civilians to extract information about rebel movements. When Taylor granted Amos Sawyer amnesty, Sawyer said, "Justice must be institutionalized. It shouldn't depend on the good will of the leader."

During Taylor's reign, an educated African-Liberian told me, "A taxi driver in Monrovia passed a car carrying Taylor's wife. Her chauffeur stopped him and said, "What you think you're doin'? Do you know who's in this car? This is the president's wife! Do you think I'm a small boy?' The taxi driver said, 'Boss man. I'm sorry. I didn't know.' The chauffeur took out his gun and shot him."

Civil war erupted again in 1999 when two rebel groups combined to depose Taylor. Rebels in LURD (Liberians United for Reconciliation & Democracy) controlled the North. Rebels in MODEL (Movement for Democracy in Liberia) controlled the South. In 2003, Taylor was convinced to step down and was given asylum in Nigeria. In the conflict before and after Taylor, Liberia had no army with loyalty to the nation. Government troops were loyal to Doe or Taylor. In the push to depose Taylor, the soldiers protecting him were the "real" rebels, while the "rebels" fighting them became Liberia's emancipators.

Doe killed Liberians. Taylor killed Liberia by destroying the youth and whatever was left. Both Doe and Taylor were reigns of terror legitimized by a national referendum. Under both, Liberia was owned by a handful of criminals who called themselves a government.

Today, Liberia is more divided than ever. Everyone is ambivalent, not knowing who to believe or trust. Although the Americo-Liberians hate the African-Liberians for their "paradise lost," they're cautious. If they could regain the upper hand, they would. The end of Americo-Liberian rule never meant African-Liberians were equal. The Americo-Liberians say amongst themselves, "Doe didn't know anything. Taylor was worse. Everything's gone down. There's no electricity. Roads are impassible. They can't even go to their areas."

The African-Liberian longing for Americo-Liberian acceptance has dissipated. African-Liberians still call Americo-Liberians, "Congo people." They're guarded with them, even though they're no longer in control.

The disparity in African-Liberians ranges from those educated abroad to those in the village. Such a difference in position and world view generates an inevitable clash. African-Liberians educated abroad, in their political and economic aspirations, stick together and hold their own. They distinguish themselves from those educated at home who don't trust them either. Added to this mix are traditional African-Liberians who trust those educated at home because they're humble.

An educated Loma told me, "A highly qualified friend of mine was recruited to set up finances in Liberia. He told me, 'When we talk, we look like strangers to them. It's like they're saying, "Who are these guys?" I'm only one in a committee of fifteen. You have to try to win their hearts for them to know what you're talking about.' "

In addition to tribalism, *modern tribalism* represents an enduring division between Christianity, and Islam and animism; between Western urban peoples and traditional rural peoples; and between the young and the old since the young preyed upon the old during the war. In Liberia's complete devastation, the greatest conflict is between rich and poor. Liberia remains "every man for himself" as everyone strives to acquire the Western goods displayed to them. With Liberia's economy in shambles, it's an impossible dream.

Competition generates divisiveness. As educated African-Liberians go home and start up businesses, they make their profit by using barely refined African-Liberians and paying them low wages. They justify this, saying they would have nothing at all if they weren't working for them.

Those who stayed resent those who fled during the hard times. Gudi Bryant was chosen as interim president because he remained during the conflict and was seen as a consensus builder. When Liberians return, people say, "Oh, so now you're coming back!"

Liberia's presidential election of 2005, had an abundance of political candidates. Political loyalty was based on *modern tribalism* as well as tribalism. Educated candidates appealed to educated African-Liberians. An educated Loma told me, "Everyone wants to be president. There are currently forty-three candidates and I don't trust any of them who were in the Doe or Taylor regime."

Former rebels are difficult to fully incorporate into Liberian society. Although they are unified in their guilt and war experience, they remain as disenfranchised as ever with no prospects for the future. In a video about Taylor's overthrow, a fourteen-year-old soldier caressed his gun, saying, "This is my mother and father." Former rebels harassed others, saying, "Nothing can touch me! I came through the war. I can do anything!" Until Taylor was captured after his escape from Nigeria, there was the fear that if he returned to Liberia, disenfranchised rebels would rally to his cause.

National unity remains a challenge. The only common ground is "survival." Since no one has clean hands, there's no trust in anyone. There's no basis for national unity because of vastly different world views that stem from different cultural backgrounds and experiences. As a result, Liberians continue to gravitate towards a leader.

The African-Liberians failed miserably. They don't understand why because they don't understand themselves. Liberia was destroyed by Liberians. Rebels displayed the height of futility. They had no constructive power to achieve anything. When they killed each other, their destructive power died with them. They thought they were somebody when they didn't have anything to eat or know where they were going to sleep. In jealousy, they killed the educated — those who could do something for Liberia. They grasped to fill a void that couldn't be filled the way they wanted.

Liberia has plunged backwards at least a hundred years. Instead of being a beacon to Africa, Liberia represents the "heart of darkness." During the civil wars, people wondered if Liberia was indeed a Christian country. Europeans said, "They're sitting around chopping off people's heads. They're savages, just savages."

Everyone has exploited Liberia, especially her own citizens. No one thinks of Liberia as a viable country. Monrovia still has no overall electricity, running water, or sanitation. Several years ago, my Kru friend told me, "Monrovia stinks because people are urinating all over." In the countryside, clusters of fruit trees delineate burned out villages. Roads are impassable.

It has all come to nothing. Doe built a three million dollar house in Zedro that was eaten by termites. Taylor is now on trial at The Hague as a war criminal.

Imitation of Superiority

> "The only way I'd give her up is for her to have a chance for a better education."
> — an African-Liberian woman in America, speaking about her baby to Anita, 2001

Liberia displays the themes of colonialism even though it was ruled by Negroes and independent since 1847. As an opposing white culture, the Americo-Liberians were a major change agent. Natives were under white influence in missionary activity and the foreign concessions. Their Western role models included the Americo-Liberians, Negro and white missionaries, and white foreign businessmen.

During the 1930s and 40s, while natives saw the Americo-Liberians realistically, they simultaneously idealized them, respecting them for their glamour and status. The Americo-Liberians were superior because of their relations with whites. They were "right" because of their Western culture. They were capable because of their power like whites. In the Western Province, when the horn announced the arrival of the district commissioner in a Gbande village, soldiers ran around him like he was something great.

The Americo-Liberians appeared to hold the promise of a better life. Adopting Western culture meant greater chances. Parents gave their children in the hope that they would be "better off than our people" — that they would succeed and become government leaders.

Loma soldiers particularly gave their children because of their greater contact with the Americo-Liberians. Whenever several Gbande went to Monrovia, parents asked them to check on their children. Sometimes they stayed an extra week to contact everyone. If the situation wasn't good, parents put their children in mission school. Those children who were never educated returned to the village unchanged.

An educated Kpelle described his life in an upriver Americo-Liberian home during the late 1940s and early 50s, "I was an outside child of my father from Arthington. My Kpelle mother and her people felt it was to my advantage to get an education any way I could. When I was six, I was taken into my father's sister's family. By the time I was nine, I was getting up at 4 a.m. to do household chores. First, I emptied the night chamber pots in the outhouse and scrubbed them. Then I cleaned the chicken manure and spread it on the garden. I brought water and got the fire going. While I waited for the water to heat, I raked the yard and polished shoes. We did all the laundry, our own as well.

By 6:00 a.m., we were on our way to the rubber farm. We rushed from tree to tree, not thinking. It took us two hours to do two hundred trees. We were trained to work fast. We knew we'd get a whipping if we didn't finish. Breakfast was a large pancake and a cup of tea.

"We hurried to get ready for school. We had to walk two miles. We dared not be late or we got a whipping. The morning session lasted until 12:30 p.m. Lunch was a bowl of cooked buckwheat with oil and a cup of powdered milk, from food donations from America. We put the powdered milk in our pockets and licked it later. It only made us hungrier because it gave us diarrhea.

"We walked home at midday break to collect the latex. After we poured it in the concrete pit, we put in acid to congeal it. By the time we got back to school, it was usually 3 p.m. There was only forty five minutes of school left. Many times, we didn't make it back. We stayed home one afternoon a week to collect palm cabbage to feed the hogs so we wouldn't have to do it every day.

"From 6 p.m. to sunset, we worked in the fields. The only time we didn't do some kind of farm work was when it rained heavy or there was lightning. In the summer, we were out of school a month to do farm work. When we got home from school, my uncle said, 'You ate at school. Go on out to the farm.' We chewed on sugar cane or ate raw cassava. At supper, we never got seconds because that was wasteful. It was time for homework but we were too tired to do anything. On days of heavy farm work, we didn't get to bed till midnight.

"We never thought about clothes. We had none to speak of — just a pair of pants and a shirt. We just wore pants most of the time and went barefoot. My aunt got our clothes from the Methodist and Baptist churches that got clothing from America. We better not tear our pants too much or we got a whipping. Even then, our clothes had so many patches, they looked like Joseph's robe of many colors.

"We were just asking for trouble if we didn't do our chores or do them well enough. I must have gotten a hundred whippings. My uncle made us lie down on the bed with our pants down. We had to grip the edge of the bed. If we let go, he started whipping us all over again.

"When my mother or other Kpelle people visited, my aunt and uncle were real nice to them. They had a fine dinner and I was dressed better. They talked nice to me. When I dared to talk privately to my mother, she told me I had no other chance so I better take this one. I'm sure she never really understood.

"My uncle molested the girls. A girl would be chosen as a playmate for their daughter but there was a hidden agenda. When we were out on the farm, he'd tell the girl he wanted to show her something. We knew better than to leave our work. But one day, my curiosity got the better of me. I sneaked over to see what they were doing. He heard me and shouted, "What did you see!"

"I said, 'I didn't see anything!' I knew I'd be beaten if I ran my mouth. He knew I saw them, though. He was kinder to me after that. He was afraid I'd tell my aunt.

"Christmas was the greatest time. They butchered a hog that must have weighed three hundred and fifty pounds. We cooked the intestines and had our own supply of rice. Boy did we eat! We were excited because we knew we'd get a new set of clothes and a pair of shoes for the next year. The shoes we got were worn out or torn. We repaired them, thinking we really had something.

"My experience was modern-day slavery. I had no other options. Where could I go? It was only my determination that got me through. I considered myself blessed just to be able to go to school. I wanted to be 'somebody' so I wouldn't have to spend my whole life doing farm work."

Serving in the Frontier Force was a way to be a part of government. From the 1930s to the 1950s, it was a major source of upward mobility. Most of the soldiers were Loma. So many Loma were soldiers, the Loma swore by saying, "May gun kill me."

Soldiers functioned as middlemen between the government and tribes in the interior. They recommended chiefs for election. They enforced tax collection by beating those who didn't pay. They relayed the district commissioner's orders and arranged for government officials to be carried in hammocks.

They also served as Liberia's pony express. They carried letters from the Secretary of the Interior to the district commissioners. When they reached the end of the main path, native runners went from village to village carrying the letter in a forked stick, crying out, "Big Letter! Big Letter!"

Western culture held a certain fascination. When I was a boy, two Gbande men returned from Monrovia with an old-fashioned alarm clock that had two bells and a clapper on top. It became quite a novelty. People in Somalahun called the men wingee because of it.

As the men wound the clock, people said, "They're talking to the clock so it can talk back to them." When it was the season for chasing rice birds from the fields, boys stood outside the door of the hut with the alarm clock. When it went off at 5 a.m., they told each other, "Come on, man! The thing says it's time to go!"

Sometimes the men set the clock to go off at noon. People stood around saying, "It will soon be talking! Don't eat yet, man. It's not half of the day gone." The women took the clock to the rice farm kitchen. When it went off at noon, they called to the men, "It's making noise calling you people! Come and rest a bit." People in Somalahun marveled, "Oh, these white people! They have things to do everything for them!"

While natives didn't necessarily see Western culture as superior, it was something they wanted. It was a new way of doing things — living in the city and having access to things such as health care. When Gbande visitors to Monrovia first saw electric lights, they told people back home, "They have big light so they can see what you're doing." They said, "The Americo-Liberians poo poo in a 'house.' You sit down and poo poo. It stinks plenty bad but there's a roof over so you don't get wet."

Firestone Rubber Plantation was a major change agent. It introduced natives to a Western economy with white business standards and efficiency. As an outside foreign company, it gave natives an independent opportunity for inclusion. As they became part of Liberia's modern cash sector, they had a regular income of set wages.

Firestone mitigated tribal values. As an industrial site or company town, it was completely unlike the tribal setting. Natives were exposed to foreigners. They had to learn Liberian English, new skills, and a new way of life in the camps. They were exposed to other tribes. Although they thought their employment was temporary, they ended up staying, which meant tribes were no longer self-contained and self-sufficient.

As wage earners, natives became dependent on Firestone. They had to buy rice on credit at the company store. At payday, they remained in debt. Each month, they owed progressively more.

Natives had a love/hate relationship with whites. As whites discounted the culture and language natives took so much pride in, natives came to realize they were all in the same plight. They simultaneously came to accept on some level that whites were superior.

One day at Duside Hospital, a light-skinned Vai tailor, who made the hospital uniforms, called to me as I was walking down the hall, "Come quickly. Don't let anyone see you." He led me into a room where a corpse lay under a sheet on an autopsy table. He lifted the sheet showing me the face of a dead white man and said, "Here, look at this. This one is dead. The way they talk to us, I thought they couldn't die."

When natives were used to build the wharf in Monrovia during World War II, they said, "They're bringin' in a whole lotta white people to build this dock. Now we have all kinds of strange diseases. White people are full of disease. If they don't kill us with their power and exploitation, they'll kill us with disease." At the same time, natives in Monrovia admired whites. One day I was doing something, a Loma boy told me, "You do this so good — just like the white people!"

Negro and white missionaries were major change agents in the interior as they introduced Western education in mission schools. Missionaries were synonymous with Western education since the Americo-Liberian required them to set up schools. Until the 1960s, most natives were educated in mission schools, wherever they were. During the 1930s and 40s, foreign missionaries were a greater Western influence on natives in the interior than the Americo-Liberians. The majority were Negro Baptists or Methodists. They were zealous to civilize the natives to "make the best out of the Negro."

In the Western Province, natives were educated by white missionaries at the Episcopal Holy Cross Mission in Bolahun, established in 1922. At first, parents were reluctant. This was something new and they were afraid. In their oral history, they knew whites had taken Africans into slavery to a far, far country. They trusted the Americo-Liberians more than white missionaries. When the priests told the chiefs they intended to start a school, the chiefs said, "You want our children. Where are your children?"

A priest said, "We don't have children. We're not allowed to marry while we're priests."

After some deliberation, the chiefs said, "We can't give you our children. If you don't have children yourselves, how can you take care of other people's children?"

The Gbande believe that no man can resist women altogether. They assumed the priests were deceiving them since the nuns at the hospital were good-looking. Because the priests and nuns lived in a secluded compound, the rumor was that the nuns were having babies but disposing of them.

Whites from the mission liked to swim in the deep part of the creek near Masambolahun. The Gbande told their children, "They're water people. That's why they look so pale. When they go to swim, don't go in with them because they'll take you down with them. They can live in the water but you can't." When they heard that whites drowned when a Firestone barge capsized, they dismissed it.

The Loma and Gbande used rags for dirty things and threw them away. When they saw whites wash their dishes with rags and eat off of them, they said, "They should clean things with their hands, like we do."

When I failed at hunting as a boy, Komah told me, "You shouldn't go back to that place. They're spoiling you. No woman will respect you if you can't hunt. What kinda people live there anyway? No wonder they look so pale."

Morlu said, "Be very careful in the white people's country. They have diseases for which we have no medicine. Be careful with their women because they spread disease so quickly."

When Komah got gonorrhea, he went to the Bolahun Hospital for treatment. People in Somalahun said, "Why is he going to the white people for treatment when they brought the disease?" When he returned, he explained how white people brought the disease. "You see that dog over there with pus dripping from its penis? A man who works for whites told me white people keep dogs so their women can have sex with them. That's how they get the disease. That's why white people sleep with their dogs and take them wherever they go."

In Vahun, the Mende said whites looked like the chimpanzee because of its face and thin lips. They said, "They look so strange, like ghosts. They don't have anyone to talk with."

When the chiefs decided to encourage their people to send their children to school, the people said, "You send your son and we'll see what happens." Since the first to become Western educated were the sons of chiefs, Western education came to represent privilege and prestige. As a small core, they were the first to go abroad for education.

Natives came to realize that foreigners were the only ones who did anything positive for them. Children deferred to missionaries, calling them "Ma" and "Pa." The Gbande called whites and Americo-Liberians wingee. The Mende called them "pumoi" (Western person).

Mission education meant a foreign staff of qualified teachers. Schools had accountability. Whites and American Negroes regularly visited to see how things were going. There was a consistent program with standards and expectations. Teachers were strict. Students at Bolahun lived on campus. There were no excused absences, except for regular vacations. No one passed without mastering each grade's material. Students continued their learning under missionary teachers at the College in West Africa in Monrovia.

Although natives had less access to education, those who had access were successful. The Americo-Liberians were kwii. The only way to become kwii was to become educated. Students were disciplined and serious. Hard work and excellence were tribal values. They were determined not to shame themselves or let their family down.

Most of the educated natives from the Western Province only completed the eighth grade. Since they had learned English in school, they spoke polished English. While they adapted to Western culture and adopted Western values, they never left their traditional culture. They had minimal contact with the Americo-Liberians and were critical of their lifestyle. Although they were literate, they leaned more towards traditional values. The majority became teachers of their own people. Some taught at the Holy Cross Mission. Some became tax collectors or dispensers at health clinics in the area.

Christianity was a major change agent. Natives directly experienced the glaring influence of white and American Negro hypocrisy. In Liberia, white profit and missionary activity went hand in hand, just as in all of Africa. White missionaries were permeated with racism which superseded their theology. Both white and Negro missionaries assumed they knew what was best for natives. They never understood African cultures or tribal practices, since they had no interest in what was inferior.

As a boy, I heard a story that circulated in Monrovia about a Kru chief and a white missionary. The chief became good friends with the missionary and invited him to his home. When the missionary met the chief's two wives, he told him, "I want you to keep coming to church, but there's a problem. The Bible says a man should have only one wife. Chief, you have to get rid of one of your wives."

The chief got tired of hearing the missionary complain about this, so one day he took his younger wife, who had no children, out into the Atlantic Ocean in his canoe and dumped her overboard.

The next Sunday in church, he told the missionary, "I got rid of one wife."

The missionary said, "What'd they say?"

He said, "Who?"

"Her people."

"Oh, Pa, I didn't take her to her people."

"Then where'd you send her?"?

"I took her for big water. She's gone to glory."

The white and Negro missionaries' aura of superiority contradicted their message and influence. They evangelized natives but didn't socialize with them. In paternalism, they saw them as students and servants.

A Loma friend, educated at the Suehn Baptist Mission, told me, "The teachers were chain smokers. They didn't want to litter when the school grounds were swept. They put their cigarettes out on our heads and handed us the butt to throw away. I thought it was the way Americans treated people." He showed me scars on his scalp and said, "I was a water boy at Suehn. Once they burned me so bad, the nurse had to dress my head. After that, I had to use a pad of old rags on my head to carry water."

Missionaries promoted Christianity as "culture." They were more interested in making natives civilized, than in making them Christian. The first things taught and adopted were Western dress and eating with a knife and fork. Natives worshipped God in Western liturgy and hymns. A white missionary told me the people said they wanted to worship as whites do.

Natives displayed hypocrisy since missionaries didn't practice what they preached. The hypocrisy of the Americo-Liberians confirmed Christianity as a morally corrupt religion.

Christianized natives weren't committed to Christianity alone. They accepted it without rejecting traditional beliefs such as witchcraft, fortune-telling, wearing talismans, and making sacrifices to the ancestor spirits. They adopted Muslim beliefs as well. Islam had an advantage in Liberia, since Muslims embraced people of every race, color, and culture. Becoming Muslim didn't require giving up traditional beliefs. In contrast, Christianity was associated with slavery and racism. It required cultural change.

Natives, as a whole, adopted Christianity for what it could do for them. They saw that missionaries and Americo-Liberians looked favorably upon those who became Christian. It was a rite of passage to become civilized. A Gbande aunt told me, "I thought people became Christian to become wingee. I'm just a poor country woman."

Migration into Monrovia was a major change agent. The majority of natives in Monrovia were barely refined, speaking a rough Liberian English. Those who weren't servant children or soldiers, were policemen when literacy wasn't required, or watchmen in Lebanese stores and Americo-Liberian homes. Some worked on government road crews. Some did market or "wood" business. Some were tailors.

Refined, literate natives worked as store clerks, lawyer's apprentices, and messengers delivering letters for the government, banks, or businesses. Several of them had a trucking business. The two electricians at the power plant were a Loma and a Vai.

Educated natives with a high school or college education worked as government clerks or officials. One example is Henry Fanbulleh, a coastal Vai, who was President C.D.B. King's right hand man. Nat Massaquoi, also a Vai, was the consular general in Hamburg, Germany, when my father served in the consulate in Berlin. De Twe was the Kru governor of Kru Town and the first native district commissioner. Dr. Togbah, a Kru, was educated at Meharry Medical School in Nashville. Rudy Roberts's father worked in the treasury department.

Peter Bono Jallah is a classic example of a native who made "good" in Monrovia during the 1940s. As the son of Chief Jallah, he received his elementary education at the Bolahun Holy Cross Mission. After his father died, he went to live in Monrovia at the Cooper house, where his brother George was a houseboy. Peter's room on the ground level could barely hold his small wooden bed and table. After his daily chores, he spent most of his time studying. His was skilled at memorization, the traditional form of learning. A professor at Liberia College mentored him and he graduated with a bachelor's degree.

Peter became one of the most successful lawyers in Monrovia. When Tubman appointed him justice of the peace, all native cases were assigned to him. Since his courtroom was always packed, he handled cases "quick, quick" without a jury. He didn't want to drag things out to milk people like the Americo-Liberian lawyers and judges did. Natives from the Western Province gravitated to him. He spoke English with a strong Loma accent and they considered him fair and just.

Most cases involved woman palaver, where a woman called her lover's name and he was obligated to pay her husband a fine. In a typical court case, a man would bring in his wife and another man and tell Peter, "Judge, this man f— my wife."

Peter pounded his gavel and said, "Come to the bench, right now. Everybody listen. You don't speak that language in my court. Just say it be woman palaver."

"Eh, Boss, I beg you, oh. It be woman palaver. And this man here, he do it!"

"How do you know?"

"Judge, I tell you the truth, oh. You see this woman? It be my woman. And it be he, my wife call his name. I no lie, oh. Woman, talk for the judge now. It be he, you told me ..."

Peter asked the woman, "Is that true?"

"Oh, Judge, it be true, oh. He did. Ask him."

"O.K. Sit down."

Peter then addressed the accused man, "Get up, man! You hear, eh? Look the woman in the face."

As the man did, Peter told the woman, "Say it again. It be he make the woman palaver with you."

She said, "It be he."

Before the accused could say anything, Peter said, "You guilty. Pay woman palaver."

"But, boss man, I don't have any money."

Peter asked the husband, "How much you want for woman palaver?"

The husband said, "My woman be fine, fine. Oh, too fine. Plenty fine, oh. Look at her." Shaking his head, he said, "I think ten dollar not be too much."

The accused man said, "You speak right. Your woman too fine. But I go fish and catch nothing. Please, I beg you, oh. Make five dollar. I go pay before moon finish."

Peter told him, "You bring five dollar and you bring altogether eight dollar — three dollar for court costs. So, go. Fish, now. Finish, go!"

Peter told the bailiff, "You see this man. Go find his house. You go there on the appointed day. If he don't pay, you bring him here."

Peter warned the accused man, "If you no pay, we go find you. You go to jail."

With the fines he charged, Peter's large volume of work made him prosperous. He built a house on Camp Johnson Road. He purchased the adjacent property and built two more houses. The bulk of his cost was materials since Loma and other native carpenters and masons paid off their fines by working on his houses. The area became known as Loma Town. He married an upriver Americo-Liberian woman from the town of Virginia. His three sons were well educated in the United States.

In the *cycle of racism*, imitating the superior group becomes emptier as the original cultural model becomes more remote. Natives in Monrovia had only a parody of Western culture to imitate. As a result, they became an even greater caricature. To distinguish themselves, they wanted to be different. Being Western brought status. They suffered a double whammy. Not only did they have a pseudo Western model, they had limited exposure and restricted inclusion. They copied something they didn't understand. They absorbed a Western lifestyle without being able to see it in its genuine or broad context.

They imitated the Americo-Liberians in trappings of dress, lifestyle, and Christianity — the necessary elements of being civilized. They loved symbols of anything Western. The Frontier Force loved parades and drill, pageantry and a big show. Natives strutted proudly in imported garments. Refined natives wore a singlet undershirt to bed. Educated natives wore pajamas. As a boy, I admired two Gbande young men who worked as overseers on the Cooper farm because they wore boots and "knee buckles" with leather chaps. The Gbande said they looked kwii.

Westernized natives learned the wrong lessons from their masters. Rascality was Liberia's way of life. Regardless of education, they succeeded by illegitimate means.

In most cases, in the African setting, education didn't go beyond literacy. Natives who migrated to Monrovia, became dependent on a Western way of life they weren't qualified to succeed in. As classic marginal men, they were ineffective in both cultures since they no longer fully understood either one. Literacy made them dissatisfied with traditional culture. And yet, they were helpless to compete in modern culture as they had assumed. In Monrovia, they faced the double whammy of restricted inclusion and lack of ability. Nor could they successfully return to the village. They survived by rascality — exploiting others. Many became con-artists.

President Tubman appointed Sam Gibson to patrol the road between Monrovia and Kakata, since he had a truck route. Sam was given a motorcycle for his job and his brother took over driving his truck. Sam fined every truck driver fifty cents, except his brother. Trucks could only go thirty miles an hour. Even then, Sam fined them for going too fast. Passengers in the back of a truck warned the driver, "Motorcycle comin'!" When the driver slowed down, Sam fined him for going too slow.

The other truck owners complained to Tubman. They said amongst themselves, "That raw Bassa man's not even givin' all that money to government. He's buildin' a big house. He's gettin' rich chopping [stealing] our money!"

Several weeks later, when Sam broke his leg in a motorcycle accident, everyone rejoiced. They said, "Hallelujah! God no be sleep. Oh, He got him. He broke Sam's leg!"

One day, at Duside Hospital, a white superintendent pulled up in his pickup truck. In the back, was a native being held for some reason. As soon as the superintendent walked into the hospital, the native ran away.

When the white superintendent came out, he assumed his prisoner had gone to the bathroom. When he called around for him, one of the Gbande men standing there said, "He be big medicine man, oh. He disappears when he wants to. He be right in the truck but you can't see him. Be very nice to him. Don't talk bad or he may grab the steering wheel."

Another Gbande said, "He go back to his house. If he like his work, you go find him there."

Two natives told a Kru surgical assistant at Duside that they found diamonds and needed money to dig for them. The Kru man fell for it and gave them money. Three months later, they returned. One of them said, "We built a dam to dig for diamonds but it broke and the area flooded. We need more money for equipment to build a stronger dam." The other added, "I need medicine. My back hurts too bad." Again, he gave them money.

After they left, I said, "Did you see how smooth their hands were? It didn't look to me like they were doing any hard work."

He said, "Maybe they're the headmen." We never saw them again.

Western education was seen as an avenue to wealth since it was the way to succeed and compete in the larger world. Literacy gave the power to communicate words on paper. Western education implied status. Since there weren't many Western educated natives, they were an elite group.

An educated Loma who attended Bolahun during the 1950s, told me, "At graduation, the missionaries gave a few of us extra recognition. The chief excused us from farm work so we could accompany the missionaries as interpreters when they visited the surrounding towns.

"In my town near Fissibu, Old Man Babu made sure we went to school and to the midweek prayer service. Every evening, he made the rounds asking us, 'Did you do your school work? If you didn't, I'm going to beat you. This is an honor for our village. These people came all the way here to show us new ways.' He was stricter than the missionaries. The missionaries didn't care if you held a girl to dance. Old Man Babu didn't like it. He escorted us out saying that was 'too mature for the girl.' When he was there, boys and girls had to dance by themselves.

"The old people understood there was something beneficial and important about school. Those who went were better off than those who didn't. Parents couldn't interrupt you if you were doing your homework. Any work the missionaries wanted done, the whole town completed — whether kids were in school or not. They suspended farm work so every able-bodied townsman could 'brush' the school compound. The elders sat and watched to see that it was done properly."

An educated Gbande woman told me about her graduation from Cuttington College during the 1960s, "There was great rejoicing in my village because I was one of the first women to reach such a level. The people danced and sang. They carried me in a chief's hammock all around the village.

"At first, my people didn't want women educated because they knew they'd never become a wife and mother in the traditional way. Girls who went to the third or fourth grade no longer wanted to be a part of the village. They usually ended up becoming the concubine of a government official and having children by him. Rarely did they marry. The men of my village didn't want that for their daughters.

"Gradually my people came to look favorably upon education for women. They realized the only way to uplift the country was to educate all the children. Each year in my village, one girl was chosen to go to school. Girls actually hid at that time because there was so much pressure to succeed. When my father decided I should go, I wanted to be the very best. I was eager to read every book there was. I couldn't wait to get home to do my homework. I worked hard to get a double promotion."

Educated African-Liberians felt justified in using every trick in the book. A classic example was Sumo, a Loma graduate student at Michigan State during the 1960s. Sumo was well-schooled in Americo-Liberian machinations since he had been given to Tubman as a boy.

One day, he saw a newspaper ad for a car "with no money down" so he went and got a car. When the dealership took him to court for not paying, he asked the members of the African Student Association to attend for support. As the judge began explaining the case, my Nigerian friend, Emanuel, said, "Who's that coming!" We jerked our heads to see someone in a large African gown, wearing dark sunglasses and a red fez, slowly and deliberately march up the center aisle, his gown trailing behind. Everyone stood, including the judge.

At the dais, Sumo said slowly, "I am Sumo Jones, a student at Michigan State University from the Republic of Liberia, West Africa. I have held many positions in the Liberian government and I'm on a full scholarship from your country to help me treat Liberians as Americans treat people. I took them at their word when they said I could get a car with no money. The salesman showed me cars and I took one. Now they're humbugging me to pay money. That's the whole truth, your honor. You see all those people sitting there? They're my countrymen from Africa. Some of them are working on their doctorate degrees. They can all vouch for me."

The judge said, "Do you have the car here?"

Sumo said, "Yes, your honor, it's in the parking lot."

Emanuel whispered loudly, "Sumo's shaming all of us! We ought to beat him up when we get out of here! He's giving us all a bad name."

The judge told Sumo, "Mr. Jones, just give me the car keys. In a case like this, we're supposed to go through a trial and you would have to pay court costs. I'm sure your friends here know this is not a give-away if they've been here any length of time. I'm going to dismiss this case, assuming you've newly arrived and you don't know our customs and culture. We're sorry to embarrass you. We respect you, Liberia, and your friends as Africa's leaders of tomorrow."

He handed the car keys to the bailiff and told the dealership's attorney, "Here's your car back." Pounding the gavel, he said, "Case dismissed."

Sumo said, "Thank you, Your Honor," and reached up to shake the judge's hand. The judge stood and said, "Thank you, Sir. This is a classic case of cultural misunderstanding. Things like this can sometimes even cause war." Slightly bowing, he told Sumo, "Thank you for your understanding."

Several months later, Sumo was back in court. This time, he ran a red light on campus in an old clunker he bought. There were only three Liberians in the courtroom. As an obviously pregnant woman walked up the center aisle, my Vai friend, Gus, whispered loudly, "So that's who Sumo hit!"

A witness said, "This woman had the light. I couldn't believe it. I saw this guy coming and he just plowed right into her car."

Sumo said, "My car's not damaged. How did her car get so damaged?"

The witness said, "Because you ran into it!"

Sumo said, "You just don't like Africans. That's why you're saying that."

The witness said, "I didn't even know you were an African. I'm just telling the truth."

The pregnant woman stood and told Sumo, "What did you want to do to me? Look at me!"

The judge said, "Have you checked with your doctor?"

She said, "Yes, everything's OK. I'm just glad I wasn't harmed and my baby wasn't. I don't want to go into a lawsuit. I just want him to repair my car. The baby's due and the quarter's almost over. I've got to prepare for exams."

The judge told Sumo, "You're a very lucky man. This woman and her husband should have sued you. You have two weeks to get her car repaired. I'm suspending your license for the next two quarters. I will instruct the campus police to help you with your driving skills. When I receive their report, I'll decide whether to give your driver's license back."

Sumo showed the black officers of the campus police his Liberian police badge and bought them beer. They gave him a good report.

When educated African-Liberians returned home, they could only go forward in the Americo-Liberian mode of Western culture. In their drive for status, they wanted everything the Americo-Liberians wanted. They replicated their hypocrisy and decadence to get it. Status was everything. Having status justified doing anything to get it. In one-upmanship, they strived to outdo the Americo-Liberians, becoming more "Americo-Liberian" than the Americo-Liberians. By doing better and having more, their "superior" imitation made them superior to the Americo-Liberians. Those allowed to join the government displayed the same "every man for himself" mentality. Their excuse was, "Everybody's doing it."

During the 1960s, at Michigan State, my friend Gus constantly railed against the Americo-Liberians. While Tubman was his particular target, he said they were all corrupted. Every day, his theme was, "Ben, we have to go and change the government. It's a disgrace. Liberia has resources but her leaders are completely immoral. Think about it, Ben."

While he criticized Americo-Liberian extravagance, he wanted the same things. When he got a high government post, he built a lavish house and other houses for rental. He ran around with women.

In 1976, I ran into him at Robertsfield International Airport and said, "Gus, I thought you told me we should come home and reform Liberia. I hear you've built all kinds of houses. What's going on?"

He said, "Ha! Ha! Ha! Ben, when in Rome, do like the Romans! The big people here do nothing. We're doing all the work. When you're in government, these foreigners doing business here bribe you with money and building materials. You may as well get in on it. Besides, one man can't make a difference."

The purpose of education is to make a meaningful contribution to bring about change. Educated African-Liberians were either put into government posts unrelated to their expertise, or they worked under Americo-Liberian heads of government. As a result, their education was only "image." While they saw the Americo-Liberians with new eyes, the lure of Liberia was great. They participated in Americo-Liberian decadence to get their piece of the pie.

They became even more lavish. As my barely refined Kru friend said, "They like big shot business too much." One day, in 1978, a Liberian colleague at the University of Michigan-Flint, walked me out to my car. When he saw it, he exclaimed, "Doc! I could never imagine you driving a (compact) car like this!"

The few educated African-Liberians who were given access to government corruption, indulged at the expense of their people. As they exploited their people, traditional African-Liberians now had three groups of predators: Americo-Liberians, foreigners, and educated African-Liberians.

An educated Loma told me, "Sumo treated us worse than any Americo-Liberian I know. He confiscated all of a Loma man's furniture from his house in Monrovia. When he served as Superintendent of Lofa County, he built a lavish house in Voinjama. Then he had the three small houses nearby demolished because he said they lowered the value of his house. One of the houses even belonged to his bodyguard. He had a Loma doctor's rice field burned because he was jealous of his popularity. When these complaints were brought to President Tolbert and investigated, Sumo was sacked (fired)."

Throughout her history, Liberia had her share of well-meaning, but unsteady white missionaries. Many times, those willing to go to foreign lands were loners who didn't fit into the American society. They were losers who couldn't succeed. In Liberia, as well as in Africa, they became the "great white father" among naïve natives who had nothing. In their arrogance, they never understood the culture or learned the local language. Converts had to learn English. When they went on furlough, they were touted as martyrs for their sacrifice of living in a savage place. In reality, they had servants waiting on them. In their isolation, they had a free hand.

African-Liberians saw Christianity as a stepping stone to modernity and success — having access to Western goods. Becoming a preacher or teacher was a way to get something from God and white Christians. African-Liberian pastors trained in America were no longer willing to live in the village and preach to their people. When they returned home, they used their education to further themselves in Monrovia.

Image was everything. Educated African-Liberians built mansions in Monrovia. They replicated the Americo-Liberian lifestyle, with traditional relatives as house boys. Taxi drivers drew attention by painting slogans on their taxis and signaling each other with their horns. African-Liberians said to each other, "Do you think I'm a small boy?" During rainy season, young men pulled up their pants cuffs as they walked so they wouldn't get them muddy. Membership in the lodge indicated Americo-Liberian acceptance. In 1972, a Mende brother who joined the Odd Fellows told me, "This is great! None of my other brothers are in the lodge, not even Patrick, who's educated." In 1973, an educated African-Liberian showed me his farm — just a patch of nothing. Even so, its very existence indicated status.

During our year in Vahun in 1983-84, my brother Patrick chided me about doing things the correct way. He was Mende in the British sense, since he had served as a police chief in Freetown, Sierra Leone. He rarely dressed before noon and regularly walked over to my house in his pajamas. Since he was the only one in Vahun, besides me, who wore pajamas, they gave him status.

One morning I walked over to his house instead. There I found him, as the local magistrate, holding court on his front porch — in his pajamas. When I told Anita, she privately dubbed him the pajama judge.

In 1985, I heard a former Gbande brother-in-law yell to his daughter, "Come take off my shoes so I can take a nap!" During the civil war, it was said that Doe's troops didn't want to lie in the grass to shoot because they didn't want to get their uniforms dirty.

In 2006, an educated Loma woman raised in Monrovia told me, "My father already had a college degree and he's a successful businessman. But he's always wanted to be a lawyer. Even though he's old, he just got his law degree from the University of Liberia."

Westernized African-Liberians replicated Americo-Liberian promiscuity. An educated Loma told me, "When I got engaged, my future brother-in-law told me, 'I'll give you a spare key to my apartment across town so you'll always have a back up.'"

"I asked him, 'What do you mean, back up?'

"He said, 'Well, even though you're marrying my sister, you should always have a girlfriend somewhere as a back up.'"

"I told him, 'I waited for your sister so she could finish her college education. And now you're suggesting this? What will happen if your sister and I have a problem? How will you advise us? No, I don't need any key for that.'"

He went on, "He's in his fifties now and has three children by his wife, one by a girlfriend, and who knows how many more. When his wife complained that he focused too much attention on his girlfriend and her child, he told her, 'If you complain any more I won't do anything more for your children.' His electricity was cut off because he didn't pay the bill. But he thought nothing of spending seven thousand dollars on a girlfriend. He's still fathering children younger than his own grandchildren. I asked him, 'Who's going to look after these children?' He told me, 'That's up to my children. They have the same name.'"

Westernized African-Liberians became alcoholics partly because it was such a large element of being civilized. "Drinking with the guys" was essential to being accepted. The two Gbande young men I brought to America were alcoholics and heavy smokers.

Samuel Doe and his cohorts were marginal men. Since they lived in Monrovia, they had no genuine understanding of traditional ways. On top of that, social change had modified tribal culture. Even if they questioned the Western or Americo-Liberian way, they had no other option but to replicate Americo-Liberian ways. The Americo-Liberian model provided the only unity for soldiers of different tribes, since their unity of opposition had dissipated with the success of the coup.

The coup's success gave African-Liberians a new confidence. They were in charge. At the same time, they were insecure since they had no idea how to govern. They wanted change but they didn't know what kind of change or how to achieve it. In their cultural marginality, they couldn't successfully go backward or forward. Since the Americo-Liberians were an empty image, African-Liberians were, in essence, pursuing something that wasn't there.

The soldiers in charge didn't even have the solidarity or limited expertise of the Americo-Liberians. Their unity of opposing the Americo-Liberians was gone. Their status as rulers was empty. Since they were incompetent, they were manipulated by Americo-Liberians behind the scenes. There was a fast training for Doe and his cohorts. Although Doe became "Dr. Doe," it didn't grant genuine status, for him or for Liberia.

Barely refined or refined African-Liberians were unemployable along Western lines. If they were literate, they weren't educated. As a result, they resented those who were educated. Liberia had two standards of knowledge — Liberian standards and Western standards. Those knowledgeable by Liberian standards weren't knowledgeable by Western standards.

When the African-Liberians gained control, it was power based on emotion, not rationality. Once the soldiers got power, it was irrelevant what happened next. Doe's aim was to overthrow Tolbert. Taylor's aim was to overthrow Doe. African-Liberians either didn't know or weren't interested in managing power for good. They could only succeed through illegitimate means, corruption and exploitation.

African-Liberians wanted to be anything other than what the Americo-Liberians had made them. Educated African-Liberians, with a renewed pride in their African heritage, wanted to be African in a Western way. Status now lay with tribal ties. Cabinet members had tribal names. Marginal Americo-Liberians claimed their African roots, saying, for example, "I have some Gbande in me too." Doe was accepted into Poro. He wore a tribal gown and carried a scepter.

Doe looked to the past for legitimacy. He resurrected Tubman's legacy by designating his birthday a national holiday. Schoolchildren lined the streets for Doe's presidential cavalcade. He gave out money like Tubman. He arrested people and then released them. He wore a swearing-in-suit like Tolbert. During his presidential campaign in 1985, he was accepted into the Masonic Lodge.

Doe said what people wanted him to say. After the coup, he said, "We seek to build a new society in which there is justice, human dignity, and equal opportunities and fair treatment for all. For too long did the masses of our people live in their own country only to be treated like slaves on a plantation." There was a vast discrepancy between the words and deeds of the People's Redemption Council.

African-Liberians succeeded by exploitation. Doe led a group of soldiers, hungry for power and determined to make up for past losses. Although he increased the salaries of the military, soldiers looted and extorted money and goods from traditional African-Liberians at checkpoints. The coup replaced one elite with another. Wealth remained in the hands of a few, just a different few. A Nigerian said, "The coup was not in the cause of the people but in the cause of Doe and his collaborators." Government and party politics remained the major source of wealth. Doe's focus on himself and his Krahn tribe created a new class of rich African-Liberians who were loyal to him, along with the few Americo-Liberians who fit into the system.

Taylor had more expertise than Tubman, Tolbert, and Doe. As a result, he took exploitation to an even higher level. My barely refined Kru friend told me, "Jiggers live by toes. He went to redeem his people but he's doing worse. They talk all kinda sweet talk but when they get in there, they do the same thing."

As Taylor exploited in a more sophisticated way, the pie was divided among the "educated". Revenue from the ship registry was tied to the purchase and transport of arms to Liberia. Taylor sold diamonds to Al-Qaida to support his war and the war in Sierra Leone. At Christmas, a little money was doled out to government employees in lieu of pay.

Taylor's soldiers lived by the spoils of war. As they took people's clothing at checkpoints, they said, "We're protecting you." Border guards extracted a payment of fifty Liberian dollars from African-Liberians fleeing into Sierra Leone.

After Taylor was deposed, Liberia's interim government was an "old man in new clothes." An educated Loma told me, "Doc, these guys are building mansions with satellite disks. A friend of mine has a huge compound with a golf course maintained by the Chinese. When you go into these compounds, you can't even tell you are in Liberia. A lot of people walk around Monrovia with cell phones.

"The U.S. is giving too much money too soon. The Speaker of the House ordered one hundred Mercedes Benz's and there are only seventy-six members of the House and Senate. These guys make twenty thousand dollars and they're given a seventy-thousand-dollar car. Some of them have numerous cars from the Taylor regime, but they're still demanding a new car."

"I checked on the internet and I found out that Gudi Bryant ordered two custom made bullet-proof cars from Germany. These cars cost five hundred thousand dollars each. And they're talking about raising the price of rice from twenty dollars a bag to thirty, so they'll have money to fix the roads. When they were warned that the people would strike, they said, 'If they want to strike, we've got the UN here.' Doc, the UN is not there to protect them from the Liberian people."

African-Liberians aspire to a life of ease. My barely refined Kru friend told me, "Sit down in the city. Don't want to go back in the country to work. Life in Liberia is now in the street. People eat and sleep in the street. Drink water. You do it in the street. Ain't got nothin'. Where will you go? No place, no food. All the rascals."

The civil war has exacerbated a dependency on foreigners. There are generations of Liberians uneducated because of the conflict. An educated Loma told me, "They're restructuring the army and the police force. They've set higher standards. Rebel soldiers aren't eligible. People will never trust those who put the gun to their head. They know the rebels must be given something to do. Their camps even have mental health counselors. On last Independence Day, the rebel soldiers said they were sorry. They would never again fight the Liberian people.

"JFK is up and running with doctors from India and Cuba. I can't blame America. Liberia's war was self-inflicted. No one came and attacked us. You mean you can get mad and break down your house and expect someone else to come and rebuild it for you?"

In the Liberian Diaspora, rascality continues as "loser" African-Liberians live off of women. An educated Loma told me, "Liberian communities in America have become colonies of parasitic Liberian men who cat around and use women to support them. They use charm and their good looks to prey on the loneliness and vulnerability of women, whether it's their wives, girlfriends, or new girlfriends.

They're leeches on women who are working and struggling hard to survive. They rely on the honor of extended family members to raise and support their children. When their children grow up, they manipulate and exploit them as well, preying on their longing for acceptance."

Liberia is the most classic illustration of the *cycle of racism*. The Americo-Liberians "ruined" the natives just as whites had ruined them. Hypocrisy remains an incurable disease. African-Liberians are loyal to any denomination or person who can help them, financially or otherwise. Prosperity theology has great appeal in a war torn country. Chain letter emails promising good luck circulate among Liberians.

Monrovia is a den of robbers. An educated Gbande told me, "Uncle, I was in a car in Monrovia and I sent the driver to get some bottled water. While I was waiting, some boys came running, yelling, 'Boss Man! Boss Man! Something wrong with your car!' When I got out to look, one of the guys jumped in the front seat and stole my cell phone."

Liberians who return are "devoured by ants." The wife of a Mende nephew told me, "The corruption starts the minute you get to Liberia. There are very few people you can rely upon, including your own family. That's what war does to you. The people are a mess and it's not just one family. It's everyone in Liberia. Everyone's fighting for their own household. No one does anything for nothing. If someone gives you a cup of cold water, you'll compensate for it in some way or another. They never thank you for anything. They told me, 'You too American now,' because I wouldn't play their game. You have to deal with them as you see them, Doc. It's not the Liberia you left. Everyone is looking to you for what you cannot do."

Ellen Johnson-Sirleaf, Liberia's president since 2006, faces a cultural standard of hypocrisy, dependency, and decadence — essentially, success by manipulation and exploitation. I fear it will prove a greater challenge than rebuilding Liberia's infrastructure.

Part II. Racism's Impact on National Character in America

America is false to the past, false to the present, and solemnly binds itself to be false to the future. Go where you may. Search where you will. Roam all the monarchies and despotism of the Old World. Travel through South America.

Search out every abuse, and when you have found the last, lay your facts by the side of the everyday practices of this nation and you will say with me that for revolting barbarity and shameless hypocrisy, America reigns without a rival.

— Frederick Douglass

Chapter Seven: Identity

The Inferiority Complex

> You degrade us and then ask us why we are degraded?
> — Frederick Douglass, 1847

America's story of slavery and racism is essentially, "The Making of the American Negro." Whatever Negroes became was a reaction to white thought and behavior. Black historians focus on slaves that revolted, escaped, learned to read, and became artisans, because these exceptions say, "Not all Negroes were stereotypical Sambos." However, the greater truth is that slavery and racism made Negroes, as individuals and as a people, more alike than different.

Racism was a force that shaped reality. Although whites had a racial image of rationality, they were primarily emotional in the area of race because of the need to justify. The power of racism lay not only in myth, but in the enforcement of that myth. To prove themselves right, whites made Negroes inferior. Since racism is based on emotion, it's impervious to rationality or reality.

The end of slavery never meant the end of white supremacy and racism. The ramifications of slavery lasted long after it ended as coping patterns of thought and behavior were passed from one generation to another. During the 1950s, Negroes displayed the lingering themes of slavery.

In 1953, in a Negro barber shop in St. Louis, a regular customer who made his living moving furniture with his truck, walked in impeccably dressed in the latest style. He wore a hat and his shoes were polished. A man waiting for a haircut said, "Sam? You move furniture and dress like this? I hear your wife doesn't come home from work sometimes. She stays at her white boss' house. Is it true he's a bachelor?"

Sam said, "Shut up, Nigger, let me tell you. He's good to Sarah. She came home the other night and you know what she put on the table? Seven hundred and fifty dollars! I was tired but when I saw it, my sleep went away."

The man said, "Seven hundred and fifty dollars? What for, Sam?"

Sam said, "Her birthday's this week and I was worried what to get her. She told me this was just a little of her birthday gift. There's more comin'."

The man said, "And you don't say nothin' about it? Nigger you must be crazy!"

Sam said, "Listen, Nigger. Sarah's a good wife. She tells me everything."

The man said, "Even about goin' to bed with that peckerwood and you don't get angry?"

Sam said, "Nigger, your head must be screwed on wrong. You know what your woman's doin' bringin' that kinda money. Take a good look at me. If you come to my house at any time, you're gonna find bread on the table. That's why I allow this. Your wife's probably screwin' someone but she doesn't tell you. And that's why you're strugglin'. Nigger, you don't know nothin'."

After Sam left, the man said, "White folks like nigger girls. That white playboy is very regular with that sister. That's gone on for a long time, right here in St. Louis."

Negroes were not only made inferior in slavery, they were kept inferior in freedom. They believed everything their Negro teachers taught them but their teachers didn't know anything. In 1956, when I was a graduate student at Fisk University in Nashville, I visited Humbo, Tennessee, the home of my first wife, Ruth, who was Negro. The local Negro school principal invited me to speak at their one-room schoolhouse, saying the children had never seen an African. The next morning, we walked to the school through a field of weeds. Inside the school, the floor was half wood plank, half dirt. Some of the wooden benches were broken. The few books were scattered on the floor, with pages torn out. Most of the students were barefoot.

Out of fifty children, there were three questions about Africa. The first was, "Do they have big snakes in Africa?" Then second was, "Do you have lotsa lions?" And the third was, "Since you got a lotta rivers, do you have that big something called a hippopotamus?" (They could hardly pronounce it.)

After answering those questions, I said, "Is there anything else you'd like to know about Africa?" They stared at me with blank faces. When the teacher rang the bell for recess, they clapped for me and ran outside.

They spent most of the day running up and down the field surrounding the school. When they were inside, they did their own thing. The only systematic thing I saw was the pledge of allegiance that morning.

I was disturbed, so I asked the principal, "When do the children do reading, math, and English?"

She said, "It's the law that we have school, but those things wouldn't be helpful to them. Tomorrow, it'll be a different group of kids. They'll all end up workin' on the farm sharecroppin' anyway."

Negroes were perpetually insecure, in many ways, as helpless in freedom as they had been in slavery. In 1956, as a graduate student at Washington University, I took some African college students on a tour of the South. At a little town in Tennessee, we stopped for gas and got out to stretch. Suddenly, Oyo came from around the back of the gas station and said, "Come here!" Lying on the ground was a dead Negro. When we demanded to know what happened, everyone ignored us, including Negroes passing by who just looked at us.

When we reached Humbo, John and Penny explained that the dead man was an enterprising mechanic in the area. A white policeman had repeatedly raped his beautiful wife. She couldn't take it anymore so she told her husband. When he warned the policeman to keep away from her, the policeman said, "No you're gonna stay away from her," and he shot him in broad daylight. Whites laughed about it and dared anyone to retrieve the body.

Negroes couldn't be anything or have anything. If they succeeded, poor whites had no excuse for their failure. In 1956, Ruth and I attended the funeral of her brother-in-law. Although Willie had a little farm on the outskirts of Humbo, he made his living as a mechanic. Since he was good at it, he lived better than poor whites in the area. His brand new Ford drove the nails into his coffin.

Since country roads are narrow, one car has to pull off for another to pass. Willie's neighbors knew when he went into town. One day, a white man waited in his truck by the side of the road near Willie's farm while the other white man followed Willie home in his truck. As Willie came down a hill near his home, the man waiting by the side of the road speeded straight towards him while the other truck followed close behind. Willie's car completely crushed, his death was ruled an accident.

He was very popular in the Negro community. At his funeral, the little countryside Negro church was so crowded, people stood along the back wall. We had to park a half mile away. As we walked to the church, I lamented, "What a tragedy! Look at the crowds coming. He was such a good man."

An elderly white woman standing in the yard heard me. She shook her head and said, "I knew this was gonna happen. He was the best mechanic we had 'round here and a good blacksmith too. But he was just too uppity."

One Sunday, a mulatto girl at Fisk took me with her to church. As Helen and I boarded the bus near campus, the back was already full with Negroes. The front had only four whites, so Helen led me to a seat one row behind the bus driver.

We were busy talking when I heard, "Nigger, move back!" I ignored it. A minute later, I heard, "I said Nigger, move back!" I looked up to see the white middle-aged bus driver get up, take off his uniform cap, and walk up to me.

He grabbed me by the shirt collar and lifted me up into the air. As my legs dangled, I struggled to breathe. I was furious. He was not only messing up my suit, he was humiliating me before Helen. Inches from my face, he yelled, "Nigger, I'm gonna get you out!" I clenched my teeth and butted him with my forehead the way I hit soccer balls. Blood gushed from his mouth and nose. He stumbled backwards and fell down the bus steps out onto the sidewalk. There he lay on his back, out cold.

After a moment of dead silence, all the Negroes on the bus instantly sprang to life, scattering out onto the sidewalk. Only one remained — an elderly, heavy set woman rocking in her seat, saying, "Lord help us. He done done it. Lord help him. He done done it."

The whites on the bus waited on the sidewalk. Helen and I stood by the bus driver. Negroes walking by stopped and watched from a distance. A police car pulled up. Four white officers came over and asked the whites standing there what happened. They couldn't say.

A policeman frisked me and said, "Are you the one? What did ya hit 'im with? Where's your weapon?"

I said, "I hit him with my head."

"You're lyin', Nigger. You must have a secret weapon. Take off your coat." He checked my coat pockets and said, "Take off your pants."

"I'm not going to take my pants off in the street! I told you I used my head. I can demonstrate it on you."

He backed up and raised his hands, saying, "Oh, no."

As the elderly woman got off the bus, he said, "What'd this nigger do to the bus driver?"

She said, "I saw the bus driver collar 'im and all I know the bus driver was down on his back."

The police helped the bus driver up. Since his front teeth were knocked out, he struggled to say, "I don't know. It happened all of a sudden."

The policeman turned back to me, "Where do you live, Boy?"

I struggled to control my anger as I said, "I'm a graduate student at Fisk."

Another police car arrived. An officer got out and said, "Let's take him to jail. We'll finish questioning him there."

When I heard this, I told a Negro friend in the crowd, "Go and tell President Johnson they want to take me to jail." I was hoping Johnson hadn't left for church. When Johnson arrived, I told the police officer, "This is President Johnson. He can vouch for me."

The policeman said to Johnson, "Boy, is this one o' your boys?"

I whispered to Johnson, "I apologize for having to call you here."

He said, "Never mind about that, Ben. We'll work this out."

I told the policeman, "According to the law, I have the right to make one telephone call."

He said, "Use the payphone on the sidewalk."

I called David Thomas, the attaché to the Liberian ambassador in Washington, and told him to contact my sister Angie Brooks at the United Nations and tell her what happened. I said, "You've got to do something quick. They want to take me to jail and they just might kill me."

Thomas said, "Give me the phone numbers of the governor and President Johnson." A Negro friend in the crowd worked at the state capitol and gave me the governor's number. President Johnson gave me his.

Thomas said, "We'll call right back."

Twenty minutes later, another police car pulled up. An officer got out and said, "We gotta a big problem on our hands. Let that nigger go. He's a Liberian national. People from the UN and the Liberian embassy are sending representatives to look into the case."

As I waited for Helen, the policeman turned to her and said, "What're you doin' with this nigger?"

She said, "I'm Negro myself."

"You got proof o' this?"

She showed him her birth certificate; mulattos always carried them with them.

At Fisk, the Negro students said, "Those Africans behave like real men! If you attack 'em, they retaliate right then and there. He stayed and admitted he did it. We've lost everything. A nigger would never do that! If he did something, he'd run away. And the rest of us would suffer for it." Whites in Nashville branded me "that African at Fisk University." The students warned me, "Don't go anywhere alone. Those people will be lookin' for you. White people in the South are ruthless. Be careful."

The incident reminded me of what a Negro GI told me in Liberia in 1945, "You gotta be very careful in America cause whites can do anything to you. If a white man kills you, accident or not, you're not considered a human being. If he kills you in a remote place, it's not reported, even if it's an accident. If your family protests, they'll kill 'em too. They have some good whites but when it comes to savin' a white man's skin, they'll never be on your side even when you're right."

Negroes lived in fear. In 1956, in St. Louis, Ruth and I took her mother, Penny, to a restaurant to eat. When Penny saw the restaurant full of white people, she hesitated at the door. After we sat down, she asked me, "Do you know any of these people here? They're all white."

I said, "No."

"An' you comin' here to eat, just you and Ruth and me? We better get outta here. Aren't you scared, Boy? I ain't hungry. Let's go."

"Penny, we've already ordered. When your dinner comes, just look at your plate. Don't look at the white people. Are they looking at you?"

"No, but I'm on my guard. I'm watchin' 'em like a hawk."

"They're just human beings."

"Yeah, but they're different human beings. They ain't like us."

Ruth said, "Ma, it's O.K. Ben wouldn't put you in any danger."

Penny said, "He come from Africa. He don't know nothin'!"

I said, "Penny, I know a whole lot."

Penny said, "I ain't talkin' 'bout books, I'm talkin' 'bout white people! What do you do when you see 'em?"

I said, "When I lived in Germany, we talked with whites and ate with them. All the servants at the consulate were white."

Penny said, "Ben, you done done everything! Lord, have mercy. I can't believe it. And you lived through it."

When I paid the bill, the white waitress said, "Thank you. Come back again." As we walked to the car, Penny said, "I ain't goin' back there. The good Lord was with us. Lord, have mercy. I'm not gonna yield to temptation."

In their poverty, Negroes were manipulated to serve whites. They knew they lived in a white world and they had to play the white man's game. They coped by conforming, staying in their place.

In St. Louis, as Ruth and I walked by a store, a white couple came out of the door. Ruth instantly elbowed me into a snow bank in the street. I slipped and almost fell. She saw I was angry so she said, "You wanna get us in trouble? Don't you know when you see white people comin', you gotta get off the sidewalk? You may be a king in Africa but it's the custom in this country. Here we're all just niggers."

I said, "They didn't say anything to us."

She said, "White people don't talk to niggers."

I said, "Ruth, I've never gotten off the sidewalk for anyone, whether he's pink or blue. The sidewalk's wide. We could have easily passed each other. From now on, you walk on the street side. If anyone touches me, I'll kick him. He'll never forget it."

She said, "You gotta whole lot to learn. This ain't Africa. This is white folks' country. White people are mean. They'll hurt you just for not gettin' off the sidewalk."

Ruth told Penny, "Times have changed. Benjamin'd be dead a long time ago. When we see white people comin', he refuses to get off the sidewalk."

Penny said, "Ben, you gotta be careful 'specially if it's a white woman."

I said, "If she doesn't want to come close to me, she can get off the sidewalk. Why do I have to do it?"

Penny said, "Lord, God! He don't know nothin' 'bout this country! Lord, have mercy on him!" And she went into a big prayer.

I said, "Nobody said anything to me."

Penny said, "That ain't mean nothin'. They'll get you next time. You have to follow the rules here."

Each time I spoke with white people and looked them straight in the eye, Ruth told me later, "You're supposed to let white people talk to you first and look down. Everybody knows that. You don't have any common sense!"

In 1950, when I was a freshman at the University of Kansas, I visited a Negro Baptist pastor and his family in Topeka. We had just finished lunch when we saw a car swerve in the street, cross the median, go into the yard next door, and come to a stop in their back yard. The pastor's son said, "It's a white woman and she's by herself." I thought she must have had a seizure, so I started to run out to check on her.

Rev. Hicks stopped me, "Don't go there, Benjamin! That's a white woman. You don't just go there. If you do, the problem is what she's doin' here. We haven't observed her yet."

I said, "To find that out, we have to go there. It looks like she's dying. She's not moving."

Mrs. Hicks said, "If you go there, she may say you took her into our backyard to rape her. And she'd have a good case. After all, what's she doin' in a Negro neighborhood? We'll call the police so she won't be able to blame us."

Two white policeman went to the car. After they talked to her, they pulled her car out of the yard, and told us, "She's drunk. We're takin' her home."

After they left, the Hicks were visibly relieved. Rev. Hicks lectured me, "Many good-hearted Negro men have been lynched for tryin' to help a white woman. Whenever you see a white person in trouble or an older white woman where people can see you, don't go by yourself. Take someone with you and be very gentle. But if it's a young white woman, she'll feel ashamed and lie and say you forced her into that situation. Benjamin, the only way you'll make it in this country is to pretend you don't see a white woman. This isn't Africa."

I said, "Rev. Hicks, with all due respect, you're a man of God. What about the story of the Good Samaritan?"

He said, "You can't be a good Samaritan to whites, especially if it's a young white woman. Whites know the story of the Good Samaritan too, but they'll hang you for it. Take my word, Benjamin. I was born here."

Negroes were locked into race, forced to play the role. Anything they achieved was in spite of white supremacy and racism. Since they were highly visible, they were easily denied access, kept out of everything. Because whites were irrational in the area of race, Negroes were rejected no matter what they did. They were not only condemned for not succeeding, they were punished when they succeeded. They were not only disparaged for fulfilling stereotype, they were persecuted when they broke out of it.

Upper and middle class Negroes played by the rules, assuming they'd be assimilated into the American society. White insecurity and jealousy made that an empty dream. Whites wanted Negroes to conform to their standards, not succeed or excel. Negroes who became doctors, lawyers, and teachers could only serve the Negro community. When they got doctorate degrees from Ivy League schools, they couldn't teach at them.

They were only allowed to rise in areas that fit stereotype such as, sports and the arts. Since they were "clumsy and slow," they weren't allowed to compete with whites. Only model Negroes, such as Joe Louis and Jackie Robinson, were allowed to excel. Boxing was an avenue of success for lower class Negroes. Negro athletes were only praised by the Negro community. The two exceptions were Joe Louis and Jesse Owens because their success shamed Hitler.

Entertaining whites was an acceptable role. Negroes were first recognized and admired by whites as musicians. When they performed in blackface, their features were grotesque. Light-skinned Negroes amused whites at the Cotton Club in Harlem. Negro actors could only play stereotypical roles. Hattie McDaniel was the first Negro to win an Oscar in 1940, for her role as mammy in "Gone with the Wind." When Negroes broke some rules, others were rigidly enforced. They could perform in a hotel but not stay in it. Negro musicians on the road had to be hosted by the Negro community.

Lower class Negroes were servants and manual laborers, work that didn't require training. They did the dirtiest and most dangerous work that whites didn't want. In the military, they served as cooks and stewards. Negro servants had to fit the image. Negro railroad porters wore full clothing. They had to have a big smile on their face to show they were "happy to serve whites."

Negroes were ambivalent towards whites. They were afraid of them but they had no respect for them. One day in Humbo, when Penny and I were alone in the house, she whispered, "We grow cotton but the white folks don't pay us much for it. They cheat us. They don't give John near the money he should get. And they go to church too. You know, Benjamin? God'll punish 'em for that 'cause He's just. That's what the good book says. I'd like to see 'em on that Judgment Day. I'll say, 'Lord, these white people tried to drive John and me and the children out.' I'll report 'em all and the Lord knows. They can't deny it."

In a Negro barber shop in St. Louis, I heard someone say, "Laugh. Then you can tell 'em anything. They'll believe you cause they're stupid as a Billy goat. They're all dirty, even those who pretend they're Christian. When you see those who seem to be liberal, be on your guard. They're gonna burn you. They're so used to cheatin' Negroes, it's just a part of their livin'. The white man'll never change. We know they're just givin' us leftovers. Those peckerwoods will drain you. They'll do anything to get a nigger to do somethin'."

In 1957, in Lansing, Michigan, a Negro friend told me, "I could mess 'em up very easy and they wouldn't know anything. But God doesn't like that. The only thing I don't have and many of 'em don't have, is a college degree. That's why I'm goin' to school."

In 1953, in St. Louis, when a white man walked into a corner store, the Negroes there instantly stopped talking. They stood at attention watching him intently. After he left, I asked them, "Do you know him? Did you think he was going to do something?"

There was a long pause. They looked at each other and then they looked at me and burst out laughing. One of them said, "Man, he's from Africa!" He told me, "You can't trust a white man till you know what he do's."

In a barber shop in Kansas City, someone said, "Here comes a peckerwood!" A white man walked in and asked if anyone there knew where a certain Negro repairman was. Everyone was dead silent. Finally, the barber said, "I don't recognize the name." After the man left, everyone laughed.

Someone said, "What he wanna do that for? Maybe he's not really lookin' for anything."

Another said, "I know the guy he's lookin' for but I'm not gonna help a peckerwood look for a nigger."

Someone else said, "I know 'im too." He told the guy next to him, "You know 'im too," and he described the guy to him.

The other man said, "Oh, I know him. They way he said his name, I didn't know he was talkin' 'bout him."

Finally, someone said, "You never trust a peckerwood."

The effect of racism made Negroes perpetually insecure. Freeing slaves made them "human," not equal. It wasn't just being ascribed to be inferior; it was the nature of the inferiority. Racial inferiority was genetic and thus unchangeable. Negroes could do nothing to alter their status. Racism universally degraded every Negro. Since it varied in degree, not substance, it generated a commonality in all Negroes — regardless of differences in the Negro experience.

As social creatures, our self-image depends on the perception and attitudes of others. Negroes took racism seriously because whites did. Each time whites called Negroes, "Boy," "Nigger," "George," etc., they reinforced Negro inferiority.

In 1956, at Fisk University, a mulatto friend and I were driving to lunch, when an elderly white couple stopped in front of us. The man rolled down his window and called back, "Hey George! Which way to Jackson Street?"

My friend said, "How'd you know my name?"

The man said, "I guessed it."

My friend said, "Well, if you're that good at guessing, damn you, guess your own way to Jackson St.! You're blocking us. Get outta my way!"

The car sped off. At lunch, I asked him, "Why'd you get so angry at those old white people?"

My friend said, "Ben, I'm from New York and white people never respect Negroes. They call us 'Boy' or 'George.' If someone's old, it's 'Uncle.' If they don't call a woman 'Girl,' they call her 'Aunt.' If I would've been close to him, you would've seen more. I might have busted his nose."

I said, "He didn't mean anything."

My friend said, "Oh yeah, he meant everything. He'd never call a white man that. He would've said, 'Sir' or 'Mister.'"

Negroes were perpetually insecure in their longing to be accepted by whites because it could never be fulfilled. They lived lives of constant rejection. During my years at Lincoln University in Jefferson City, Missouri, I spent my summers in St. Louis. When I went to the movies with my girlfriend Rebecca, I thought we sat in the balcony so we could see better. One evening, I went by myself and decided to try the main floor. The theatre was dark. They were already showing the previews.

As I sat down, the previews stopped and the lights came on. Someone in the audience called to the usher, "He's about midway!" The usher shined his flash-light in my face and said, "Come with me."

Negroes were perpetually insecure in their loss of identity. Although racism was a lie, they were subject to its all pervading influence. They were made in the white man's image because they lost any identity that derived from themselves. They had no identity or cultural perspective to counteract racism. Since they were outside the realm of history, there was no one to applaud their value. They had nothing but slavery to judge themselves.

They had only a past of shame, slavery justified by racial inferiority. Negroes were truly alone in the world — so lost, they didn't know how lost they were. They were the lowest of the low, a people with no place in history or the American society. Since they had no nationality to truly call their own, they had no genuine civic pride. Their only myth of glory was "survival."

In self-hatred, they blamed themselves and their African heritage for their suffering. They regretted the African in them. They didn't lament the loss of African culture since it represented an uncivilized past. With no interest in Africa, they were grossly ignorant.

During my first trip to America in 1949, I was talking with a Negro woman in the Philadelphia train station when she said, "You say you're African. I don't see any ring in your nose or openin' in your lip."

I said, "I may not have a nose ring, but I'm an African."

She turned to her friend and said, "He ain't from Africa!"

In 1957, I was waiting in the Chicago train station when a Negro sitting next to me said, "Where you goin'?"

I said, "I'm going to Michigan State University in East Lansing."

He said, "Where you come from?"

"From St. Louis, Missouri."

"No, where do you come from really? You speak funny."

"I'm from Africa."

"Africa? How'd you get here?"

"Well, I've been here for quite some time now."

"You walked all the way here from Africa? That shor' musta taken a long time! How many days did it take you?"

I said, "Walk from Africa?"

He said, "Yah, they don't have any roads. They don't have any cars. And they don't have any trains. And here you are. You musta walked to get here. How'd ya manage to do it?"

I said, "Well, Sir, you could do it too. Nothing's impossible when you're really determined."

He told the other Negroes sitting there, "Listen to this! This is incredible! You see this young man here? Can you believe he walked all the way from Africa to America?"

He told me, "Walkin' from Chicago to East Lansing must be a piece a cake. I bet you could do that too if you wanted to."

I said, "Well, why should I if the train's here?"

The Negroes sitting there nodded. The man said, "Power to you! Ain't you see? The white man done spoiled us. We can't even walk to the grocery store or the beer store!"

In 1951, during my first year at Lincoln, none of the girls would date me even though I was one of the best students. One day, I heard some girls say among themselves, "It's foolish for any decent Negro girl to date an African. Africa's responsible for our status of inferiority. Why would anyone want to identify with them?" As I walked across campus, boys sometimes called out, "Say! Where do you live? In a tree? How do you make tree houses?" Sometimes they said, "Do you really travel from tree to tree like Tarzan?" One day a boy told those with him, "He can speak English! Tarzan's been all over the country!"

One day, after gym class, I was taking a shower and I heard whispering. I turned around to see a group of boys staring at my behind. I said, "What're you guys looking for?"

They laughed nervously. One of them said, "We were told you had a tail. What happened to it?"

I said, "If I had one, you'd have seen it by now. I'm just like you. Get out of here!"

Word spread around campus that I didn't have a tail. Even then, some of the students said, "He may not have a tail but he's just one African. Maybe the others do."

Negroes longed for identity. Negro institutions longed for status and glory. There were Negroes as well who yearned for a positive feeling about Africa. They took pride in what they imagined Africa to be.

In 1956, when I was a graduate student at Washington University, I supervised a team of interviewers for the St. Louis Metropolitan Survey. For the survey to be authentic, homes were randomly chosen. None could be skipped or substituted.

One day, a white young woman on my team was unable to get an interview, so I assigned a white young man to accompany her. They came back and told me the minute they got to the door, an old Negro man had run them off with a shotgun, saying, "I know you, young lady. Whatcha bringin' this one for? Get offa my property or I'll blow your heads off!" When the young man refused to go back by himself, the director suggested that I go.

With some trepidation, I knocked on the door. The man abruptly opened it and looked at me sullenly. I said, "Good morning, Sir!" He left the door open and walked to a chair facing the doorway. Laying his shotgun on his lap, he said, "If you're comin' for the same thing those white people come for, you can forget it."

I said, "I'm from Africa and yes, I'd like to talk to you about the same thing."

He said, "From Africa? You talk funny. You tryin' to fool me with some funny language?"

"I can prove it to you. See the tribal marks on my face?"

"Lord, I declare. You really are from Africa. How'd they put that on your face?"

"I was too little to remember."

"Whatcha doin' here with those white people?"

"I'm a graduate student at Washington University. Those white people you chased away were working for me."

"I didn't know Negroes went to Washington University!"

He asked me in. As I sat down, he walked into another room and brought back a bottle of whiskey. Leaning his gun next to his chair, he sat down and said, "Oh, I'd like to go back to the ole country. Here, them white people never let us rest. And to think I mighta blown you up. Lord, forgive me. Come drink with me."

I said, "Well, it's early and I'm still working."

He said, "The Bible says a little for the stomach's sake. Now ask me anything you want to."

At the conclusion of the survey, I was honored for conducting the most difficult interview. Several weeks later, I stopped by to see him. He told his friend with him, "This brother's from the real country. He's from Africa. Man, I tell you, he's even goin' to Washington University! And white folks workin' for him!" As they clapped their hands and tapped their feet, the other man said, "Ain't that right!"

Negroes sensed that Africans had something they didn't. When I was at Washington University, I took a group of African college students on a summer tour of the South. Wearing our African gowns, we were well received everywhere we went. While staying in a hotel in Louisiana, I overheard a Negro cleaning woman say to her co-worker, "Girl, you know that's what we'd be if we weren't born in this country."

As racism generated self-hatred and self-rejection, it made Negroes their own worst enemy. They were forced to accept a pattern of thought contrary to what they inherently knew — they weren't what whites said they were. In their inferiority complex, they saw themselves and their racial group as whites did. Their stereotypes of Negroes were the same as whites, or even worse.

Since Negroes had no possibility of changing white perception, they conformed to white expectation. They expected to be inferior. Self-hatred made them dissatisfied with themselves. They hated their physical features. I heard in the Negro barbershop, "If you call someone black, you better be able to fight like Joe Louis or run like Jesse Owens." There was a significant market for skin-lightening creams and hair-straightening products in the Negro community. Negro performers either wore wigs or they straightened their hair with lye.

Negroes wanted to be "anything but an American Negro." They claimed Indian ancestry or white blood. The quadroons and octoroons in New Orleans were classified by how much white they had in them.

Negroes were classic examples of the insecure personality. While whites could be insecure as individuals, Negroes were fundamentally and perpetually insecure, not only as individuals, but as a people. To diffuse their pain, they used self-deprecating humor. One of the jokes I heard was about a Negro mortician who picked up a body. As he began to work on him, the man suddenly revived. He told him, "Niggers never cooperate! Lay down! You supposed to be dead!"

Negroes hated stereotype. They criticized and made fun of those who fulfilled it. When they called each other nigger in camaraderie, it meant "We're all in the same boat." They simultaneously used nigger as a criticism of stereotype, as in, "You ain't nothin' but a nigger!" I heard in the Negro barber shop, "Look at you, Nigger. What you wanna do? You can't do that. You're just gonna be a nigger like the rest of us." At Lincoln University, Dr. Maxwell told the chemistry students, "When you use a chemical, put the cap back on and put it back. Don't do like a nigger."

Negroes compensated by imagining they were somebody. They said, "We may not be educated, but we have mother wit." Those in the middle class said, "Be self-reliant. Save your own butt. I'm not gonna beg. I'm gonna work for my children." Negroes who were "higher up," said of others, "I wouldn't do that for anything." Parents shielded their children. They made sure they ate and went to the bathroom before taking them shopping.

Insecurity generated status consciousness in Negroes. They were obsessed with the impression they made on others, especially whites. Since they had so very little to be proud of, any little success or recognition was blown up. Jet and Ebony magazines exaggerated the social importance of Negroes in America and worldwide. Because there were so few heroes in the Negro community, Negro sports and entertainment figures were venerated.

Insecurity made Negroes sensitive to criticism. They couldn't reveal that they "didn't know." In their fear of failure, they said, "I'm not gonna humiliate myself." They were authoritarian. Everything was "black or white, right or wrong." They insisted on others agreeing with them, talking loud and long enough to win any argument. If they were challenged, they had to have the last word.

In self-centeredness, they looked for what they could get out of a relationship. If a man couldn't control a woman, he wasn't interested in her. Negroes displaced their anger and frustration on those closest to them. Negro parents were harsh in disciplining their children, the only thing they could control.

Negroes watched as African nations became independent and were recognized by the United Nations. They saw African diplomats in Washington, D.C. and African students on college campuses. After World War II, they said, "If we can fight and die in a war that liberated Europe, what about our own liberation in America?" Rosa Park's refusal to move to the back of the bus sparked a powder keg of black indignation. The issue of civil rights became a raging river that couldn't be contained. It swept everyone along, including its leader Martin Luther, Jr.

During the movement, Negroes were still denied their sense of being fully human. Andrew Young said, "At the heart of racism, a Negro is not a man." In 1968, during the Memphis sanitation strike, marchers wore signs declaring, "I am a man."

Negroes were forced to play the role. Non-violence is a role of subservience. They couldn't retaliate. If they had, it would have justified Southern mob action against them and cost them the broad support of white liberals.

For the first time, Negroes defined themselves. In a new image of confidence, they were "black." In "Black is beautiful," they celebrated their Negro features in Afro's. Jesse Jackson said, "I am somebody," and "I'm black and I'm proud." Nina Simone wrote "Young, Gifted, and Black." Rev. Martin Luther King Jr. said, "I have a dream."

As black rage transcended fear, blacks expressed what was there all along. It wasn't just "Black is beautiful," but "Black power." Blacks wanted self-determination, power over themselves rather than power over whites per se. They intended to achieve their rights with power as in, "Kill the pigs," and "Kill whitey." Whites considered Malcolm X and the Black Panthers wild and lawless because of their vehement protest.

At the same time, blacks remain insecure since civil rights never ended white supremacy or racism. Blacks with recollections of "Can't cross here," play it safe. A black friend in Florida told me, "I never venture far from I-75." Blacks are still controlled in a subtle way.

A black friend who worked in the corporate world during the 1970s and 80s, told me, "Whites lower their expectations and then force blacks to fulfill them.

They say, 'We'll give you this day but we don't really want to. We'll keep you in your place.' Whites concede things only to cool things down. They hold out the rose and then snatch it away. They flatter the uppity nigger to get him up there and then they kick the blocks out.

"There's a perception of fairness in the hierarchy but the majority rules. Whites promote and hire in their own image. It's the nature of the beast. If they can't fire a black man, they lay him off or take away all of his responsibility. When I first became line supervisor, second in the history of the company, there was a white guy of Armenian descent who didn't like me. When he became my boss, since he couldn't fire me, he stripped me of all authority. No one worked for me. No one reported to me. I had so little to do, I read three newspapers each day. I got all my raises on time but I didn't get promoted. It didn't hurt me but it didn't help me.

"They manipulate you to get done what they want done. Whites don't care what blacks achieve as long as it's not power. Blacks can get anything but power. Whites dilute black leadership by integrating potentially powerful blacks, who have no power of their own, into white corporations. The idea for these blacks is, 'Play your own game and let your people support you.'

"They watch any black who turns out to be a leader activist because he can stir people up. They try to get him on their team. As he slowly goes up the ranks, he becomes isolated from the blacks he represents. Once you're let into the corporate ranks, with all the white trappings of money, prestige, and honor, there's no longer empathy for black people. You no longer feel for the people you're leading. And the younger you are, the more you're affected by these trappings. You're afraid to jeopardize your earnings which puts you in a position where they have economic control. You're part of the organization. The white man will let you play but he won't let you win.

"The reason they put me on the fast track was to get me on their side since a core of blacks listened to me. If the dominant white establishment can't control you, they won't inflame you, they'll dilute your influence. Looking back on it, I realize they did that to the firebrand union people. The company promoted them to management because they saw they had leadership skills. These union men were formidable opponents. But when the vice president of the union got a personnel job, he left the others behind.

"Whites get blacks on their side by making them beholden to whites. The good nigger becomes a symbol, a black 'first.' As long as whites tell you you're different and they see that you succeed, you begin to believe you're different. These blacks have been made captive to their white identity. They've been told, 'You're not like the others,' so they give no credit to Affirmative Action.

"Clarence Thomas is dark-skinned. Whites use him by saying, 'I'm not prejudiced. Look at Clarence Thomas. He's my friend.' But Thomas is the black servant in the house. They don't look at him with the same eyes. And he can't see what they've done to him. He's no Thurgood Marshall who had to fight all the way up and who used his power to help black folk. Although Marshal was light-skinned, he wasn't ashamed of being black. Thomas is a black man in a totally white environment, a victim of his own stigma in his own shell.

"Adam Clayton Powell used power the same way whites did and he rubbed it in their faces. Since he was light-skinned, they couldn't call him a black 'son of a bitch' and wound him. It wouldn't have the same psychological impact as it would on a Clarence Thomas.

"The power of the black community has been diluted and siphoned off. One of the things black colleges did for black folk was that blacks were successful amongst blacks. Black leaders came out of black colleges. Think of all the guys who are doctors. The economist Andrew Bremer, in the Federal Reserve under Ginsberg, is a product of an all-black college. Those who were with Martin Luther King, Andrew Young and Jesse Jackson, can't forget the struggle.

"The reason whites want to do away with black colleges is they can't control the thought process. Whites influence black colleges through money. Fisk was a hotbed of activism. But it almost went broke last year. Whites now let blacks go to prestigious white colleges. Black athletes and those with leadership potential at white colleges have no allegiance to the black experience. They have no obligation to the black community."

Subtle forms of oppression such as, denial and neglect, have the same effect as overt oppression. Lower class blacks see neglect and failure all around them in the ghetto. And whenever they leave the ghetto, they face frustration and rejection.

Blacks remain cynical since racism has only been driven underground. In 1986, in my "Race and Ethnic Relations" class at the University of Michigan-Flint, I mentioned the introduction in our textbook written by Lyndon Johnson. I asked the students, "How do you feel about such a public statement against racism by a president of the United States? Do you have any doubts about it?" Many of the students, white and black, agreed that it was a profound statement.

Two of the black students in the class always sat together. They kept to themselves and watched me intently as I taught. One of them raised his hand and said, "Dr. D., he's a Southerner."

I said, "What's your point?"

He said, "With all due respect, you can never believe a Southerner. He's just sayin' these things to throw you off guard. They've done this all the time. The minute you trust 'em, you're their prey. You're done for."

Some of the white students insisted it was genuine. When some of the black students agreed, he told them, "Yeah, he succeeded. He deceived you. You're black just like me and you listen to that garbage? No wonder they call us fools.

Man, you don't trust no white man, especially a president. I bet his father had more slaves than anyone else."

Blacks say, "Integration was just another trick of the white man. Since whites have a history of oppression, what makes us think they'll ever change?" Concerning the apology for slavery, blacks said, "Why did it take so long to even bring it up? Can a leopard change its spots?" Blacks know there's no meat in the apology since it didn't involve reparations.

In 2004, Anita and I were visiting in the home of a Liberian married to a black woman. When we mentioned the apology for slavery, she said, "It won't make any difference. Yes, we can go to college and get a job and eat in a restaurant. But the apology for slavery won't change what the white man thinks of me. It won't change the way I'm watched in a store to make sure I won't steal anything. The white man will never change."

Despite differences in social class, blacks share a common racial experience. In their social marginality, they still suffer rejection — whether it's open or subtle, as in microagression. They expect to be rejected, which is as powerful as reality. In 2003, a black security guard at Florida Gulf Coast University joked, "Oh, do they let us into Naples?"

Upper and middle class blacks remain insecure despite their success and achievements. Their status in the black community doesn't translate to the white world, for the most part. When they are socially included and socialize with whites, they assume an "empty" status because white acceptance is superficial.

Educated blacks are rejected because the issue isn't competence. It's race. Upper and middle class blacks are always watching whites. If whites reach out, they oblige. However, if blacks reach out and they are ignored or rebuffed, they feel the rejection keenly. In 2006, we were walking out the front door of a black friend's house when he called out a friendly greeting to a white neighbor jogging by. The jogger had earphones and never responded. Nonetheless, my friend stared intently at him to see if he was deliberately ignoring him.

Blacks still feel the things whites aren't saying. In, "Racism is and racism ain't," blacks walk on eggshells wondering if they're reacting or overreacting to slights. My son Joe told me how he copes with life in Chicago, "If racism is obvious, deal with it. If it's not obvious, don't assume it's there." Blacks are never sure if or how racism operates in any given situation. If they are fired, the easiest guess is racism because it absolves them. Educated blacks who are losers, say, "Well, I was qualified but they didn't want blacks."

Joe told me about a forty-year-old black man he worked with at Citicorp in Tampa in 2004. He said, "Frank's face always had a look of quiet rage. When I told him I wanted to get into management, he said, 'The black man will never succeed. The only way you'll get into management is for the company to gain points by filling some Affirmative Action quota.' When I told him I was looking for another job, he said, 'I'd like to move to Los Angeles or Atlanta. I like Tampa, but I'm not gonna fight the Civil War all over again.' When I told him how much I liked my car, he said, 'Just wait till the warranty runs out, then you'll be paying all kinds of bills you hadn't planned on.'

"On casual dress day one Friday, I wore a Liberian shirt to work. Several whites in the office complimented me on it. Two days later, a black girl in the office told me that Frank said, 'Joe's an uppity little bastard, thinking he's better than others just because he's mixed race and a first-generation Liberian.' A week later, when the supervisor took us all out to lunch for a job well done, and I told her I was half-Liberian and half German-American, Frank said, 'I'm not just black. I've got some Creole mixed up in there and some German and some other groups that aren't obvious.' "

Neither Emancipation nor civil rights granted blacks the mental freedom to analyze why they think and behave as they do. As they face the same insecurity, challenges, and struggles associated with racism, the focus remains on survival. Shirley Chisholm said in 1972, "Blacks can't even conceive of a black being president." In 2008, despite Barak Obama's bid for the presidency, there's still a limit to black dreams. A notable black author said, "You can see people on the mountain and admire them but not aspire to the mountain. There were only certain roles that I could yearn for."

Self-acceptance means accepting myself as I am — not as I wish to be, or in comparison with someone else. Without their own perspective of themselves, blacks remain encased in a white perspective. They're still captive to the power of a history of shame. Black girls don't want dolls dressed as slaves. A black woman said, "Blacks want to be descendants of Africans, not descendants of slaves. There's a big difference." Blacks compensate by saying slavery was worth it. A Tuskegee airman said in 2006, "Slavery may have brought me here but this is still the best country in the world."

Black circumstantial inferiority makes black humor ring true. Blacks tell each other, "You're no Kunte Kinte!" In the black movie, "Kings of Comedy," a black comedian talked about blacks goin' on long breaks; blacks "runnin' away when they hear the slightest noise; and blacks saying, "No, I can't pay but I can put somethin' down on it." And there's an element of truth in all of these.

Blacks remain examples of the insecure personality. A black friend told me, "Everyone thinks you're inferior. You get to believe it too. You see others with wealth and you think something is missing. You get to thinking we must be what whites say we are." When I told him about the situation in Liberia, he said, "We niggers don't appreciate anything. We always spoil everything."

Blacks still want to be anything but an American Negro. In 2005, a black friend in Florida joked about how whites compliment her on her great tan or warn her about getting too much sun. A black friend told me that when he and his wife were introduced to another black couple at the flea market, the man told him, "I'm Haitian; she's black."

Educated blacks want to get the better of whites by proving them wrong. Whenever I mentioned my book to blacks, they said, "Let the truth come out." Some blacks still have to be right and they don't mind telling others they're wrong. Black pastors, in their fiery rhetoric, "speak truth to power."

Blacks remain sensitive about their image. They resent any re-enactment of Negro actors on stage. Spike Lee objected to the movie "Barbershop" because he considered a comment in it, to be disrespectful of Rosa Parks.

Upper and middle class blacks have never gotten the recognition they deserve. As "wanna be's" in a white world, they have to be in the spotlight. Some are big talkers. Some distinguish themselves by an African name or by wearing African clothing. Some call themselves prophets and quote the Bible. Some make bold statements in the media. Diddy uses an air horn at parties. Blacks in sports use bravado. Black football players do a dance when they make a touchdown.

Black leaders exaggerate their importance and influence. They make world trips as intercessors. In reality, they are manipulated by world powers that want to showcase America's less than united front. These black leaders have respect primarily amongst lower class blacks, not amongst whites.

While improvement requires self-criticism, blacks don't want to air their dirty laundry. Blacks crucified Bill Cosby for publicly criticizing black lower class parents. The black columnist, Thomas Sowell, wrote, "In too many black communities, dedicating yourself to getting an education is called 'acting white.' These are painful realities and they do not become any less real or any less painful by hushing them up. Nobody enjoys being made to look bad in public. But too many in the black community are preoccupied with how things will look to white people...."

Blacks don't want anyone "in their business." In 2005, in Ft. Myers, Anita and I mentored a black teenager whose father was in prison. Things were OK as long as we gave him things and did things for him. When we wanted to talk to him about his behavior with his mother present, he distanced us. We later found out he dropped out of school and is now in prison, just like his father.

While blacks are fully American, they remain culturally marginal. They have only a half-history since they can't go farther back than slavery. Even going back to slavery is a blur. Blacks still long for identity and a cultural heritage. One element of black pride during the Civil Rights Movement was African ancestry. During the 1970s and 80s, Alex Haley's *Roots* gave blacks pride in Kunte Kinte, the slave who refused the white man's definition of himself. Blacks wore African dress. They called themselves "Afro-Americans."

During the 1980s, there was a groundswell of interest in Africa by black students on college campuses. One day, after my "Africans and Their Cultures" class at the University of Michigan-Flint, a black girl followed me back to my office. During our conversation, she told me, "Dr. Dennis, this class on Africa is so good. I'm really enjoyin' it. Africa's so great. We thought we were nobody."

Black married students asked me for African names to give their children. I said, "How will this help?" They said, "We want our children to grow up thinking of Africa. Nobody will tell them we denied them."

Today, blacks are "African-Americans" even though there are only trace elements of African culture in blacks. Despite a greater awareness than ever before, blacks can only identify with Africa in a general way. They can't trace their family, tribe, or even their country. The linkage is race, not culture. In 1973, during my Summer Study Abroad trip to Liberia, the black students wore Afro's. As they got off the plane, they kissed the ground of Mother Africa. As they were well received by the Liberian people, they saw a new image of Africa. Despite their enthusiasm, they were fully American. At the Methodist Youth Hostel, in a basketball match between Americans and Liberians, the black students appeared to side with the Liberians at first. When push came to shove, they united with the white students to beat the Liberians.

Today, as blacks today display African art in their homes, their pride in Africa is based on imagination. The focus is on ancient African kingdoms since Africa is in chaos and poverty.

In 2003, in Ft. Myers, I was exercising at the Lee Memorial Fitness Center, when a young black woman came up to use the machine. After I demonstrated the machine for her with the weights I was using, she said, "I bet I can do as well as you." When she couldn't budge the weights, she said, "Wow."

I was sitting on a bench outside waiting for Anita to pick me up, when I saw her walking out with a friend. I overheard them talking. She told her friend, "You see that guy over there? He may be small but he's strong as a bull. He says he's from Africa."

The other girl nodded and said, "Girl, that's where our strength comes from."

In 2005, in Ft. Myers, I was at Southwest Regional Hospital going in for surgery, when a black nurse noticed my tribal marks. She told the white nurse, "You see those marks on his cheeks? Those are tribal marks. He's real. He's from Africa."

The white nurse said, "What's that again?"

The black nurse said, "Tribal marks! I don't even know my tribe or where I came from. Slavery took all that away from us. White people here put tattoos on their arms and legs but it's meaningless. This is the real thing. It means something."

She asked me, "What tribe do you come from?"

I said, "The Mende and Gbande tribes of Liberia."

She said, "Oh, the Amistad! That's the tribe that overthrew that slave ship. They were real warriors."

Blacks remain socially marginal in their different racial perspective. Since race continues to determine experience and thus viewpoint, everything in America is perceived racially. America's shared experience is superficial because whites experience life as "whites," blacks as "blacks." Only recently has America's history been presented from a black and Indian perspective. Certain markets appeal to whites, others to blacks. White movies appeal to white and black audiences, black movies to black audiences. Because whites and blacks are not peers in the truest sense, I think whites should have an all-white jury and blacks, an all-black jury.

Whites see the world as the dominant group, blacks as the subordinate group. And therein lies the great divide. White and black interests diverge, rather than converge. Since there are only so many pieces of the pie, something positive for whites is not necessarily something positive for blacks and vice versa.

Whites see the police as their "friend." Blacks see the police as "patrol and control." A black friend told me, "I can't trust the police. I shined shoes at the Philadelphia Police Station when I was a boy. I watched them beat up black suspects all the time and get away with it. Blacks who were arrested had no recourse. Nothing was ever said about it."

Blacks and whites can find no common ground until they acknowledge and deal with their differing racial perspectives. Whites inherently look to their own interests. They can't even imagine black interests, or what it's like to be black.

A black friend told me, "At work, they were talking about a member of the Pennsylvania Human Relations Commission and I mentioned that I was involved in some things that involved hiring blacks. My white boss said, 'Why are you involved in that?'

"I told him, 'I feel I can be of help in the struggle.'

"He said, 'What struggle?'

"I said, 'Things happen to black folks that don't happen to whites in hiring and housing.'

"He looked at me and said, 'Ed, I thought you were just like me. You don't act like them.'"

Blacks have no choice but to be "black." They primarily look to white interests since they have to. Black interests are secondary.

Today, students shoot their classmates because of rejection or intimidation. Workers kill their co-workers. The United Farm Workers Union struggles to improve the grueling conditions of migrant farm labor. And yet, all of this pales in comparison to what Negroes endured.

During the 1950s, Negroes were in a "no-win" situation. While they had to solve racism by proving themselves worthy, whites were keeping them from succeeding and proving them wrong. During the Civil Rights Movement, whites pointed to a few select Negroes who had succeeded in the professions and business as sufficient proof of equal opportunity. The greater truth was that the vast majority of Negroes suffered degradation.

No people in human history have suffered such a complete loss of identity and culture. Slavery in America involved a complete social and cultural disorganization with nothing to replace it. And the ramifications of that loss have never been fully explored.

Imitation of Supremacy

> If you're light, you're all right.
> If you're brown, you're down.
> If you're black, get back.

Oppression and racism simultaneously united and divided Negroes. During the 1950s, Negroes cooperated for success, knowing they were in the same boat. They shared a common suffering, a racial identity, a white "enemy," and a goal to prove themselves worthy. Since upper and middle class Negroes were an extreme minority, there was no great disparity in the Negro community.

Segregation fostered Negro unity. Negroes didn't belong in white society. They belonged in Negro neighborhoods, schools, and churches. They were served by a Negro professional and business class; cared for in Negro hospitals; and buried in Negro graveyards. The Negro barber shop was a significant gathering place. Negroes of every social class went there, especially on Saturday. They shared amongst themselves, as participant and audience. The barber shop was a socializing agent as the boys listened to the men talking.

Negro neighborhoods were close-knit, as if to say, "You're part of us." Negroes only had genuine status within their community. Their neighborhood was the one place they were free to use their abilities and encouraged to do so. They cooperated with each other and praised one another. They corrected each other's children. There was a strong respect for old people and people in authority in the community.

If kids said, "Yes," to an older person, someone would prompt, "What you say, Boy?"

When the child said, "Yes, Ma'am," or "Yes, Sir," the person said, "That's better."

Negroes were reluctant to intermarry as a betrayal of race. The presence of a white person at family gatherings would keep Negroes from freely interacting. When a Negro married a white woman, Negroes said, "What's he marryin' her for? You mean we don't have enough Negro women? She ain't even pretty. All she has is her white skin. I bet she's a reject from the white race." They said, "That nigger's just wastin' time with that white girl. Even her own people don't want her."

The Negro neighborhood was a source of race pride. Streets were clean. There was very little crime. In Topeka, Kansas, a barber told me, "Ben, I see some of these yards. They make us look like no good niggers."

He told a man sitting there, "I passed by your yard, man. Don't you have a lawn mower? I'll give you free haircuts until you can buy one. Don't you know all those white folks are watchin' you?"

The next summer I asked the barber, "Say, did Jimmy ever fix up his yard?"

The barber said, "That place is a showplace. I'll take you by there. He's got flowers planted he doesn't even know the names of. It looks real good. Benjamin, I'd rather be talkin' to him than have white folks talkin' to him."

Negro neighborhoods were a place of safety. Negroes could walk freely without fear of danger, even after dark. Neighborhoods were a place of protection. Every door was open to any Negro fleeing whites that were after him on foot or in cars. People said, "Come on in, child, and then we'll talk. What's the matter? What happened?"

White neighborhoods were dangerous. I was warned in Jefferson City, Missouri, "Ben, this isn't Europe or Africa. Lots of these whites livin' here have never even been all over Missouri. They're very prejudiced. You don't have to give 'em any cause to do somethin' to you. When they see a nigger walkin' by himself in their neighborhood, they think he's there lookin' for a white woman, especially niggers from the big city or foreigners. Don't go out by yourself, especially at night. They're like wolves or hound dogs. They'll attack. But they're really afraid. When they see three or four niggers together, boy, they're shakin' in their boots."

The only thing Negroes had or could depend upon was each other. Those who were better off helped the others. There were mutual aid societies and homes for delinquent girls. Orphans were adopted. Funds were collected to care for the sick and bury the poor.

The most consistent employment for Negroes was working for other Negroes. Segregation fostered the rise of the Negro upper and middle classes by giving the Negro professional and business class a guaranteed clientele. The positive influence of these upper classes gave stability to the Negro neighborhood. Upper and middle class Negroes provided connections and opportunity for those in the lower class. For example, they purchased old buildings and had Negro construction workers fix them up.

Lower class Negroes provided services to those higher in status as part of an implied relationship. When I stayed with Rev. Huntley of Central Baptist Church in St. Louis, men came by his house and asked him, "Got anything I can do? Your yard needs mowin'." They periodically mowed the yard with their push mower. They carried out the trash and burned it. They swept the street in front of the house. In turn, they asked Rev. Huntley for a little something. As a sign of deference, they said, "Just gimme twenty-five cent." He kept a bowl of change just for this. Sometimes he said, "Well, the bowl's empty," and they said, "Another time, Rev." At a church meeting, I heard a deacon say, "Listen, folks, don't go botherin' the preacher, beggin' all the time. It's good to beg but not too much."

Middle class Negroes, in their longing to be accepted by the upper class, served as the worker bees of the community. For example, when there was a problem with trash collection in St. Louis, they arranged for, "Our people to take the trash away." The middle class empathized with the lower class, saying, "Brother, I been there. I understand what you're goin' through."

Negroes shopped at Negro grocery and clothing stores, the only place they could get credit. When a storekeeper didn't have what a customer wanted, he referred him to another Negro business.

White supremacy fostered reciprocity between mulattos and dark-skinned Negroes. In white stores, Negroes couldn't pick up anything or try anything on. They were served last. High mulattos passing for white, that worked as store clerks, waited on Negroes and gave them advance notice of sales.

One day, I asked a mulatto teenager about her friend, "How is it you're such good friends with a white girl?"

She said, "She's a nigger just like me. I use her to go into white stores and try on dresses. We're the same size."

Negro camaraderie affirmed and nurtured Negroes, even though it didn't stem from true self-love. Since Negroes were powerless to change things, they diffused their frustration and despair with bravado — empty pride and exaggeration. They turned the joke on themselves to neutralize the pain of white ridicule and disdain. Using nigger on each other, diffused its power. As a group joke, it was used affectionately and received that way.

Negroes had a racial solidarity with all other Negroes. In St. Louis, I was driving with a Nigerian and we got so busy talking, I inadvertently ran a red light. I told the Negro police officer who stopped us, "I'm very sorry. I don't usually do something like this."

The Nigerian said, "He was concentrating on what I was saying."

The officer said, "Where you come from?"

I said, "We're both from Africa. I'm a graduate student at Washington University."

He said, "Wow! Well, just be careful. You're too precious to us. I won't give you a ticket. These peckerwoods do it for their own people all the time."

The Negro church was a symbol of unity. Christianity was their only comfort. They had nothing else to rely on. They believed in God's justice, that men reaped what they sowed, if not in this world, then the next. They believed in God's providence, that God could bring good out of tragedy. They took comfort in knowing God wouldn't give them more than they could bear.

Gospel music simultaneously reflected their suffering and hope, sadness and joy. For the most part, everyone went to church, from the upper class to the downtrodden. Church services were the only time Negroes got together since they worked long hours. It was the only place they could freely express their emotions. They jumped and clapped. They fell out in the spirit and were revived by "nurses" in uniforms. People shouted, cried, and sang a solo in their own way.

Everyone had a voice. For once in their lives, Negroes had an audience. They didn't have to be careful about diction or language. They were affirmed in an assembly of their peers by applause and "Amen's." Christianity helped Negroes bear the brunt of racism. The church wasn't only a place of spiritual salvation. It was a place of psychic healing, a refuge from the rejection they faced. In Sunday school and prayer requests during the service, they shared their frustration and expressed their hurts freely.

Most of the work Negroes got was through the church. When a newcomer or new church member requested a job, those in the community a long time, competed amongst themselves to get him one.

Everything revolved around the church. The first question Negroes asked each other was, "What church do you go to?" The church's many avenues for expression and status gave dignity and respect. There was a spirit of competition among the many choirs.

The church was a place where the leader was a Negro man. Negro pastors were significant as the church's voice in the community. The church was a place where leadership was developed.

During my first visit to Central Baptist, so many people came to shake my hand, that Rev. Huntley said, "I'm going to bring him up here with me. Otherwise, we'll never start the service. Benjamin, I'm going to make a preacher out of you." He told the congregation, "My son will preach next Sunday. I want every one of you to come." The first time I got into the pulpit, I said, "Good morning." The congregation answered, "Good morning." Rev. Huntley said, "You can do better than that." Everyone said, "Good Morning!"

As I began speaking, the assistant pastor's mother received the spirit. She shouted, "Hallelujah!" and fell down. Several "nurses" rushed to pick her up. I looked at Rev. Huntley. He nodded as if to say, "Just wait."

After the service, the deaconesses wanted to call a meeting to ordain me. Rev. Dubney's mother, who was now revived, hugged me. Rev. Huntley said, "It's an affirmation of the women!"

I said, "Do I have to shake hands with everyone?"

He said, "You particularly have to."

People fussed over me, saying, "He has to come to dinner with us today." That Sunday, I was booked for dinner for the next three months.

Pastors were a great source of pride. Churches competed in honoring them. The first summer I stayed with the Huntleys, the church raised three thousand dollars. People told me, "We bought the reverend that Chrysler."

I said to him, "Wow! Where'd they get all that money?"

He said, "The women work and the only thing they spend money for is bus fare. They save everything for this day."

Deacons competed in doing things for the Huntleys so that people would say, "You see Rev. Huntley's house? He's the pastor of Central Baptist Church."

One day, Mrs. Huntley called me downstairs to meet the deacon of the month. As I ran down the steps, he said, "This boy is runnin' down too fast. We need to change these stairs and make the railin' smooth, shinin' like ivory."

I said, "The stairs are fine. I didn't trip."

Mrs. Huntley said, "Benjamin, he's a professional carpenter who works for white people. That's his job."

The deacon said, "When you go to play at Forest Park this Saturday, when you come back, it'll be finished. I'll measure now and bring my crew. By the time you come home, all you'll see is a gorgeous new stairway."

That evening, as Rev. Huntley opened the door, we smelled varnish. He said, "Benjamin, come and see! I'm going to ring him up so you can apologize for your skepticism."

The deacon said, "I told you we'd finish! You're a Baptist and you're gonna be a preacher. That's the way you're gonna be treated. Benjamin, I'm deacon for this month and I do for my preacher what I can do."

Deaconesses competed in cleaning the Huntleys' house as if it was their God-given duty. I heard one of the women say, "Some of these people didn't do too well. This place has to be done right. Our souls are hungry and Rev. Huntley gives us good spiritual food."

That summer, I spoke at several congregations for Rev. Huntley. In August, at a pastoral conference, a group of deacons told me, "We know you'll soon be going back to Lincoln. Here's a small donation from the deacons, deaconesses, and members of Central Baptist Church. You're our son."

When I opened the envelope and saw five hundred dollars, I knew how hard they had worked for this money. I said, "This is so much money. It's hard for me to accept it."

One of the deacons said, "If we take it back, our wives will crucify us. They've been talkin' 'bout this for a while now. It wasn't a spur of the moment thing. We're your family in this country. It's the least we can do. We wish we could do more. We're ashamed to even give you such a small gift."

Negro schools and colleges were a source of strength and affirmation. Negro teachers wanted their students to succeed. At the University of Michigan-Flint, one of my black students described his elementary school teacher by saying, "Miss Van Zandt was straight, Dr. Dennis. You couldn't get away with anything."

At Lincoln and other Negro colleges, fraternities and sororities were a great source of camaraderie. In 1952, during my sophomore year at Lincoln, I was asked to pledge Alpha Phi Alpha. Since I was hungry for friends, I was impressed when they took me to the "Greasy Spoon" down the hill and bought me beer.

One night, they paired me with another pledge and took us somewhere blind-folded. Finding our way back was supposed to make us strong. When we took off our blindfolds, my partner, who was in the agricultural program, knew exactly where we were — in an old chicken coop on the outskirts of campus. We waited a while to make it look like we were having a hard time. On our way back, it started raining. We were soaking wet as we walked in.

Charlie, the head of Alpha Phi Alpha, said, "They're here! Hey, Dog, how'd you get so lost?"

I said, "I don't know."

He said, "Dog, what you say?"

I said, "I don't know, Sir."

He said, "That's better. Since you're all wet, go on home. Tomorrow night will be another test."

Charlie knew that a girl he liked was sweet on me. The next night, it was sleeting and very nasty outside. Charlie said, "Hey Dog! You know I'm a big man and I like to eat. Go get me somethin'. You think you can do that, Dog?"

I said, "Yes Sir!"

Charlie said, "I'll make it very easy for you. You know the doughnut shop down the hill by the capitol building?"

"Yes Sir!"

"Dog, go get me some doughnuts."

I paused as I looked out and saw the sleet coming down. Charlie said, "Go on Dog!! Get outta here!"

The ground was a sheet of ice. I went down the hill more on my behind than on my feet. When I got to the shop, I was soaking wet, my eyes and nose running. The Negro clerk looked at me a long time and said, "Son, you came out in this bad weather for donuts?"

I said, "Ma'am, it's for my big brother at my fraternity."

She said, "Lord, help us. They oughta outlaw that stuff. I wouldn't send my dog out in this kinda weather."

She gave me a bag of six doughnuts and said, "Take it. You don't have to pay me. They wouldn't do that to an American boy. He'd tell 'em to kiss his ass. This kinda weather?"

When I got back, I could hardly see Charlie through my fogged glasses. I handed him the bag of donuts and said, "Sir, here's your doughnuts."

Charlie opened the bag and said, "You see what this Dog has done? I asked for a doughnut and he brought me six. Maybe he's still in the African bush and doesn't understand English. I meant one doughnut, Dog." He threw the bag of doughnuts on the floor and stomped on it, saying, "These don't count! You gotta follow instructions."

I looked outside. It was sleeting even worse. I walked home. Since I lived with President Scruggs that year, I told him about it the next morning. He said, "I'm an Alpha man myself. Well, you stood your ground. I respect you for that. You're a real Alpha man. You don't need that, Ben."

Race pride unified Negroes since they were seen as a racial group. A desire for success was a vital part of the Negro community. Whatever one Negro accomplished made every Negro feel good, not only because of race pride, but because the success of one implied the possibility for all.

Successful Negroes were role models. I heard someone say, "Look at him. They were poor like grasshoppers. He finished college and now he's a lawyer. Look what he's doin' for our people." Negro day workers bragged about the successful Negroes they worked for, "Oh, they're pretty good. They're really gettin' up there."

Sports and entertainment played a big role in the Negro community since Negroes had so few heroes. Famous Negroes were a source of pride and joy. They visited the Lincoln campus all the time. The walls of Negro barber shops were covered with pictures of athletes and performers.

Negro sports figures were idolized — larger than life. In boxing, whites and Negroes fought on equal terms. Since Negroes could fight back, boxing was significant as an example of Negro power over a white man.

In 1950, in Topeka, Kansas, Dr. Cotton, a prominent high mulatto, asked me, "Wanna see Joe Louis fight?"

I said, "Sure!"

At the arena, I saw that Joe's white opponent was larger and taller. The announcer said, "This is just an exhibition fight." I knew there weren't many Negroes in Topeka, so I was surprised to see the upper balcony packed full.

During the fight, the announcer said, "Joe Louis usually disposes of them in the third round but this is already the end of that round. The guy's stalking Joe. Maybe the champ will have trouble tonight." Just before the fourth round, Joe told his handler something. Someone in the crowd yelled, "What'd he say?"

The handler said, "Joe knows people paid money to see the fight. He'll go one more round and the next will be the last." This spread by word of mouth to the balcony.

During the fourth round, the white boxer chased Joe all around. When the fifth round opened, the white boxer hit Joe with a right. Joe followed with the old one-two — one with his left and a big one with his right. The second punch was so fast, we didn't even see it. Suddenly, we saw the white boxer fall backwards, his feet up in the air. He landed on his back and lay so still I thought he was dead.

Joe walked over to his corner and held out his hands for his handler to take off his gloves. Pandemonium broke out in the balcony. It sounded like the place was being demolished. Negroes yelled, "He done finished! He's dead now!"

Whites in the audience yelled at the white boxer, "Get up! You can't do that! Get up!"

I asked Dr. Cotton, "Do you think he's dead?"

He said, "No, he's knocked out. That's why they call it a 'knock out.'"

The announcer said, "Is there a doctor in the house? This is the end of the fight."

As Joe climbed out of the ring and we started to leave, whites ran up to the balcony yelling, "Get outta here, Niggers!" Everyone ignored them and kept on rejoicing.

At the Cottons', we heard on the radio, "Police are rushing into Negro areas. Topeka is tense, very, very tense. It looks like we have the honor of having the champ, but there's trouble in our community."

The next morning, I walked over to the Negro barbershop to see what was going on. I saw the police checking any small gathering of Negroes on street corners. At the barber shop, a white policeman suddenly walked in. Everyone was quiet, their transistor radios turned off and in their pockets. He walked around slowly. The barbers glanced at him and went on with what they were doing.

After the policeman left and the door closed, everyone burst out laughing. Someone said, "Joe Louis beat that white man's butt! Nothin's gonna change that!"

Another said, "He shore did! I saw it myself!" There was great pride and satisfaction in their laughter that followed.

White supremacy and racism simultaneously generated divisiveness. While racism united whites, its effect divided Negroes. Self-hatred made Negroes ambivalent towards each other in a love/hate relationship of trust/distrust. There was togetherness in the Negro community, but no genuine or lasting unity. Racism made Negroes reject their only group of acceptance and support.

Every Negro saw every other Negro as a reflection of his inferiority, his inability, and his lack of status and opportunity. Negroes despised others of their racial group because they "knew" them. Their Negro-ness kept them from doing things. They could almost make it if it wasn't for their skin color. They could succeed as a group if it wasn't for the flaws of their race.

Racism pitted the individual against the group. In order to be seen positively by whites, a Negro had to be distinct from his racial group — an exception to the rule. The only "status" he could achieve in the eyes of whites was in comparison with other Negroes.

In 1959, I brought my Negro family to East Lansing, where I was already working on my doctorate at Michigan State University. Our daughter, Winona, was six weeks old. We were pulling a U-Haul with our furniture. It was extremely cold. Snow was drifting over the highway. Winona started crying so I stopped at the next roadside restaurant. As we pulled into the parking lot, Ruth said, "We gotta find another place to stop. This looks like all white people."

I said, "We have to feed Winona." Ruth waited in the car while I went in to warm Winona's bottle. When the waitress returned, I said, "It's too cold to feed our baby out in the car."

She said, "Well, you can't stay in here. If she's hungry enough, she'll eat."

I asked to speak to the manager. I told her, "I want to feed my baby in here where it's warm. The waitress says I can't do it." I yelled to Ruth, "Bring Winona in here!" When Ruth came in, she looked only at me.

Winona was still crying. I told the manager, "See how miserable she is? She's wet and she's hungry. It's freezing cold out there. The car is cramped because we're moving. I'm not asking for anything for myself but do you mean to tell me we can't even feed our baby in here?"

She paused for a minute and said, "Let me have her. She's so tiny. Isn't she a doll? Where do you come from? What kind of work do you do?"

I said, "I was a graduate student at Washington University and I'm now at Michigan State finishing my doctorate."

"Where are you from originally?"

"West Africa."

"Oh, come on in. You all can feed the baby."

Everyone in the restaurant stared as Ruth changed and fed Winona.

Upper and middle class Negroes especially resented Negro stereotype being fulfilled or being applied to them. Those who succeeded forgot about and shunned the "inferior" of their race. Those, who could, passed for white.

The upper and middle classes went to the lower class for everything, feigning sympathy to manipulate and exploit them. In large cities in the North, they excluded the lower class from their social activities. In order to improve their status, middle class Negroes gave the upper class preferential treatment and served them. While they reciprocated with the lower class, they aligned themselves socially with the upper class so their children could marry up.

Upper and middle class Negroes hated those who fulfilled stereotype because they made them ashamed to be Negro. As an ego defense, they perpetually criticized their racial group. When they saw someone laughing and talking, they got angry and said, "Look at that nigger. Looks like he hasn't seen the time of day. Looks like he hasn't evolved." They said, "Only a nigger can act like that. That's why we can't go anywhere." Negroes who were higher up assured themselves they were better by saying, "I'm not like that nigger!"

In the Negro barber shop, I heard, "You can always tell a nigger by the way he does things. Look the way he walks, swingin' his arms. Looks like he just come down from the tree! Ain't that a nigger!"

One day, a man was talking loud and laughing boisterously in the pool hall adjacent to the barber shop. After he left, someone in the barber shop said, "He's nothin' but voice — a noise box. He musta come from a large family. That nigger can talk. Looks like he's talkin' to people 'cross the river and there ain't no river here. I bet you, white folks think all niggers talk like that."

For the most part, Negroes criticized each other about racial attributes, not personal qualities. In the barber shop, I heard someone say after a man left, "He looks like Sambo. Musta come from the Congo."

Everyone laughed. Someone else said, "He shore looks like a nigger! Look at his eyes, all sittin' up there like a bull frog, shinin' like an Eastern star."

In Topeka, Kansas, everyone called a dark-skinned football star "Pretty." One day, as he walked into the barber shop, someone said, "Here comes Pretty lookin' like midnight."

Pretty laughed and said, "Only niggers can have that kinda feelin'."

Sometimes, the men said with pride, "Pretty's playin' today."

Negroes perpetually criticized every one of their leaders, including: Frederick Douglass, Marcus Garvey, W. E. B. Dubois, George Washington Carver, Booker T. Washington, etc. E. Franklin Frazier, the Negro sociologist and author of *Black Bourgeoisie*, was so criticized that he kept to himself on the Howard University campus. Joe Louis criticized Muhammad Ali for not serving his country. Negroes said of Martin Luther King, Jr., "He's gone too far. He shouldn't do that."

White supremacy pitted the individual against the group. Negroes had to compete for the very few avenues of success or elevation available to them. They could only succeed as individuals, not as a racial group. Since everyone was trying hard to survive, personal interest was primary. In their own helplessness, Negroes couldn't help others. In "Every man for himself," they were so focused on their own success to attain status, they couldn't consider their racial group.

Insecurity kept Negroes apart. Their hunger for personal affirmation made them self-focused. They had to be in the spotlight even when it was detrimental to their racial group. They so desperately wanted approval themselves, they couldn't give it to others unless it enhanced their own position. They disparaged their racial group to distinguish themselves from it.

In their need for personal recognition, Negroes who weren't educated, strived to excel in sports, music, or the homemaking arts. They attracted attention by talking loud and excessively to show they knew it all. They compensated for their lack of education by saying it wouldn't matter anyway.

In a Negro barber shop in Jefferson City, Missouri, I heard the barber say to a student at Lincoln, "What you tryin' to do? Behave like white people? You're nothin' but a nigger. I don't care how much book learnin' you get, you're not gonna do nothin' but nigger work. It makes no difference whether you're educated. They'll give you what they want to give you."

The Negro community was rife with class division and competition. Negroes could only succeed as individuals because insecurity fueled a perpetual undercurrent of rivalry and positioning. Like crabs in a barrel, they pulled each other down as each scrambled to the top. There could only be "one nigger in charge." In their fear of any kind of competition, every other Negro was seen as a rival. In their suspicion, they said, "Don't get in my business!"

Despite a shared condition of race, there was never a uniform Negro voice. Negroes defined and articulated their problems but they could never agree on a solution or work together as a racial group to solve them. Malcolm X's own people killed him.

Everyone had to be on the same level. Since one Negro's success implied the possibility for all, it made the rest of them failures. Negroes didn't want anyone above them and they were jealous of those who were. Jealously brought down any successful, cultured Negro who spoke English with good diction, and was accepted by whites on some level. Their stinging criticism which implied betrayal was, "What you think you are? White? What you tryin' to do? Be white?" Anyone who behaved properly or acted like a gentleman was ridiculed by the expression, "What you wanna do? That's white people's behavior! Ain't no nigger acts like that!"

In the Negro barber shop, I heard, "That nigger's behavin' just like peckerwoods. See how he talks and shines his shoes? He ain't no different. He ain't nothin' but a nigger."

Negroes compensated by criticizing mulattos. In St. Louis, when a well-dressed mulatto came into the barber shop, everyone gave him a friendly greeting. After he left, the barber said, "Sure can tell someone messed with his mother or grandmother. He don't belong to us. He sure ain't a nigger. That's the thing about this country. Somethin's missin'. I'm sorry for him. You can have everything in the world but if you don't know who your daddy is, you can never define yourself. That's why fathers are so important. I'd rather be a nigger and know my parents. I may be dark but I know who my Daddy is."

I heard a barber say good-naturedly to a cultured, well-dressed mulatto, "You may look good and get all those good things and go to places I can't. But you and I are in the same boat. You're scared to death someone may recognize you, but I'm free. No one'll mistake me for anything else but a nigger. And when you come down to it, you're just a nigger like me."

Everyone laughed and said, "Ain't that right!"

Negroes resented those who tried to succeed. At the same time, race pride made them admire them when they did. In St. Louis, I knew a young man who was training to be a nurse at Homer Phillips Hospital, the segregated Negro hospital. One day after he left the barber shop, a man said, "Here's that little nigger comin' here talkin' 'bout he wanna be what?"

Another man said, "He wanna be a nurse."

The first man said, "Lord, have mercy! I ain't goin' to that hospital! They gonna have that nigger be a nurse? That's a sure way to die quickly!"

Everyone laughed. Someone else said, "I told that nigger he was just a nigger before he started. That's all niggers are good for. Big ideas and nothin' come of it."

When the young man became successful as a nurse, someone in the barber shop said, "He shore did it!" Everyone laughed. After that, parents told their sons, "You can be a nurse like Alan."

The possibility for Negro success was precarious, not only because of white opposition, but because of Negro jealousy. Any Negro who strived to be something was not only rejected by whites as "too uppity," he was rejected by Negroes for "tryin' to be somethin' he ain't." Success required forfeiting the good will of a large segment of the Negro community. Solidarity required the sabotage of any successful Negro. Those who bettered themselves were told, "Shut up, man. You talk too much. You're nothin' but a nigger." The only successful Negroes who weren't resented were colossal sports and entertainment figures.

If everyone had nothing, Negroes looked bad as a whole. If a Negro succeeded, it made the others look bad because whites said, "If he can do it, why can't they all?" One individual's success made it harder for the rest because their failure became personal rather than racial.

To compensate, Negroes attributed success to "kissing up to the white man" — something other than ability. And there was an element of truth in this. When successful Negroes were called "Uncle Tom," it allowed the rest to attribute their failure to white supremacy and racism. And there was an element of truth in that as well.

Successful Negroes became scapegoats, "traitors to their race." There was an element of truth in this since many of those who were "accepted" by whites looked down on other Negroes and no longer cared about them. Negroes said Uncle Toms didn't know the score since they had no interest in the Negro community.

In the barber shop, Negroes said, "When you see him behavin' like he has no education or money, he behaves that way to white people. He's got money, man. He's a real Uncle Tom. He doesn't respect hisself. When white people talk, he's jumpin' outta his nigger skin."

Ruth had a cousin Billy who was a gifted mechanic and owned a garage in Traverse City, Michigan. Most of the whites in the area brought their cars to him since he was good at what he did and his prices were reasonable. In 1957, during a visit with Billy, Ruth and I were picking grapes with some Negroes in the area. One of the men said, "We gotta a good mechanic round here who can take an old car and make it new. Everyone calls him Billy. He don't mix with our folks, but boy, does he eat out of the palms of those white folks. They keep him hoppin' fixin' old junkers for 'em, day and night."

Another man said, "The guy thinks he's somethin'. He works his butt off. He's got so many cars there he doesn't know which one to work on first."

The first man said, "He's always helpin' others and those others are mostly whites. All the time you go there, he's fixin' some redneck or peckerwood's car. They get him outta his bed to haul their car in when it's rainin' or snowin'. I told him, 'I wouldn't do that, Nigger. They won't do that for you.' "

Everyone laughed. The first man went on, "White folks can make fools outta us and he's the biggest fool 'round here. He's never doing nothin' for hisself. He's never understood the rule that God helps them that helps themselves."

Ruth said, "Well, is he better off?"

The first man said, "He pays the bills and the tax people get the rest. You can't get away from these white people. One way or another they'll get you."

When we got back, I told Billy what happened. He said, "They think I'm an Uncle Tom 'cause I don't turn white people away when they come. Niggers have cars that are junkers and I fix 'em too. There's three or four at the garage right now. The difference with whites is, they use their cars. As soon as I fix 'em, they pick 'em up. They don't always pay the full price but I make 'em sign for the balance and I get it the next time they come. They pay me enough to keep me in business."

In the *cycle of racism* Negroes, viciously controlled by whites, displaced their frustration and anger on the only ones they could — each other. There was no penalty for a "nigger killin' a nigger." As compensation for not having power, they preyed on one another. In order to rise, they manipulated and exploited those in the same situation or worse, even more so than whites.

A Negro told me, "Niggers will take you even more than the white man. They come with their big laugh, wantin' to get everything for the white man. They think they're doin' good for the white man."

Another Negro who was there said, "Man, that's their job. The white man will like 'em for that."

There was no full confidence or trust in anyone. Negroes not only had to watch the white man, they had to watch other Negroes. Suspicion made them secretive and defensive. It kept them from forming close relationships.

Successful Negroes were oriented to whites. Encased in a white mental framework, they couldn't stand up for their own interests as Negroes because they didn't have their own interests. They thought only in terms of white interest and their relationship to whites. Negro children had white heroes, white dolls.

Mulattos identified more with whites than they did with dark-skinned Negroes. Upper and middle class Negroes were so focused on whites, their efforts to develop their community were futile.

Any successful Negro had to be a team player with whites. If a Negro leader couldn't get something from whites, Negroes branded him a trouble-maker. Frederick Douglass, Marcus Garvey, and W.E.B. Dubois were radical Negro leaders. Garvey, who never agreed with whites or got anything from them, was jailed and dropped out in complete obscurity. W. E. B. Dubois was an intellectual that Negroes branded a trouble-maker. He died in Ghana, West Africa. The only reason his name lives on is because he founded the NAACP.

In the *cycle of racism*, Negroes were victims of racism who unknowingly perpetuated it among themselves. Miscegenation made Negroes "all the shades of black." Only mulattos had any chance since they were seen as less of a threat. Because of their social advantage, they excelled more in education and had some small avenue to achieve distinction. They were the Negro elite in New York, Philadelphia, and Chicago. They could get jobs "inside" while dark-skinned Negroes could only get jobs "outside." The prestige of mulattos in the Negro community was based on their advantage and white "acceptance." However, their status with whites was pseudo since whites saw all Negroes as more or less alike.

Negro racism was a white mentality in Negro minds. Negroes valued what whites valued. Skin color was as important to them as it was to whites. Negro color consciousness within their race was the result of white color consciousness. Their social hierarchy was based on how much "white" they had in them — the lighter the skin and softer the hair, the higher the status.

Mulattos replicated the very thing they hated — discrimination based on skin color. In their exclusivity from the "inferior" of their race, they saw dark-skinned Negroes as the "enemy." Those "more white" looked down on those "more Negro." To maintain their status, mulattos rigidly intermarried. In large cities in the North, they nurtured their status by socially excluding dark-skinned Negroes. To be feted in a cotillion, a girl had to have light skin and soft hair. If she was dark-skinned, her parents were from the Negro professional class. Negro sororities and fraternities were highly color conscious. In the "brown paper bag test," those who were darker couldn't join.

If a Negro couldn't marry a white woman, a light-skinned woman was the next best thing. As long as a woman had light skin, it didn't matter if she was smart or pretty. Men assessed women solely on skin color. They said they were "dark, with good features," or they said, "Damn, she's dark." A light-skinned woman, called a "skillet blond," was considered a conquest or prize.

At Fisk University, Negro men preferred mulatto women. Although Nashville was highly segregated, mulattos passed for white all the time. It was a rite of passage affirming their superiority. The top fraternity, Alpha Phi Alpha, was comprised of mulattos and a few dark-skinned men who were studying to be doctors or lawyers. The corresponding sorority, Alpha Kappa Alpha, had mostly light or very light-skinned women, along with a very few dark-skinned women from prominent families.

In 1956, when I taught a few courses at Fisk as a graduate student, I had a student named Wilma who was light-skinned but not mulatto. When a dark-skinned medical student became interested in her, I told him, "Wilma's a very nice girl."

One day, Wilma told me, "Victor's havin' another girlfriend. Please talk to him. I love him so much."

When I spoke with Victor, he said, "The girl I'm goin' with now is from Chattanooga. You can't even tell her from a white girl. Even on campus, they think she's white. She's got to tell 'em she's Negro."

Several days later, when we were all eating together in the cafeteria, Victor told Wilma she should look for another guy since he was in love with this girl. Wilma went home and slit her wrists. Her roommate found her in a pool of blood and she was rushed to the hospital. As soon as she recovered, she packed her bags and returned to New York.

What mattered most to light-skinned women was money, or the potential for it. One day at Fisk, I asked a mulatto friend, "Why do the mulatto girls at Fisk date the dark-skinned guys at Meharry?"

He said, "It's the profession! To be a doctor in the Negro community is a big thing. Doctors are prominent. Everyone knows you. Even though Negroes pay less, these doctors get rich because they have a large volume of patients. The big thing for these girls is to get a degree and marry a successful person. What other options do they have?"

Dark-skinned Negroes admired mulattos and wanted to be like them. They were socially marginal since they suffered discrimination from both whites and mulattos. To be considered a marriage partner, a dark-skinned man had to have exceptional ability or economic promise. A dark-skinned woman was "second best."

At Lincoln, I was sweet on Nancy, a chemistry major, who was the smartest student I ever tutored. One day, a guy told me, "You're the only one takin' that girl out and you're from Africa."

I said, "She's pretty."

He said, "She's ten times darker than even you."

I said, "She's pretty and she's smart."

Mulattos were socially marginal — rejected by whites and rejecting dark-skinned Negroes. In turn, since dark-skinned Negroes couldn't be like mulattos, they hated and ignored them unless they could do something for them.

Those who passed for white were socially isolated. They not only had to conceal their identity from whites, they never fully belonged in the Negro community. They lived in two worlds — active in the Negro community and passive in the white community. Their endless dilemma was, "Who am I? Where do I fit?" Although they were racially white, they were socially Negro.

In the Negro barber shop, I heard a high mulatto say, "When they see you with fair skin, man, they don't ask any questions. They just take you like a sister or brother. I tell you, they're stupid, just stupid. Have you ever found a Negro mistakin' another Negro for somethin' else?"

The others in the barber shop said, "Ain't that the truth!"

One of the men said, "Nigger, if I looked like you, I'd really fool 'em and get everything from 'em. They think they're smart but I'd take 'em for a ride if I were you."

He said, "Shut up, Nigger. What you think I'm doin'? I talk like 'em. I don't talk like I'm talkin' here. And I'm takin' 'em for a big ride. Look at my shoes. Look at my shirt. It's one of the best shirts you can buy."

Passing for white required a lifetime of continuous conspiracy. High mulattos lived secluded lives. Each day, they worked for whites. Each night, they returned to the Negro neighborhood. They lived with the constant fear and worry they might be discovered. In the South, they could be lynched.

The conspiracy went into action whenever Negroes shopped at stores with clerks who passed for white. I once heard a mulatto girl joke with an older woman, "I know what you were doin' when you came up to me, sayin', 'Yes, Ma'am.' I saw you winkin' and you saw me wink back."

The woman said, "Here you better call me, 'Yes, Ma'am,' or I'll have your behind whipped!" Everyone laughed.

There were scary moments. I heard a high mulatto say, "Edna came to the store with her three children and they all know me. The kids just ran to me yellin', 'Barbara! Barbara!' Edna had to pull 'em away, scolding, 'You don't know that white woman!'

"The kids said, 'Yes, Ma, we know 'er!'

"I moved quickly to the back of the store and Edna left. I didn't think anyone noticed but as I was leaving work, one of the white clerks said, 'Where do you know that woman and her children?'

"I thought fast and said, 'She used to work for my parents.'"

In St. Louis, my mulatto friend Milford had blue eyes and passed for white. He was a manager at Anheuser Busch. Some whites who worked with him attended one of our African dances and saw him dancing with a lot of Negro girls. The next day they reported to the head manager that Milford was a "nigger lover."

Milford told the head manager, "Two months ago you awarded me 'Best Division Manager' because I sold more beer than anyone else. How do you think I did that? Negro folks like their beer. The only way I can sell to them is to be friendly with them." The head manager was so convinced, he told the others, "You ought to practice what Milford is doing."

Because of envy and resentment, high mulattos faced hostility in the Negro community. Dark-skinned Negroes told them, "You think you're better cause you're high yellow."

One day, I had lunch with Milford in a Negro restaurant. At the next table, some Negroes were talking loud and laughing. Milford said, "Those people are behavin' just like niggers. Look at that waitress twistin' her butt yellin', 'I'm comin' baby!' I can tell you this, Ben, but if I told 'em that, they'd skin me alive."

I said, "Why's that, Milford?"

He said, "Look at me, Ben. Look at my skin."

The Civil Rights Movement was an example of black unity and courage — a source of race pride. Blacks had served in two world wars. They had higher expectations. They believed their success was limited only by a lack of opportunity. Knowing they were in the same boat, they were together in their determination. While they disagreed on the way to go about it, they were unified in their desire for civil rights. They agreed to go to jail and risk their lives.

In 1955, in St. Louis, Rev. Huntley introduced me to Rev. Martin King Jr. when he spoke at Kiel Auditorium. In 1956, when I was at Cornell University, I transferred to Fisk to work with the Fisk Institute on Race Relations in its investigation of the Montgomery Bus Boycott. In the spring of 1956, when I arrived in Atlanta, King told the director of the project, "He can stay with me." King introduced me to his group, saying, "Have you ever heard of Liberia? It's an independent country founded by Negroes from here."

The movement was equally characterized by black disunity. There were generational differences. Black children were willing to fight for civil rights while their parents hesitated or were opposed to it. Many black pastors didn't speak out for civil rights. In the beginning, there were not many with King. But in time, his leadership garnered support. People said, "Martin, we're gonna do this together."

The movement's just cause gave it dignity and power. In Atlanta and later in Montgomery, King led his group in morning and evening devotions. He began by praying that the Lord would forgive and guide the white community. He prayed that the Lord would make us humble and guide us. Each evening, he thanked the Lord for protecting us all, whites and blacks.

On the day we marched in Montgomery, King told us before we left the church, "Racism is a divisive scheme. It not only divides whites and Negroes, it divides whites and it divides Negroes. Not all white people are racists. And not all Negroes want non-violence. They're against us too."

A man in our group said, "We've had to take these things from whites all these years. This is playin' the old role. You only die once. Before I die, I'm gonna take some of 'em down with me."

Martin was firm. He said, "We have to do it with non-violence. Otherwise I can't lead. The whole country, and indeed the world, is watching us. Our success depends on our holding together. They may kill some of us, but they can't kill all of us. Some of us will live on to carry the torch of truth. And in the end, we'll win. Just keep marching. Don't look at them. If they block our way, stand. Don't run into them. Be firm. Just watch me."

We left the church holding hands and looking straight ahead. When I glanced sideways, I saw white policemen with clubs walking back and forth between us and the white mob on the sidewalk. Women holding babies screamed profanities. Men brandished sticks and clubs. I saw a toothless old man waving an ax. I panicked until I looked ahead and saw Martin marching calmly and resolutely. It gave me courage.

We had just started singing when we saw whites blocking our path up ahead. Linking arms, we turned onto a side street just before we reached them and eventually returned to the church.

Integration came at a price. While it solved some problems, it created others. The downside was the destruction of the unity and cohesive values of the Negro neighborhood. With a choice of housing, blacks chose white neighborhoods. With a choice of goods and services, blacks chose white stores and white professionals, assuming they were better. This resulted in a loss of the Negro professional and business class, which ultimately led to a decline in the black community.

Blacks became anonymous in neighborhoods in a state of flux. Parents no longer felt responsible or corrected other children. Blacks bore the brunt of school integration since their schools were closed and their children bused out to white schools. Black teachers weren't "qualified" for integrated schools. Today, whites still prefer having their children taught by whites. Blacks must now compete with whites at white colleges without the old Negro support system.

The ghetto is a source of danger as blacks displace their rage and frustration on each other. Instead of helping each other, they prey on each other. Today, in Ft. Myers, in the black Dunbar community, if someone gets a ride from someone, they have to pay.

There's a rivalry amongst blacks for the few good jobs available. Some blacks have risen without the background or qualifications. A black man told me, "Since they can't do it and you can, they make things hard for you so you won't get their job."

Since civil rights never ended white supremacy or racism, the themes of Negro insecurity are played out in blacks. Although the negatives of racism have lessened, they haven't disappeared. During the 1970s, a prominent black leader in Flint, told me, "I'm going to send Bob to your class. These are the people dragging us down." In 1996, in Ft. Myers, a black guest at a party at our house dominated every conversation. After he left, a black friend told me, "I know his kind."

Blacks want to be anything but what they are. They bleach their hair blond. Michael Jackson looks like a white woman. It's not about being black. It's about being Haitian, Puerto Rican, Hindu, etc. During the race riots of Watts in Los Angeles in 1965, and Detroit in 1967, blacks destroyed their own neighborhoods.

Blacks criticize each other. Chris Rock said, "I love black people, but I hate niggas, brother. I hate niggas." Blacks say to educated blacks, "You're bougie," (meaning bourgeois.) In 2005, in Ft. Myers, Anita heard some blacks say to other blacks, "You all must be doin' so good with your fancy hairdos and expensive purses. We just tryin' to make it."

Whites and blacks criticize black leaders. Blacks say that once their leaders are "accepted," they forget the rest and just want to feather their own nest. And there's an element of truth in this. During George W. Bush's re-election in 2004, black pastors, "diverted from the issue of race," were accused of a greater kinship with white evangelicals than with black elected officials and leaders. Black conservatives, who are praised and superficially accepted by whites, are seen as "agreeing with the enemy." Blacks call them Uncle Toms, saying, "The house slaves are still with us."

The black community has no commonality except race. During the 1950s, Negroes were in the same economic boat for the most part, since there were so few professionals. Today, as the economic gap among blacks increases exponentially, class differences generate all kinds of social, political, and religious divisions within the black community.

The black upper and middle classes no longer have anything in common with lower class blacks. Black professionals don't relate to the black community the way Negro professionals did.

Widening class differences have resulted in cultural disparity. The upper and middle classes are united in their focus on conformity. The lower class is united in its focus on non-conformity.

Elite blacks, who have abandoned the black community, are isolated. There is now the issue of whether a black is "authentically black," as in the case with Barack Obama. Elite blacks, who have made it, no longer have the impetus to use their talent to lift the black lower class. In their primary orientation to whites, they are unable to think of what's best for themselves as a people. Michael Dyson says, "These blacks assume they occupy a place other niggers don't. Has the black middle class lost its mind? Nigger, don't just wait till you're in trouble to discover you're a nigger."

Successful blacks are socially marginal. They're not fully accepted by whites nor do they have any identity or emotional connection with other blacks. Success has required giving up their roots, their solidarity with the black community. Lower class blacks are even more socially marginal. Not only are they rejected by whites, they have lost the support of blacks who could help them. In the generation gap, black children today are removed from the Civil Rights Movement. Older people make statements without asking young people what they think.

There's a conflict between the black leaders of civil rights days and those of the younger generation. The conservative Independent Black Majority says blacks today are misled by traditional civil rights leaders who are "grievance merchants" that over-emphasize racism. Younger leaders are focused on economic empowerment — economic viability instead of victimization. They say blacks today care more about education, crime, and the economy, than race relations and voting rights.

Today social class predominates. Since integration opened the door to all blacks, there are both light- and dark-skinned blacks who have become wealthy. At the same time, there remains an elitism based on skin tone. Mulattos still have greater advantage, greater job opportunities in visible areas. They have a greater generational accumulation of wealth. If there are no intervening variables to quell it, blacks with white in them still feel superior to dark-skinned blacks.

In 1985, as I was coming out of my office at the University of Michigan-Flint, I ran into one of my black students. I had seen her with a young black man on campus and knew both of them, so I said, "He's a bright, ambitious young man. You'd make a nice couple."

She said, "Oh, I can't marry him. He's too dark. My parents wouldn't approve."

The ability to pass for white remains a source of pride. In 2003, a high mulatto friend told me that when her mother was in the hospital, her white roommate thought she was Italian. When my friend's father walked into the room, the white roommate yelled, "Oh my God! She's married to a black man!"

A black friend told me, "Skin color is important to the eye. It's just not talked about anymore. There were light and dark Alpha's. The Delta's were dark males and females. Spike Lee is dark and homely. Prince is light and baby faced. He's got lots of acceptability."

Since everyone was needed to lift the race, divisiveness and Negro racism guaranteed Negro failure. Self-focus and jealousy generated a constant tension in the Negro community. It facilitated white control, keeping Negroes vulnerable and powerless. Only joint ventures of Negroes and whites had any status or clout with whites, since whites were a part of them and controlled them.

The class divide in the black community is permanent. In subtle racism, blacks have no sheltering community. Black progress remains "one step forward, two steps back." What is needed today is a creation of wealth within the black community. Black small businesses can't compete with the large chains.

Upper and middle class blacks are only elite within the black community. A black friend told me, "We're middle class, but we're black middle class. And we'll never be anything but black middle class." Cornell West said, "Before the Civil Rights Movement, blacks liked to shine their shoes. White policemen stepped all over them, scuffing them, and blacks could do nothing about it. Now folks with a little money think they have honor. Things have not really changed."

Blacks are culturally marginal. They no longer hold the old Negro values nor can they forge a new community that nurtures. Today blacks don't know how to achieve unity nor do they fully understand why.

Chapter Nine: Image vs. Reality

Imitation of Superiority

> Success is to be measured not so much by the position one has reached in life, as by the obstacles which he has overcome.
> — Booker T. Washington

During the 1950s, white thought and behavior were crucial and important for Negro survival and success. As Negroes formed an emotional bond with whites, they came to see everything in the eyes of whites. They couldn't imagine any path to status than being like whites.

Negro day workers, privy to white foibles, exhibited a classic love/hate relationship with whites. They reveled in exposing white flaws since it meant things weren't really as whites said they were. On the steps of Central Baptist Church in St. Louis, I listened to them talking before and after church.

One woman said, "They think we're dumb bunnies. Girl, we know more about them than they'll ever learn in a generation about us. My boss is so nice, but do you know she can't even make toast? She burns it every time. Her husband tells me secretly, 'Thelma, you make the toast. Don't let Mary touch it.'"

Another woman said, "Girl, white people are wasteful! Those teenagers put a lotta food on their plate. They take two bites and want desert. There's seven in the family and they leave enough food to feed an army. My boss says, 'Gwen, please take what's in the pot. Otherwise, it'll just get thrown away.' One or two times a week I take food home and we can't even finish eatin' it."

Another woman said, "Girl, that house looks like a hurricane has been in it every mornin' you go there. There's underwear from the bathroom to the bedroom — things scattered all over. I have to put all that stuff in the hamper before I can do anything. Those people should go into the trash business. All the baskets are full. Sometimes I say, 'Do you mean to throw this away?' They throw clothes out just because they have a little spot on 'em. One day my boss gave me a dress. When I took the spot out and took it back to her, she said, 'Are you sure that's the same dress?' Girl, I tell you they're all a bunch o' dummies. But don't tell 'em that. Let 'em believe they're smart.'"

Another woman said, "I spend most of my time takin' care of the baby. My boss is in her thirties. They wanted this baby so much but she doesn't know how to take care of it. When I went in yesterday, the baby was cryin' his head off. She told me, 'He's been cryin' since my husband left for work. I gave him a pacifier and warmed a bottle but he just keeps cryin'.' Girl, you know what was wrong?

185

That baby was dirty! I smelled it right away! Maybe her long nose can't smell. I cleaned him up and gave him his bottle. In five minutes, he started cooin'. My boss said, 'You're a lifesaver.' Girl, I tell you, these white folks are so stupid."

While Negroes hated and distrusted whites, they simultaneously admired them for their power and success. They longed for their acceptance and approval. They were always torn between how they knew whites saw them and how they wanted whites to see them. Since whites were "superior," pleasing them and being like them was more important. Day workers were a classic example of this as well.

One Sunday, a day worker said, "Girl, I was so surprised to see Mrs. Sherman comin' to my house the other day. You could see her jaw drop. She said, 'Where'd you get all these good things? Everything's so clean and orderly. And you have five children in the house?' I told her, 'Yes, Ma'am. Those who are eight years and up have their chores. Even the babies pick up stuff.' "

Another day worker said, "My boss took me home last week and I told him, 'Come on in and see where I live.' When he did, he said, 'What're you working for? You must have money stored somewhere.' I told him, 'We're so busy workin' just to get by, we fight hard to keep things in good order. We can't afford any new thing. These children have to eat.' "

Someone else said, "Girl, I almost fell over. My boss came just as I was about to leave and said, 'Girl, where're you goin'? Oh, no you're not.' I told her, 'Well, Ma, I'm through. Your brother and his wife are comin' over so I'd better get outta here. I'll do the dishes tomorrow mornin'.' You know what she told me? 'You're part of the guests this evening! I want my brother and his wife to meet you.' Girl, I tell you. They didn't put me in the kitchen. I ate with 'em."

One of the women said, "What'd you do? How'd ya eat?"

She said, "I was watchin' 'em like a hawk. The same thing they did, I did. The way they ate, I ate. Girl, I was kinda nervous at first. But nothin' to it! I tell you, they eat just like we eat!"

Negroes wanted to be white. One of my sons told me, "Dad, when I was in grade school, I wanted to be white." If all else could be equal, Negroes would have chosen to be white because of the social, economic, and political advantages.

They wanted to look like whites. They straightened their hair and used skin-lightening cream. Mulattos socially rejected what whites disdained — dark skin and nappy hair. Those who could, passed for white.

In 1952, the first summer I stayed with the Huntleys' in St. Louis, Rev. Huntley took me to a local Negro barber shop and told the barber, "This is my son from Africa. Remember him. The bill's on me. Cut his hair good. He's a good looking boy. He's going to Lincoln, one of our good universities."

As the barber started cutting my hair, he said, "Your hair's not like nigger hair." He called over the other barber and said, "Feel his hair. This must be the real

African hair. Workin' in the swamps of Mississippi and Louisiana with armies of mosquitoes layin' their eggs in our hair is what made it so kinky. The only ones here with soft hair like this are those whose blood has been tainted by the slave master."

The other barber said, "I'd like to pair you with my daughter so we can have some of that good hair in the family."

Someone said, "But John, you haven't asked Benjamin how he feels about the whole thing. Whatcha say, Benjamin? She's a nice-lookin' girl."

I said, "First things first — education first and then we'll talk about that."

John said, "You see? He's a real book man. If you tell a nigger here somethin' like that, that you'll give 'em your daughter? They're like hungry dogs. They'll leave everything and follow that. And they won't have anything to feed 'er."

Negroes were judged by how well they resembled whites. They were only valued for thinking like whites. Imitating whites gave them a certain satisfaction and prestige they couldn't receive from their peers. They were determined to get out of stereotype since there was no status in being Negro.

Negro day workers were determined to show themselves the opposite of stereotype. When a seasoned day worker broke in a new girl from the South, she instructed the new girl, "Girl, if you're supposed to clean, clean until you can see yourself. Wipe your hand to make sure you feel no dirt. Don't take a break till they ask you to sit down and rest a little bit. Even then, say, 'Ma'am, I've got so much to do I wanna catch up.' And you must never, never, girl, take anything whether it's food or even trash you can use, till they give it to you. Cause they're gonna be watchin' you like a hawk. If you find anything in the trash basket that looks good, ask 'em before you empty it. Say, 'Do you mean to throw this away, Ma'am?' Wait till they say, 'Take it.' The next day they'll have something similar as a gift for you. Always look 'em straight in the eye and smile and say, 'Thank you, Ma'am.' Let us know how you're doin'."

Because success meant "Be white," Negroes looked to their racial group only for survival. The constant dilemma of upper and middle class Negroes was, "How do we get them to accept us?" The message that continually played in their minds was, "Be like whites so you can have their power and status." They assumed that by internalizing white values, they would be superior like whites. Negroes were focused on white opinion, "If I do this, what will they think of me?" They longed for dignity in the eyes of whites, acceptance as citizens and equals. Because inferiority was genetic, they could only assume status by association with whites.

In St. Louis, I had a good Negro friend named Dugan who had been a personal attendant to General Dwight D. Eisenhower during World War II. He told me, "The general was so nice! On the weekend, he said, 'Take a bottle of cognac to have a fine time with your friends. Are you short of money? Take this.' Sometimes in the evening, after I served dinner and we were by ourselves, he let me sit and drink with him. I thought to myself, 'This is General Ike and I'm drinking with him! Just he and I, the General of the Allies. Man, that's a good man. I could do anything for him, even die."

Race pride was based on white opinion. "Proving themselves worthy" was both a burden and a discipline for Negroes. In order for them to be proud of themselves or their race, they wanted and needed the approval of whites.

When I attended Lincoln, it was all-Negro. The professors and staff were dedicated to making their students "proud." The support network included special study halls and tutoring. Lincoln had an arrangement with the University of Missouri for graduate work in the sciences since it had better science facilities. Those who participated received their degree from Lincoln because Negroes couldn't enroll there.

President Scruggs hosted dinners at his home on campus to encourage these graduate students attending an all-white university. He wanted them to succeed for the pride of the race and the pride of Lincoln. Since I lived with the Scruggs my sophomore year, I attended one of these dinners and saw firsthand the deep inner pride of Negroes — their rejection of their "inferiority."

The first dinner was held before classes began. As we all sat around the table, President Scruggs began his pep talk, saying, "You know what you want to do. It's your own choosing. Do you hear me? Are there any questions?"

Everyone said, "No Dr. Scruggs!"

He said, "Young men, young ladies, you can do better than any of them. You're obligated to us. Don't make their lies come true. I want monthly reports on your progress. If you find any difficulty that indicates you can't do it, drop out. But I know you won't drop out. I'll show you an example."

He nodded to me and told them, "See that little boy sitting there? He's a pure African. None of us can be any purer than he is. Dr. Cox, Dr. Miller, Dr. Boyd, Dr. Dowdy, Dr. Maxwell, and Dr. Freeman are Harvard and Yale graduates. They all say Benjamin is the best student they've ever had. And you know why? No one has spoiled him with myths and propaganda that he's inferior. Talk to him. See what he's doing. Because that's what you've got to do."

He told me, "Tell us more about the real Africa, not the one we read about in the paper or those wild stories that missionaries and hunters bring."

I said, "Well, it's hard to talk about Africa since it's the second largest continent. As for myself, I can talk best about my Mende and Gbande tribes. We're a proud people. We hate for anyone to dominate us. We hate failure and we hate lies. In order for you to be free, you must be truthful and you must not fail."

He said, "He's young but that's a good way to sum everything up."

Negroes were the epitome of conformity as a way to assume status. In their longing to belong in white society, they derived a certain satisfaction and security in conforming to whites. Despite their treatment, they only wanted a fair and equal opportunity.

Upper and middle class Negroes were the epitome of white values. No one believed the American dream like they did. They wanted what whites wanted. They believed that if they played by the rules, they could succeed and be accepted. Ebony magazine displayed materialism as if to say, "You can get it too." The whole purpose of the Urban League was success in the white world. The NAACP was designed to make America better, not just help Negroes. In their desire to be a part of the system, Negroes didn't want to change white institutions, just their racist practices.

Negro leaders were the epitome of conformity. In order to receive white support, they had to be in close agreement with whites. Their "status" with whites accorded them status in the Negro community. W.E.B. Dubois, from the Negro upper class, advocated a classical education to be "better than the white man." He wanted Negroes to be intellectually "white" while still being Negro. Booker T. Washington, from the middle class, advised Negroes to follow the values of the white working class — to work with their hands. He advocated separation in all things social.

Negroes adopted Christianity despite white hypocrisy. It gave them a positive identity of worth and honor as children of God. They took pride in being the redeemed. They knew that nothing could separate them from the love of God. Negroes of all social classes were devout Christians, following the rules of Christianity and white society.

Negro pastors were conservative. Rev. Johnson of Jefferson City, Missouri, was a classic example of the Negro themes of the day — work hard, keep the family together, and be proud of your race. Those who were young should go to school, because "Many of our people didn't have the opportunity to do so when we were comin' up."

"Today people borrow and don't pay. And they think they're smart by doin' so. We used to work and help widows and old people but you don't see very much of that today. We don't feed the hungry. We don't take in the stranger. We don't visit the sick or the prisoner. These are the things that held the Negro community together. We looked after each other. The opposite of this is creepin' up in our society today."

In St. Louis, many lawyers, doctors, and other professionals joined Central Baptist Church because Rev. Huntley was upright. When I stayed with the Huntleys I became aware that women in the church were after him. They would call and want to see him. They'd give him expensive gifts. One day he told me, "Elizabeth knows all about these women who are after me."

She said, "Oh, yeah! They're not hiding it from me. That's why white preachers respect my husband. I know Rev. Williams who went to Lincoln with you is faithful but there's a lot of other little preachers all over who take this as something good. People say, 'Oh, he's so popular. Women are just falling after him.' I've even heard young people say, 'Man, I'm gonna be a preacher and have all those women fussing over me.' Rev. Huntley has told the youth group, 'That's the wrong reason to be a preacher. You shouldn't do that and especially if you're a preacher.'"

Familial love and duty were primary values in the Negro community. Upper class Negroes had stable families. They limited family size to garner resources and pass them on. In Puritan morality, they said, "Don't bring a child into this world unless you're prepared to care for it."

A black friend told me, "Our family was very close. Every Tuesday was family night. I'd be at my mother's for dinner no matter who I was married to or what my schedule was."

In the Negro lower class, the family was matriarchal. Negro parents worked long hours or several jobs. In many cases, there was no man in the house. Grandmothers raised the next generation. They felt it was their calling to be the morality police keeping tabs on the neighborhood. This kept the Negro community together and was one reason there was little or no crime.

Grandmothers knew every street and house. They knew every child and what family they belonged to. They told any child, "You'd better not do that! If white folks see that, they'll say niggers all behave like that. I'm gonna beat your butt!"

I heard kids say, "Don't do that. Grandma'll see you! Oh, girl, you're gonna be in big trouble."

Negroes were super patriots, even though America was a different nation to them than it was to whites. Negroes wanted so much to belong. The Negro soldier was the epitome of race pride, serving his country to prove himself worthy. In 1944, I asked a Negro GI in Monrovia, "What are you fighting for?"

He said, "Benjamin, this may just be our ticket to be free, really free. They think we're all cowards and they'll see we're not."

Negroes "fought" to serve a country that denied them their rights. A black friend who served in the military told me, "Love of country is paramount. You don't touch that. I've been in the military and for me, serving one's country is the greatest honor."

Military service exposed Negroes to the world. I first met Dugan, the friend I mentioned earlier, at our first meeting of the African Association in St. Louis. We needed cab service to bring people to the meeting and Dugan was the first cab driver to respond. He became our greatest supporter. Each week he called me to find out what we were doing. He offered to bring people and arranged the hall rental for our bi-monthly dances. He invited whites to these dances, telling us, "I want them to see Africans who are educated. These white folks only see the day workers who clean their houses."

One night, two white men at our dance began cursing and calling people, "Nigger." Dugan and his friend took them out and beat them up before I knew anything about it. He told me, "These rednecks in St. Louis haven't experienced what I have. I'm not gonna let 'em treat Africans badly. You're better off than they are. I fought to preserve this country and I'll fight again to protect my African brothers and sisters."

Negroes realized what they could do, particularly in World War II. In 1952, in Topeka, Kansas, a tall, muscular Negro friend was with me when we took a common short cut through a white neighborhood. Two young white men yelled, "Nigger, you can't walk here! You have to go back!" We ignored them. They stood right in front of us and yelled in my friend's face, "Can't you hear, Nigger? Go back! Go round!"

My friend lifted them up, slammed them together several times, and dropped them on the ground. He told me, "These peckerwoods don't understand nothin'. I been in the army fightin' for 'em, riskin' my life. We done nothin' wrong."

The eternal hope of Negroes was to work hard so their children could get an education and have better lives. Parents were willing to sacrifice since they knew their children had to be twice as good to succeed. Education was the mainstay of the Negro upper and middle classes. Negroes took advantage of any opportunity for higher education, however limited. They attended Negro colleges. Many went into the military to take advantage of the GI Bill.

In 1956, when I was at Washington University in St. Louis, I sold World Book Encyclopedias part time. In my sales pitch, I said, "I'm from Africa and I'm working on my doctorate at Washington University. Your children will have a good foundation for their education if you have a World Book Encyclopedia in your home. If I can do it, they can too. Maybe someday, they'll be working on their doctorate."

At one home, a Negro grandmother in her rocking chair nodded and told her daughter, "Ain't that true. Lord, have mercy. This young man from Africa is an example of excellence. He's at that white folk's university. Ain't no white people comin' here to sell these books to help our children. This is a blessing comin' our way. You're gonna buy this for my grandchildren. This'll be good for all our children. Let's tell our people 'bout this. I want this announced in church next Sunday."

The daughter invited me back that evening for dinner so I could speak with her husband. She told me, "Our parents didn't have the opportunity for all of this. They didn't even graduate from grade school. Those who reached fourth grade were lucky. This is a chance of a lifetime. My husband will listen to you. He didn't finish grade school. I have some college but I dropped out to get married. We want things better for our children and for our people. We're always at the tail end of everything because we can't read. We can't do things."

During the days of discrimination and segregation, acquiring an education was a source of great pride for Negro families and the Negro community. Any success in education was highly praised and an occasion for a family celebration. Family members said, "Now since you're grown, remember us. We've come a long way but we still have a long, long way to go. Remember your younger brothers and sisters and cousins. You've had this opportunity and if you fail to live up to your responsibilities, our work will be in vain. We don't need your money or material things. We want you to preserve our good name and the honor of our family."

As relatives sat around drinking and laughing, they said, "Times have changed. We have schools to go to and our own good colleges. Sometimes I think they're even better than those white colleges because there are too many of 'em. We're new to this kinda treatment, havin' our own colleges. Whenever you hear A & M, that's a Negro college! Tennessee, Georgia, Alabama, Louisiana — those are states of the Confederacy and we have schools there now! And there's our grand old school — Tuskegee Institute by Booker T. Washington. Did you know Booker T. Washington was born a slave? And don't you know most or all of the people teachin' in these colleges are Negro? Like us! And, oh, boy! Do they know their field! They're professionals! Your grandfather and great grandfather never thought such a day would ever come. I tell you, the door's open. Have you seen those athletes at our schools on the football field or the basketball court? I tell you, you'll see something different when the day comes that they let our boys play with their boys. That's the time we'll have respect cause we'll beat their butts! Don't stop short of anything. You can do it!"

The more "white" Negroes acted, the more they were accepted by whites. The theme of upper and middle class Negroes was to prove themselves worthy by becoming more "white" than whites. In the "Old School of the American Negro," they rigidly and excessively imitated the white lifestyle. Upper class Negroes had extreme standards of wealth and success. In their social organizations, they followed white etiquette to the slightest detail. Middle class Negroes were workaholics. Since they were socially "on the fence," they wanted to do everything properly.

Negroes knew their race was always on trial according to white standards. They knew they were perceived as a racial group and they faced consequences as such. If one Negro got out of hand, they all suffered in some way. They conformed to raise the image of their race.

In 1958, at Michigan State, I became friends with one of my students. Willie told me he worked for the city of Lansing. He said, "They can't say niggers are always late cause I'm the first one there and the last to leave. White people like to exaggerate what they think our shortcomings are and minimize our good qualities."

When he invited me to meet his family, the house was spotless. Before each of his children went to bed, they came one by one to tell me "Good Night." He told me the only break he took from studying was coaching softball on Saturdays. I said, "Willie, may I join the game next week?"

He said, "Well, if you insist. But when you strike out, that'll be it. You won't play again. You're too important and respectable to shame yourself by having someone strike you out. We've got four pitchers. The one next Saturday is white. I wouldn't want a white guy to strike you out. If it was a black pitcher, I'd tell 'em not to strike you out."

I said, "Willie, I don't want that. I want him to pitch to me like anyone else."

That Saturday, the stands in the park near Everett High School, were full of mostly white students. The score was tied and it was the last inning. There were two outs and two men on base. I said, "Willie, "I'm ready. I want to bat."

He said, "Bunt the ball so at least one man can get home. And that'll be a hit for you. Don't try to hit cause I'm afraid they're gonna strike you out. Please, Professor, don't let down the race." He checked my bat and said, "This one's not too heavy. You can handle this. Remember, don't let down the race. You know how I feel about that. If it was just anyone, it wouldn't make any difference. I'll be sayin' a prayer for you."

As I stood at the plate, the white students yelled at the white pitcher, "Give 'em one of your fast balls! He won't even see it! He's a professor! Give it to him! Let's go!" Willie looked at me in dead seriousness.

At the first pitch, I hit the ball over the fence into a wooded area. Everyone yelled, "It's gone!" so I ran slowly around the bases.

As I came into home plate, some students cheered and shook my hand. Willie ran up and lifted me up. He hugged me so tight, it took the wind out of me. He said, "Professor! I didn't know you had it in you! That ball was so high they didn't even try to catch it! I'm gonna take you home with me to have a celebration! Any time you want, you can play with us!"

Several months later, he asked me after class if I had a tire gauge. He said, "I heard you're drivin' to Tennessee. Niggers have a whole lotta accidents cause they don't look at their tires. When it's snowin' and their tire's low, they just go into the ditch. We don't want that to happen to you."

The next day he showed me a tire gauge and said, "I bought this for you. Let's go try it out on your car right here on campus. The students comin' in and out of the Union will see us."

That night he told Ruth, "All those white students and teachers were lookin' at us but we pretended not to notice. Nothing misses their eyes — especially a nigger checkin' his tires."

He told me, "You didn't notice those white people, but I did. I know 'em. I've lived with 'em all my life."

Upper and middle class Negroes were focused on image more than anything else. Elite Negroes assumed that imitating white taste would make whites think, "They're just like us." Clothing was a way to show they weren't an ordinary nigger. Conveying the right image through dress was important. Negro colleges polished their students. Negro performers, like Duke Ellington, were always impeccably and elegantly dressed. Negroes admired them for their appearance and style.

Elite Negroes believed "Clothes make the man." They dressed the part to be respected. They were "slaves to fashion," following dress etiquette to the "T." They competed in dressing their children.

A black friend told me, "Ben, when I was at Merck, I must have had fifty suits, top of the line. I was the best dressed guy there. Ann's cousin owned a formal wear shop so I must have had fourteen tuxedos, one in every color of the rainbow, for all the affairs we went to. I never wanted anyone to say, 'Look at those niggers. Look how they dress.'"

Accumulating property, rather than accomplishment, became the symbol of success. Elite Negroes spent their income on consumer goods. To outdo whites, they had to have the image of a lavish lifestyle. Ebony magazine displayed the lifestyles of rich and famous Negroes.

Negro homes had to display the best. The table was always set with the finest china and linens. Negro pastors and other professionals had to show off their prosperity with a good home, a nice car, etc. Their wife had to be well-dressed like white women.

Since most Negroes didn't own a home, they showed their status in the clothing they wore and the car they drove. They had to have a large, late-model, flashy car. In St. Louis, any time a Negro friend saw a mark on my car, he told me, "Ben! You can't be drivin' a car like this. I'll bring some paint to fix it up real good."

Upper and middle class Negroes were always concerned about their image. I heard a Negro pastor in St. Louis, say, "Don't go walkin' down the street like you've just picked cotton." There were oratory contests with people reciting poetry on street corners. Upper class women retained their maiden name, for example, Coretta Scott King and Elizabeth Maddox Huntley. Negroes wanted an elaborate funeral to give them, in death, the status and respect they never had in life.

Negroes displayed destructive cultural mentalities that derived from the realities of white supremacy and racism. In their insecurity, they displayed a fear of failure, "If you don't try, you won't fail." They were apathetic to even try anything because they knew they wouldn't succeed. Insecurity made them overly cautious. When they were given opportunity, they couldn't show initiative or take risks.

They were anti-intellectual, saying, "Education and success are for white folks." A professor at Lincoln told me, "Negroes want to get something good, to be in a good position — and they want it now. They want status like anyone else. But they don't want to go through what it takes. They don't want to make the sacrifice of staying up late to study. They just want 'book.' They don't want to be enlightened. That's why Lincoln's mission is to teach people to persevere. Benjamin, if you give these people one million dollars, in a year, they'll be poorer than they were before. The white man has made us our own enemy and we're proud to be our own enemy — to stay in poverty. That's why when someone does well making good grades, people say, 'Look at that dude. What you think you are — white?' "

Negroes exhibited defeatism. When I was a lab assistant in chemistry at Lincoln, I tried to help a student heat a chemical over a Bunsen burner and record its boiling point. When he simply couldn't or wouldn't do it, I said, "You'll have to come back on Saturday. You can't pass chemistry if you can't do this simple measurement."

He told me, "You're a nigger just like me. You don't know nothin'. You just come here. This is white folks' stuff. Even if I learn to do this, I ain't gonna get nothin'. I'm just gonna get a nigger job. I'm not gonna kill myself, Ben. When I finish here, I'm gonna look for a job. If there's another nigger there who never went to college and they like him, they'll hire him. Lotsa whites hire Negroes who have never been to college. They resent us as smart niggers."

At Lincoln, I was sweet on a girl, but we never made it because she was so focused on taking me to all kinds of social activities. One day, she told me, "You African! You don't know anything! You can't go anywhere. All you wanna do is study, study, study all the time. That's not gonna get you anywhere. What you think? You're white? You're just a nigger like the rest of us. It gets white people somewhere, but not us."

Elite Negroes not only wanted status in the eyes of whites, they wanted to maintain their status in the eyes of their peers, the Negro community. Since Negroes couldn't participate in white society, the Negro upper class created its own social clubs that the middle class joined. Their claim to prestige was their elaborate imitation of white etiquette and ritual that was classically displayed in their cotillion balls for young people. Their social extravaganzas were displayed in Ebony magazine, as if to say, "We can do it better." Jet Magazine's society column religiously reported on elite Negroes. Negroes focused on these social organizations as a diversion and compensation, a way to keep their sanity in their isolation from the white world.

White hypocrisy led to moral inconsistency in Negroes. Negroes were always shown the worst of whites, openly or secretly. In St. Louis, I heard a Negro barber say, "The white man is the most rotten person in the world. I don't know why God made 'em. They're cheaters. They're liars. They're rascals more than the devil himself. Let me explain this to you, brothers. All those things you see on Market Street in the white man's shops that are open to colored people are left-overs

— rejects that no white person would buy. Look at the expiration date on the groceries. They've expired months or years ago. And they still sell 'em to colored people. There's no redeeming quality in the white man as far as colored people are concerned. Man, I went two years to Stuart College, right here in St. Louis. Those two years opened my eyes to see the white man as he really is. So I left and went to barber school to make me some money. I didn't want to learn any more about the white man. I knew enough."

In another barber shop, I heard a barber say, "Those rascals can get away with anything. You know what they're doin'? My wife works for a rich guy who works for Anheuser Busch. She was standing with his wife and two other white women and man, they were they talkin'! The wife told the other two women that her husband had gotten a rotten deal and was gonna pass it on to another guy who'd get nothin' for it. And he thought that was good business."

The other barber said, "You mean to tell me a white man was gonna do that to another white man?"

The first barber said, "It was a lotta money and the guy fell for it! Six thousand dollars. That's the truth. They didn't even take my wife into account when they were talkin'. It was as though she wasn't there. She told me that within three months the guy he duped had to go back to him to bail him out. Man, if you can dupe the white man, do it! They dupe their own people!"

Everyone laughed. The first barber said, "I'm tellin' you. The white man ain't no good. Lordy, I never saw a good one in all my life and I'm forty years old."

In the *cycle of racism*, decadence is ratcheted up. Whites were hypocritical in the area of race. Hypocrisy became a way of life for Negroes, the norm of the Negro community.

Negroes ridiculed whites but they never seriously questioned them. Although whites didn't follow their own norms, power and success meant, "Be white." In a "whatever works" mentality, Negroes imitated the cunning and rascality they saw whites getting away with.

In a Negro barber shop in St. Louis, I heard one barber say to another, "Beat the white man at his own game."

The other barber said, "And he ain't even know 'bout it. He thinks you're just bein' a nigger."

The first barber said, "My wife Lilly can dupe 'em so well. I tell you, she had the whole family sick in two days. When her boss called, Lilly told her, 'I have this bad cough. I'm not feelin' well. I can't come.' Her boss told her, 'Lilly, you have to come. I'm having something at the house. My friends are coming.' My wife's a charmin' lady so she said, 'Yes, Ma'am, I'll come.' Her boss told her, 'I appreciate it so much. I know you love me, being sick and still coming. Thank you, Lillie.' You know what Lillie did? She coughed all over the food and even spit in it. Man, that was a bad flu. Lillie shot 'em down with her flu and they didn't even connect it. They're so stupid and they think they're smart. Anyone would know you catch the flu from another person."

Since Negroes were always at a disadvantage, they applauded those who could get away with things and take advantage of others. Ruth and her sisters pointed out someone and said, "Man, he's so clever! He's makin' a better livin' for him and his family than those of us sweatin' all day. Man, I tell you, he always dresses well and appropriately for the occasion. If he wants to get somethin' from a mechanic, he dresses like one. If he wants to take somethin' from a business-man, he's in a business suit. He knows more people than you and I put together. He can open any car. I don't know how he does it without the key. He sure is a smart guy."

Deceiving whites was a way of life for Negroes. In the barber shop, I heard a man say, "Nigger, man, how'd I do?"

The other man said, "You did well. They ain't know nothin'. They're stu-pid. They think they know niggers but they can't even tell niggers from other niggers."

One day, Ruth told me about a guy who could put a radio in our car. I said, "Where will he get it from?"

She said, "He's mechanical. He can do anything."

I said, "I know that. But where's the radio coming from?"

She said, "You're too technical!"

I thought the matter was closed. But when I returned from a trip, she told me, "I want to show you something." She took me out to our car and turned on the radio.

I said, "Did that guy do it? How much did it cost?

She said, "Don't worry about it. It's taken care of."

Because the Negro church was corrupted by hypocrisy, it had negative as well as positive elements. Negro religious expression was more emotion than convic-tion. While the church tried its best, it was primarily a social organization, rather than a moral force. The informal norm of the Negro community was sexual li-cense and illegitimacy. It was traditional for Negro women to seduce the pastor. Pastors were excused for their womanizing and indiscretions.

Negroes were particularly disillusioned after World War II. Their eyes were opened. They had fought in two world wars and still faced the same realities of white supremacy and racism. They defended a country that wouldn't defend them. White GIs returned as heroes. Negro GIs returned as "Negroes." America never honored Negro soldiers. They couldn't even be buried in white cemeteries.

When part of the Negro dream died, Negroes felt they should get anything they could, any way they could. The upper class had such extreme standards of conspicuous consumption, many Negroes could only garner such wealth illegitimately. To support their lavish lifestyle, they participated in drugs, gambling, and prostitution on the side.

At Lincoln, Dr. Maxwell, the head of the Chemistry department, called me into his office several days after I had taken an exam. Dr. Boyd, my Chemistry professor, was there as well. Maxwell said, "Benjamin, you're a good student. However, I have two exams here that Dr. Boyd has given me. They have one name on top and your name on the bottom. Do you have the exam that was returned to you yesterday?"

I said, "It's right here in my briefcase."

Dr. Boyd said, "I remembered that the boys whose names are on those papers sat behind you, so I've summoned them as well."

Dr. Maxwell said, "Did you arrange for them to sit behind you?"

I said, "I haven't the faintest idea what's going on. I've seen those boys on campus. They're football stars. But I don't know them."

Dr. Boyd called them in and said, "Tell us the truth or you'll be expelled." They broke down and confessed that they had copied everything on my exam, including my name.

Elite Negroes viewed education as "status." They wanted education for the image it garnered, not to do something with it. There was no genuine love of learning, no intellectual talk. The education most Negroes received was substandard. Not only that, many left school early to support their family. Teachers in small Negro colleges in the South had great prestige in the Negro community. However, since they weren't really qualified, their degree was "empty." It became the same for their students.

At Lincoln, while the vast majority of professors were top-notch, there was a great variation in student ability. When I tutored a mulatto young man in math, I struggled for months just to get him to do common algebra equations. One day in frustration, I said, "Why do you want this education?"

He said, "My parents! That's our tradition."

I even asked the dean, "Can't you just waive algebra?"

He said, "We can't. It's a requirement."

So we struggled on. Finally the dean told me, "Ben, you've done well. We're going to give him a C so he can graduate. It's not your fault. His parents want him to do this. As long as they're satisfied, we're satisfied. He's not going into teaching. We won't recommend him for graduate school or for anything."

The day he graduated, his parents gave him a brand new white Cadillac. When they took us out to dinner, he told them, "If it wasn't for him, I'd have been stuck there for years!"

It was the idea of education that was important. Simply being enrolled in college gave Negroes an aura of status. However, there were high drop-out and give-up rates. The majority of those who graduated weren't well-prepared. They were ashamed that they couldn't compete with other college graduates, white or Negro.

The Negro lower class was characterized by circumstantial inferiority — ignorance and poverty. Whites in America might be poor. Negroes were certainly poor — invisible and always last.

When I told Ruth I'd like to meet her parents, she said, "You won't like 'em. They live in the country in a house with no bathroom. They bathe in the kitchen in a large tin tub."

After I arrived by bus, Ruth walked me to the outskirts of Humbo. On a narrow country road, we arrived at an old, unpainted clapboard house with a zinc roof. Parked in the yard was an old Model T. Out back was an outhouse. Inside, the floors were wood plank. Wooden shutters covered the windows. Hung high on the wall were pictures of family ancestors and Sallman's "Head of Christ."

John and Penny were dressed in their very best, he in suspender pants and she in a cotton print dress with a bib apron. They provided for their seven children on six acres of land by sharecropping, tending an enormous garden, and raising their own hogs and chickens.

When Ruth walked me out to the back yard, she showed me the huge iron pot her parents put her under when she was a baby, while they worked in the cotton fields. Penny said, "Well, she was so little and we all had to work all day."

Lower class Negroes primarily looked just to survive and find some enjoyment in life. They didn't think in terms of social class, just richer or poorer. Their ambition was to have status in the eyes of their peers — having something more than other Negroes.

One day I asked Penny, "Why don't you sit down and rest?"

She said, "Benjamin, I'm workin' for myself. If I was workin' for white people, they'd never let you sit down one minute. I'm not gonna cheat myself."

John and Penny were illiterate. When I suggested, "Let's recite a Bible verse each time we eat dinner," the next two nights Penny recited "Jesus passing by."

On the second night, I said, "Where'd you get that verse?"

She said, "I tole you I don't know how to read but I listen to them preachers. Of all things in the Bible, the greatest is when Jesus passes you by. The poor blind man, he couldn't go to Jesus. So if Jesus hadn't passed by him, he wouldn't have gotten his sight. Jesus passed by me. Hallelujah! I'm his daughter and my husband is his son because He's in our heart."

Gross ignorance was a way of life for Negroes. Those who are completely ignorant are sure of nothing and gullible to believe anything. Those who know nothing, think they know everything. It is education that makes us realize how little we know.

In St. Louis, I heard a barber tell the others in his shop, "You see that guy, Benjamin, comin' in? He's from Africa and he's goin' to the university! You know what university means? It means you talk book-talk. You can't even talk like that. They talk big, big words. You can't even understand 'em."

One of the men said, "You mean he's from Africa and he go to, what you call that?'

The barber said, "University, Nigger! University! Nigger, you can't even understand that. This is a walkin' book right here from Africa and he's goin' back too. He ain't no nigger."

Someone told the man next to him, "He's goin' to universal. He's a universal student."

The barber laughed and said, "You niggers don't know nothin'! I said university! Boy, you can't even say 'university.' You better not go there. You won't understand a thing."

The lower class suffered even more from destructive cultural mentalities. Since we attempt those things we think we can succeed in, in learned helplessness, "If you think you can't, you can't." Since Negroes were treated unjustly, they had no respect for the law. Because they were inept, they used illegitimate means to get what they needed. In their poverty and helplessness, they displayed despair and fatalism. They had no goals since they had no resources. They couldn't plan their future since they had no control. No matter what they did, it was never enough. They expected a life of poverty. Unemployment and idleness were a way of life.

Ineptness and insecurity kept them in their own little comfortable realm of the Negro community. In their poverty syndrome, they feared risking what little they had. They said, "Be careful. You know what it's like if you don't have." Since there was no resolution to their deprivation and suffering, they carried the burdens of the world. They sang the "blues."

In their desire for instant gratification, they behaved on impulse. They couldn't make sacrifices for the future because there was no possibility of long term success. Becoming educated and successful in the white world wasn't even remotely possible. In contrast, success by rascality was possible and provided instant results. Gambling was profit based on chance, not ability. In the Negro neighborhood, it was a way of life. Decadence was the norm. Drugs and alcohol were an escape from daily frustration and despair. Violence and crime were a lifestyle.

Sexual promiscuity and illegitimacy were an integral part of the Negro community. Sexual behavior was the one thing the white man couldn't control, early sexual behavior, a form of entertainment. I heard that getting gonorrhea made a girl a woman.

Negroes disdained manual labor. They didn't want to get their hands dirty. Role models were drug dealers, pimps, and con artists who succeeded by exploiting others. Men who preyed on women to support them, were considered clever. They got what they wanted without paying for it.

Lower class Negroes who dressed well were an empty image. In a barber shop in St. Louis, Negroes were polite to a well-dressed man. The minute he left, they said, "Those are the ones who have women supporting 'em. I know a day worker who gives all her money to him. He ain't nothin' but a nigger."

My mulatto friend Milford introduced me to a man he knew. Calvin was always well-dressed with a hat. His shoes were shined. He wore dark glasses and his large, late-model, four-door Chrysler was always polished.

Ruth told Milford, "Calvin must be loaded. Where does he work?"

Milford said, "He works here and there. He spends most of his time in beer joints and pool halls. He sleeps in his car."

Late one night, Milford took me to a fairly nice Negro neighborhood and knocked on the window of Calvin's car. He said, "Hey, man. You wanna help me deliver some beer?

Several days later, I asked Calvin, "How is it that you sleep in your car?"

Calvin said, "I may not have a place to live, but I've got a good car to sleep in. If I come early, I can always find a parkin' space."

I said, "Why don't you get a place at the Y? How do you take a bath?"

Calvin said, "I got a friend now who's stayin' in the Y, so I go there. He likes his beer so I give him some when I sell beer. He says I can stay with him but he's only got one room and I can't be cooped up. Besides, you can't have a car like mine and keep it on the parkin' lot. People have to see you drivin' it. Man, these girls in East St. Louis! I can have any one I want."

I said, "How can you pay for a car like this?"

He said, "I haven't finished payin' for it yet. Sometimes I miss a month here and there, but I'm payin'. My girlfriends help me."

Sexual performance was a source of status. There was pride in conquest, particularly that of a white woman. Since white women were forbidden fruit, marrying one was an act of defiance. In so doing, a Negro got something over on the white man.

In a barber shop, I heard one man say to another, "Get it boy! That's it! They been doin' this to our women all the time. They think they're sacred cows. And the bigger and darker you are, the better it is. When they see you, their eyes will bug out, sayin', 'Look at that big buck with that tiny pretty white woman.' They'll see that lovely white woman lookin' in admiration into your big black eyes. And that's the only way white folks look up to us!"

At Billy's garage, a group of us Negro men were talking when a Negro with a white wife walked in. One of them said to him, "No white man would want that woman. She's too fat."

He said, "Well, she's good for one thing."

The rest of the conversation focused heavily on a word beginning with f, and I later expressed my surprise to Billy that they would talk about a man's wife like that.

Billy said, "Man, they toned it down 'cause you were here."

During the Civil Rights Movement, black leaders were the epitome of conformity. The movement was very American because it was based on white morality. King worked within the system, holding whites to their ideals. The purpose of civil rights was not to destroy America but to allow blacks to participate in it.

Whites took King seriously. He was not only from the black upper class, he was an authentic leader with a just cause. He used methods approved by whites.

Blacks admired King. They said, "He's educated. He's Dr. King. If you ever wanna find a real Christian, it's Martin. Many of us have been to jail for stealin' or whatever. Martin didn't even mind goin' to jail. If he was any ordinary nigger, he would've been strung up on a tree long ago. He's a poisonous snake to whites. He says things quietly in such good English, even those crackers can't understand him. He talks calmly but he does what he wants to do. Ain't nobody gonna make him change his stand. Man, they're afraid of him. They're tremblin' in their boots. White people better leave him alone. He's more dangerous than any black person alive because he's not afraid to die."

Black extremism was a replication of white extremism. Radical blacks replicated white supremacy. The Black Panthers symbolized anarchy and lawlessness, the same type of power whites used in the South.

In 1963, at Michigan State, I was in a panel discussion on integration with Malcolm X. Malcolm was bitterly opposed to it. I sided with King, saying, "The very concept of separation spells inequality. Blacks have worked to develop this country. They should have equal access to everything. Integration will allow America to serve all of her citizens, not just whites."

Malcolm laughed derisively and said, "The white man has had his day. He's on a sinking ship. If you join him, you're going to the bottom with him. It's time to take back from the white man what he's taken from us for almost three hundred years. They only want integration to save themselves."

Malcolm X was the ripe fruit of racism, a reactionary created by white society. He was an authentic leader who was brutally honest. He said, "Wake up and see who and what the white man really is. Judge him by his actions, not his words and ideals. Christ told whites to love. Lynching people, is that love? Killing people, is that love to you? Blacks are trying to exercise their right to vote and they're killing them for that. We're taxpayers too. This is our constitutional right. The only thing the white man will listen to is force. The only thing they understand is violence. They kill us but they don't want us to do it to them. Any time blacks take responsibility, whites get angry and say blacks are getting too 'uppity.' When blacks get to the point that they can do for themselves, we won't have a problem." Malcolm was both a radical and a conformist. While he railed at whites, deep down, he wanted their respect. Although he rejected the system, he wanted for blacks what whites had.

Blacks knew in their hearts that Malcolm was right. They said, "He just tells the MF's, 'you're goin' to hell.' He uses everyday words we all understand."

Despite significant social change, the themes of the Negro are still played out in blacks who live in a world of subtle racism. While blacks criticize whites, they still want to be accepted and affirmed by them. They still look to them for their identity and worth. Token blacks, who fulfill their role, have psychological security in being the "good nigger." A prominent black said, "There's niggers in this country who believe that shit."

Successful blacks try to get something over on the white man by proving whites wrong. They master chess, fencing, and golf. Blacks press for slave reparations. The black church is "prophetic" to the white church. For black entrepreneurs, it's about black economic power.

Successful blacks are neo-conformists who can only go forward in the white mode of materialism. They don't want to change the system. They want to be a part of it to get their piece of the pie. Cornell West said, "Today, money is equated with respect. The new black values are no longer a demand for dignity but a quest for material prosperity and security."

Radical blacks now fit into the system. The strength of the Black Muslim movement is diluted. Afros and Ebonics are out of style for blacks who want to succeed in the corporate world.

Conservative blacks are similar to conservative whites — liberal blacks similar to liberal whites. Successful blacks have more in common with whites of the same social class than they do with lower class blacks. Since the emotionality of the black church no longer appeals to them, they become second class Christians in a more sophisticated white church.

Elite blacks remain socially marginal. As they aim for assimilation, they leave their baggage behind. In an "every man for himself" mentality, they focus on succeeding as individuals within the system. They work for white firms with a white and black clientele. Integrated education gives them shared values with whites. Living in white communities, they're divorced from the black experience –the lower class isolated in the ghetto.

The "Oreo" is a black man who's more "white" than black. Living in a totally white environment, he's part of the elite white culture. His lifestyle has nothing in common with the vast majority of blacks. Although he's well-meaning, once he's accepted by whites, he doesn't care what happens to lower class blacks.

Conservative blacks consider themselves superior as open-minded, independent thinkers, un-swayed by the opinions of common black folk. Encased in the realm of white interests, they rail against Affirmative Action, saying, "If I can make it, other blacks can too." Since black gains are largely image rather than substance, these blacks are focused on whites at the expense of their racial group.

The old incentives for education are gone for black children. Upper and middle class children who have a chance for education, are subject to fads. The emphasis is on athletics. They want to get by with as little as they can.

Image is everything. In 1985, in Flint, Michigan, a black teacher in the community took one look at my car in the church parking lot and said, "What's this? A Ford Tempo? Professor, you should be drivin' a Cadillac!" Black women are slaves to fashion. They make a statement of identity in their hairstyles. Elite blacks wear African dress.

Blacks outdo whites in the pursuit of wealth and pleasure. The focus is on bling. Ebony Magazine showcases the lifestyles of black athletes and movie stars. Since blacks focus their spending power on consumer goods, no wealth is passed down in the black community.

Blacks not only have enormous disadvantages to overcome, they must be overly qualified. A black friend told me, "I love my work, but not the people I work with, one man especially. I work for a white law firm and the problem is, I know more about insurance than one of the attorneys there. When he asks me to do something, I say, 'Are you sure you want me to do it that way?' He gets angry, but if I do it his way, I get in trouble with the other lawyers. They tell me, 'Lou, we expect you to know better than that.' "

Lower class blacks fulfill stereotype, reinforcing white racial attitudes. As the epitome of black futility, they act like slaves even though they're free. They say, "We're victims of the system. Whites are gonna do what they're gonna do." They live for the moment. In their culture of violence, tomorrow isn't guaranteed. Since they want to experience everything, they grab the first thing. They see sports as an avenue to instant success. It's everyone's dream.

There's not much reason to hope, nothing much possible on the block. The lower class has no support system. Blacks who have no personal power, want status without personal responsibility. In their self-hatred, they think their failure is due to stupidity. Hard work won't help them. Examples of black success can't dispel this. Just because one black succeeds doesn't mean they'll succeed.

Lower class blacks are culturally marginal. The ghetto is counter culture. They know they'll never be a part of what they see on TV. To compensate, they rebel, as if to say, "If I can't have it, I don't want it." The ghetto's glorified culture of prison, drugs, and pimps is the opposite of white norms. The black counter-culture means "keeping things within our group." Ebonics is "our own language." Lower class blacks reject black music when it goes mainstream, since it no longer speaks to them or for them.

In their need to belong, blacks join gangs to garner status among their peers. The ghetto is a "revenge" culture. Blacks defend their honor by violence. Two classic examples are the murders of Tupac Shakur in 1996 and Biggie Smalls in 1997. Fellow rapper 50 Cent said, "The environment I'm from teaches you to be aggressive or be a victim." The code of survival in the ghetto is toughness. Blacks have a code of silence. They can't admit vulnerability because it's equated with femininity.

Success in the white world represents a loss of community. Those who succeed in the white world are betrayers. An authentic black identity is equated with ignorance and thuggery. Getting "As," speaking standard English, and visiting the Smithsonian Institution are "white." It's an insult to be called a "schoolboy."

It's in style to be stupid. In 2007, in Ft. Myers a black girl said, "Kids drop out of school because they see other kids dropping out. They think they're all grown up." In the ghetto, reading and writing are all that's needed. It's not cool to read.

Among teenagers, jail time makes one a celebrity. In "Jail to Yale" stories, a rise from degradation is a form of status. Gold teeth are a status symbol. Blacks spend their little income to their detriment. Only the rich can afford ostentation.

The theme of the American Negro is futility. The only way for them to be accepted by whites was not to be Negro. When they did the same things as whites, they didn't get the same things. Even those who were fully qualified were never taken seriously.

Elite Negroes were an empty extension of whites. E. Franklin Frazier called them the Black Bourgeoisie, who "played at work and worked at play." In their self-delusion, they assumed the quality of their social ritual earned them white acceptance and approval. Their affectations of white society never made them a part of the American culture in a significant or meaningful way. They had the form of education, religion, and social institutions, not the substance. They were guided by whites but never accepted by them. Negro leaders, with some minimal recognition, primarily served whites, not Negroes.

While successful blacks have an image of wealth, they lack the social background and inheritance of wealth that whites have. There's a gap in learning and saving habits. Their success is tenuous, dependent on economic swings. Upper and middle class children go into integrated colleges with lower SAT scores. With increasing college tuition, blacks remain less likely to go to college — with less preparation, less likely to graduate. In school integration, being in the same classroom with whites doesn't change white perception. When black students have difficulty and compensate by pretending they're not interested, white teachers lower their expectations.

In today's subtle racism, successful blacks don't belong anywhere except in their own company. Oreos (white inside) don't fit into either racial group. Black leaders are "pepper in the eyes of whites" — but that's all they are. They have no credibility with whites. Black social importance on the world scene is a façade. Blacks have no real power because they can't rise as a racial group. The slogan of the NAACP is, "The struggle never ends."

CHAPTER TEN: IDENTITY

The Superiority Complex

> Go West, young man. Go West.
> — Horace Greeley, 1840

The essence of racism is comparison — whites being proud of being better than others. Whites have a delicious feeling of superiority that is inherited at birth and doesn't have to be lived up to. All whites benefit from a positive racial image regardless of what they do or don't do. Racism made the "lowest" white supreme over the "highest" Negro. It gave poor whites hope in spite of their poverty and ignorance.

In 1965, when I taught at Ohio University in Athens, Ohio, one of my sociology students, a blond, heavy-set white girl, asked to see me after class. As she sat down in my office she blurted out, "I don't know how to say this but I'd like you to marry me."

I said, "What on earth are you talking about? Have I given you any impression that I'm interested in you?"

She said, "No. I just like you because you're very intelligent. This is my second year at OU. You're the first black professor I ever had. Your course is more interesting. It really means something. I come from the back woods. There's only a path to our house. We don't have a car and we sleep in one bed. The yard is full of chickens and goats and the water stinks. I just go to class and back home. I've never been anywhere outside of Athens. I told my parents about you. They threatened to take me out of school. If I married you, it would kill 'em and I'd be free."

"But, Sheila, why should I marry you? You're young and inexperienced."

"Well, I'm white."

Whites are assumed to be somebody until proven otherwise. They're powerful and capable. They know about everything, even other races and cultures. American know-how is "white." Whites succeed because of their innate intelligence and ability. If they fail, it's because of outside circumstances beyond their control.

Whites have sanctity. Since their lives have value, they deserve protection from anything bad. Their racial beauty symbolizes their superiority. For most of America's history, the white race was the sole standard of beauty. During the

1950s, only *Ebony* and *Jet*, geared to a Negro audience, featured Negro models. During the 1950s and 60s, Tarzan was a classic symbol of white superiority in Africa.

Whites free of racial assignment think of themselves primarily as individuals. When they are asked, "Who are you?" they say, "I'm a nice person," or "I'm a good student." They see their racial group in positive terms. If they have a negative view of whites, it's about an individual or a group of whites, not whites in general. "Poor white trash" applied to Southerners.

Whites ignore inconsistencies in their racial group. Since they're civilized and moral, they can do no wrong. No one can doubt their intentions. Whites that do bad things are exceptions to the rule. Lee Harvey Oswald was a loner acting on his own. Lynching in the South was a white aberration fueled by fear. White atrocities are isolated incidents.

Tolerance has never dented racial pride. Whites defend and protect their racial image. In 1986, Lynn Cheney criticized the PBS television series "The Africans," by Ali Mazrui, because it was critical of the West. In 2001, whites criticized Alice Randall's *The Wind Done Gone*, a back parody of *Gone with the Wind*. In 2005, whites in Ft. Myers were defensive about a letter to the editor criticizing Robert E. Lee. In 2006, they defended a white woman who emailed a racist cartoon to the people in her department, saying she was a good Christian woman.

The American culture is based on the white myth of glory. White racial and cultural superiority justify white supremacy. Whites deserve to rule lesser peoples since they impart no benefit to the larger world. As Christians, whites are "the powers that be ordained of God." God has favored and protected the white race as the descendants of Noah's son, Shem, the ancestor of the Messiah. God is on America's side because it's a Christian nation. God blesses America as the home of the white race.

White superiority granted whites the natural right to take. In the cycle of white success, cultural superiority and the blessing of God, made technology possible. Technology facilitated exploration and thus exploitation. Exploitation furthered advances in technology and thus more success. Whites deserve glory and recognition because they explored and claimed America. White frontiersmen tamed the West. Whites developed America.

The South's myth of glory is based on the image of aristocracy made possible by slavery. The large slave plantation, classically portrayed in *Gone with the Wind*, was the social model of the South. White slave masters were the standard of success and power every Southerner longed for. They displayed their newfound wealth and status in a mansion on a well-laid-out plantation. In formal dress, they were the epitome of the Southern gentleman, their life of leisure focused on political interests and social activities.

After the Civil War, the South's image as a "lost cause" generated white sympathy in the North which led to the end of Reconstruction. During the 1960s,

Southern homes portrayed this lost aristocracy in statues of slave boys waiting to hold the reigns of a gentleman's horse. Today Southerners cling to the Confederate flag as their symbol of past glory.

In 2002, Charley Reese, a white Southern newspaper columnist, wrote, "All we owe the people of the past is to look at them in the context of their own time, not in the context of our time. They, like us, fell out of the womb into an already existing society with already existing beliefs and institutions. Like us, they had no choice but to play the cards God dealt them."

Throughout America's history, white supremacy was based on "whites deserve to rule." In the antebellum South, since slavery and racism benefited all Southerners in some way or another, they weren't open to abolitionist ideas. Everything belonged to the white man, including Negro women. Southerners were focused on exploiting Negroes and keeping them in their place. In their hubris, they were resistant to change. Their little kingdom was destroyed during the Civil War and they have never forgiven the North for it.

After Emancipation, Southerners, in a fear of retaliation, enacted a reign of terror to keep Negroes in their place. Rich whites defended poor whites. Negroes had no place as free men. They were "punished" no matter what they did. Negro rule was a violation of the natural order of things. Negro congressmen were never accepted in the South. Negroes couldn't walk the streets alone at night. They had to ride in the back of a bus or train; come in the back door; and speak only when spoken to. They had to tip their hat and say, "Yes, Ma'am," or "Yes, Sir."

During the 1950s, whites expected to be in charge. When I visited my Negro sharecropper in-laws, I was sitting on their front porch engrossed in a book, when I heard someone say, "Boy, where's John?" Hardly raising my eyes, I said absentmindedly, "I don't know." Then I heard, "Well get up and go look for 'im, Boy. I wanna see 'im."

I looked up to see a toothless old white man in overalls. His matted hair poked out of his straw hat. His shoes looked as if you could scrape off a bucketful of mud. He stood there stoop-shouldered, one strap of his overalls hanging down. I thought he was drunk. He stood there glaring. He said, "Don't you hear me? Don't you understand me, Boy?" I wanted to choke him.

Suddenly, Penny came around the corner of the house and said, "Ben? Whatcha doin'? Who ya talkin' to?"

When she saw the man, she told him, "This is my daughter's husband. What can I do for you?"

He said, "I'm askin' him to get John."

She said, "Oh, I'll do that!"

Penny later apologized, "We're sorry, Ben. That's the way these white folks are. They just talk and expect you to do somethin'. That's the problem with this country. White folks just don't have any manners."

Segregation and discrimination in the North weren't based on personal hatred. Negroes were anonymous — living in boundary communities. Negroes said, "In the South, a white man don't care if you live next door, he just don't want you gettin' ahead in the world. In the North, a white man don't mind you gettin' ahead in the world, he just don't want you livin' next to him."

No dominant group willingly gives up or shares power. The Civil Rights Movement was not about whites sharing power. While blacks were given civil and even some political rights, they never achieved economic rights. Granting civil rights never altered the white economic power base. What whites lost legally, they retained economically. Today, as blacks participate in America's economy as workers, they don't reap the benefits of capitalism as a racial group. Whites have never agreed with black equality or equity because they fear retaliation — a loss of control.

The Kerner Commission Report of 1968 told blacks what they already knew. Whites are talk, but no action. The time is never right. Black progress remains "one step forward, two steps back" because their gains are subject to economic downturns. If whites consult blacks about something beneficial to them, it's a superficial courtesy. Whites built the St. Louis projects as high-rise buildings, despite the results of the St. Louis Metropolitan Survey. Twelve years later, the projects had to be torn down. Today, whites facilitate the new Harlem behind the scenes. Although civil rights cases are now being re-tried, justice delayed is still justice denied.

Blacks are in a continuous uphill battle to retain and regain advances in civil rights. Cornell West said in 2007, "Our rights are slipping away in a subtle way. Whites don't take us seriously. Now it's the same old lies. We need to go back to the leadership that made the boycott successful." In any exchange between whites and blacks, the dominant/subordinate relationship is there. Whites continue to say whatever comes into their minds. The difference is that blacks no longer keep quiet about it.

Racial unity facilitated white supremacy. Because of slavery's influence, racism continues to dictate America's status quo of economic, political, and social forces. White agreement in the area of race enhanced white dominance as it minimized individual and cultural differences. Whites of different religious and philosophical persuasions united as Americans to effectively dominate, control, and exploit American Indians and Negroes — their common enemy.

In 1956, I was looking for an apartment in St. Louis close to Washington University where I was a graduate student. I saw a sign in a third floor apartment and went up. The woman living there said, "You have an accent. Where do you come from?"

I said, "Africa."

She said, "My folks came from the old country. They had problems too. I'd like to rent you this apartment but the problem is my neighbors. We all had to sign a restricted covenant. We're not supposed to let in any Negroes or any other race except whites."

I said, "You mean all the people on this block have signed it?"

She said, "Not only on this block, but the whole area. We're all members of it."

Racism united whites as a racial group. When we think of racism, we think of the South. Malcolm X said, "When it comes to racism, the South means south of the Canadian border." While the North and South disagreed on slavery, they agreed on racism. Northerners felt Negroes shouldn't be enslaved, but that didn't mean they were equal. Northern philanthropists and Southern slave masters united to send Negroes back to Africa. In 1841, when John Quincy Adams argued the case of the "Amistad" before the Supreme Court and won the freedom of the Mende slaves who rebelled, the issue was slavery, not racism.

Racial unity softened the aftermath of the Civil War. Northerners accepted white Confederate soldiers who fought against them, while rejecting Negro Union soldiers who fought on their side. America's racial unity of North and South facilitated segregation and discrimination. Even the unity of "male" or "female" remains subverted to the unity of "white" or "black."

In racial camaraderie, whites assume a commonality with other whites. Even when nothing is said, they assume other whites agree with them. In 2005, in Ft. Myers, Anita was in Wal-Mart on a Friday shopping by herself. She told a white middle-aged woman that she came on Friday, because Wal-Mart was so crowded on Saturdays.

The woman said, "Well, you know all those Mexicans come on Saturday. I don't know where they all come from, really. We drove over to Lake Trafford the other day. There were Mexicans on one side of the street and blacks on the other. They looked at us like we were from another planet. I told my husband, 'Lock the doors and put the pedal to the floor. We're gettin' outta here!' My daughter works near there and she's a statuesque blond. You should see how those men look at her. One day they even followed her to work in their car. When they saw the casino guards in the parking lot, they drove off. It's a dangerous place out there."

White privilege is present in every white mind whether it's acknowledged or expressed. Whites are superior. They deserve everything. America's rightful destiny is to be a white country and serve whites. The American dream is for "whites only" and "whites first." Anything blacks or other immigrants attain implies a loss of what whites should have. While whites acclaim black athletes, they resent their success and wealth. Even when whites aren't necessarily against blacks, they must be first. Immigrants of other races don't really belong in America. They're a burden that threatens the American way of life. Europeans who immigrated to America, say, "We learned English. Why can't they?"

In 1973, I went to the Genesee Bank in Flint, Michigan, to get traveler's checks for the Summer Study Abroad Trip to Liberia. A white teller who knew me called me out of line, "Come over here, Dr. Dennis. I'll help you."

As she waited on me, a white man standing in line, said loudly, "I'm an American. I was born here. I worked hard all my life and I can't even save that kinda money. These foreigners come here and take all our money."

White privilege is the foundation of inequity in America. White America has always had a white agenda. Whites have higher paying jobs, more choice of jobs. There's name discrimination in the job hunt — "white" names evoking more responses. In a world of limited resources, there are only so many pieces of the pie. White supremacy and racism ensure that those pieces are for whites. Racism facilitates the subjugation of the poor by dividing poor whites and poor blacks. White advantage inevitably equals black disadvantage — unequal life chances and opportunities. The bottom line is, "Who benefits?" Even black crime benefits whites. Jails have become an industry.

In 2005, at Gold's Gym in Ft. Myers, I was talking with two black young men. One of them said, "Pop, if I reach your age, I'll be thankful to God. The way things are goin' in Dunbar, I don't think I'll see thirty. The white man makes niggers kill each other. They bring drugs in, sellin' 'em to key people in the black community who boss the people on the street. These niggers work hard gettin' all these people to buy from them. When they can't get their profit, they kill. The white dude's gotten his profit that's so much more than the nigger ever gets. He ain't goin' to jail cause he didn't kill. If you get into this thing, you're signin' your death warrant."

Whites resent Affirmative Action as reverse discrimination. In 1995, when Oseola McCarty, a poor black woman, endowed a $150,000 scholarship fund for black students at the University of Southern Mississippi, it was called reverse discrimination. In 2004, a white woman told Anita, "I was trying for a teaching job in Florida and I was so qualified. I had a four point average plus I was given all kinds of awards. The examiner admitted to me, 'We're looking for black females for teachers.' I walked out. White males are an endangered species. Blacks with less qualification are promoted over whites with greater qualifications."

In 2006, David Ward, the president of the American Council on Education, said, "Americans have a deeply engrained sense of fair play and individual rights. For many, Affirmative Action doesn't seem fair. If you feel you've been deprived of something by a process, it is felt very strongly." Blacks have faced this all their lives. Whites resent being marginalized in the job market. To compensate, they say blacks have unfairly taken their jobs, as if to say, "If you want my country, do what it takes, but don't try to talk me out of it."

Whites have never questioned their racial advantage. Although success is a combination of racial advantage and individual achievement, whites say, "We worked hard for what we got." In 2006, my white doctor justified his lavish house by saying, "My wife and I have worked hard all our lives." Whites say about blacks, "We pulled ourselves up with our own bootstraps, why can't they?"

In a society based on racism, identity is primarily determined by race. Racial identity determines racial perspective and thus a different set of interests. Barack Obama's campaign for the presidency classically illustrates this. Being "authentically black" entails a different perspective and set of interests. Whites denounced Rev. Jeremiah Wright as "divisive and hateful" when he dared to express an authentically black perspective at his church and at the National Press Club.

As a political candidate, Obama must be all things to all people. His dilemma is "being too black" which would alienate whites and being "too white" for blacks. A white majority will not elect an authentic black who is for black interests. Obama must merge white and black interests into a common American interest. Like Colin Powell, he's a cross-over candidate. Powell was a good prospect for the presidency. He's light-skinned and his service in the military and government validates him as a supporter of American [white] interests. Powell and Obama are acceptable because they aren't authentically black. If Obama is elected, white guilt will be resolved, as if to say, "Racism's over. The doors are wide open. If Obama can be president, any black man can."

White guilt has generated white defensiveness. The superior are never to blame. Whites are a paradox of arrogance and insecurity in the area of race. There's a role of shame in race relations since racism is a lie that never justified whites. If whites have doubts about their image, or the image of blacks, they can't bring it out because it's embarrassing to them.

White hubris is the foundation of white denial. The powerful are never held accountable. Racism made whites their own worst enemy by allowing them to keep from facing the truth. To maintain their self-image and status, they deny the truth. During slavery, whites feared retaliation. Today, they fear losing their place and advantage in the American society. Throughout America's history, whites were bold in their oppression. Their atrocities weren't committed in secret. The results of their persecution are obvious. Since everyone knows about these things, inflammatory race issues keep popping up. When they do, the response is consistent — when blacks accuse, whites deny.

Self-condemnation is impossible. Whites don't want their hypocrisy revealed. Telling the truth about racial issues is "black rage" or "blaming whites." Blacks who say what everyone knows are "playing the race card." Prominent blacks who express their anger "alienate whites who want to help." Each time, I discussed my book with whites, their response was so universally defensive, I could predict it. A white woman who read the manuscript, warned Anita, "I'm reasonable. I've got an open mind. But if you indict all whites, you're going too far." There's a knee jerk reaction to any black outcry because whites can't be made ashamed of their racial group or for "being white."

In 1997, when US Representative Tony Hall from Ohio, requested an apology for slavery, it touched the white nerve of guilt. Whites can admit slavery was wrong only in an abstract way. Accepting a national responsibility for it threatens white dominance and pride. Admitting a national guilt makes whites accountable to blacks. It makes them responsible to right the wrong through reparations. Although states have put forth their own apology, slavery remains an albatross around America's neck. Denial means that, even when we know something is true, we hope it will go away if we don't admit or acknowledge it. In 2001, America's official position at the World Conference on Racism in Durbin, South Africa, was, "Slavery was not a crime against humanity."

Whites pass the buck, saying, "Others did it too." They say, "Roman slavery was pretty cruel," or "Slavery was introduced into this country 157 years before we existed as a nation. Let the English, Spanish, and French apologize. They allowed slaves to be transported to these shores long before the U.S. was founded."

Whites accept racial generalization when it benefits them, but not when it accuses. They avoid accountability as a racial group, a society, and a nation. They say, "Surely there are tens of millions of white Americans, many from Northern states, who have little or no historical connection to pro-slavery Southerners. The assignment of guilt by heritage only infects old wounds." They hide behind individual responsibility, saying, "I didn't enslave anyone." Whites say they never personally benefited from slavery. A white man said, "John Hope Franklin's assertion that white Americans are 'the direct beneficiaries of slavery' is unbelievably grandiose."

Whites re-invent slavery to excuse themselves. I was talking about my book with a white man in my church when he interrupted me, by saying, "Oh, but remember! There were good slave masters!" Since whites are basically good, all slave masters can't be bad. Today, in political correctness, they're called slave holders.

Whites say they've already atoned for slavery. A white man said, "We paid for slavery in the Civil War, the bloodiest conflict in history. Many Union soldiers died to end slavery. Roughly three per cent of white American males died freeing the slaves, with thousands more maimed and wounded. Shouldn't blacks be grateful for the thousands of Republican-led troops who gave their lives to free the slaves? Why should there be an apology?"

Whenever whites say, "It's not about race," it usually is. In 2005, Hurricane Katrina was a classic example of whites accusing blacks of "playing the blame game." Whites said it wasn't the "white" government's fault. Katrina was a disaster like no other. Poor blacks who "refused to evacuate," are to blame for their suffering. Pat O'Reilly said the lesson for blacks in Hurricane Katrina was, "Don't be poor." Although CNN news reporters had to call attention to what was happening, whites said things were blown way out of proportion. Conservative white Christians said they were victims of the liberal media — "It's always white America that helps but is condemned." Whites say it's necessary to change the behavioral patterns of the poor, rather than simply designating money to fight poverty.

Whites agree that racists were bad back then. They say, "I'm not a racist," since it implies a hatred of blacks. Although whites cover up their racial feelings and attitudes, they know that racism exists in every family, social setting, community, and city in America. Whenever something threatens whites, racism flares up. Even so, the unspoken rule for whites is, "Don't accuse whites of racism."

In 2005, Anita brought up the subject of racism during a women's Bible study. One of the women said, "You can't say all whites are equally racist. There are lots of whites who are against prejudice. I'm not racist. My dad was so racist, I determined not to be like him. I grew up with blacks in my school and neighborhood. I don't hate blacks. I just don't have anything in common with them. We all want to stay in our own comfort zone. Just because I don't associate with black people doesn't mean I hate them."

Whites can't admit the truth about themselves, about whites as a racial group, or about America's history. Although racism is on everyone's mind, it can't be discussed, especially between the races. During Barack Obama's 2008 campaign, racism was a political elephant in the room. The buzz words were "voting by demographics" and "white working class males" with a choice between the lesser of two evils — a white woman or a black man. The Democratic primary was a classic example of racial polarity and white defensiveness. Whites deflected the white vote for Hillary Clinton by saying that blacks voted for Obama. There's a difference. Blacks united as an oppressed group to gain a foothold. Whites voted for Clinton to keep a black man from being president.

The psychic damage of racism for whites is self-delusion. Racism kept whites from facing the truth about themselves. It allowed them to be proud of what they should be ashamed of. Whites in America were "risk-takers," not predators. The Sons and Daughters of the American Revolution are proud of their ancestors even though they denied freedom and justice to others. White success in America was due to racial and cultural superiority, not the confiscation of American Indian land and African labor.

In truth, it wasn't the successful in Europe who founded America. It was losers looking for economic opportunity, along with religious and political freedom. Those disenfranchised in Europe perpetrated injustice and persecution in America with impunity. In America's independence, whites were free to colonize within their borders. America's Manifest Destiny regarding the West was the biggest land grab in history. Although whites as a racial group have slaughtered countless peoples, other races are barbarians. Whites won the West by removing the savages from it. When Indians fought back, they were preying upon whites.

Racism makes all whites superior regardless of circumstance which made poor whites particularly self-deluded. After Emancipation, during the South's rule of insecurity, the only "strength" poor whites had, was their mouth. Mob rule gave them a sense of confidence and power they never had before. They were nobly doing what must be done to save white society.

As long as there are white losers, racism will thrive as a crutch for white ego. Hating blacks gives white losers "status." Hate crimes make them somebody — defenders against black encroachment. In 2004, fairgoers in Mississippi had an opportunity to shake hands with Edgar Ray Killen, the man convicted of killing Goodman, Chaney, and Schwerner during the Civil Rights Movement. In 2005, there was a big turnout in Howell, Michigan, for an auction of KKK memorabilia.

In their self-delusion, whites can't admit they're a part of the system of racism that justified and facilitated slavery. Regardless of social class, all whites have preferential treatment to some degree. They have advantage, not only because of race, but because they're rich. They wouldn't be rich if they weren't white.

Supremacy

> The black man doesn't have to be taught to love the white man;
> The white man has to be taught to love the black man.
> — Malcolm X

The myths of Africa were the foundation of a racist view of culture. An inferior culture reflects an inferior race. An inferior race is only capable of an inferior culture. From the 1960s to the 1980s, I taught "Africans and Their Cultures" at three different universities. I began each class by telling my students that they had to first "unlearn" what they "knew" about Africa.

In 1957, as a graduate student at Michigan State, I began teaching classes on Africa as part of the emerging African Studies Program. I also taught introductory anthropology.

One day, a geography professor at MSU, who was from South Africa, sat in on my anthropology class. I described how man first domesticated himself in Africa because of its conducive climate and topology. After class, the professor asked to see me privately. In my office, he said, "Do you mean only Africans did this? Don't give all the credit to Africa. Inventions and contributions have been made by many peoples."

In 1965, when I taught anthropology at Ohio University, I was invited to speak on "The Role of Art in Traditional African Society" to the art league in Parkersburg, West Virginia.

My anthropology student, who was an art major, concluded his introduction by saying, "Doctor Dennis, Welcome!" During my talk, I couldn't help noticing an impeccably dressed elderly white woman who sat just below the podium. She watched me intently, hanging onto my every word.

At the little reception afterwards, she waited patiently until the others left, Grasping both of my hands, she said, "Oh, Dr. Dennis. I'm so happy you came! We're so blessed to have you in Parkersburg! During my childhood and even now, I've always wanted to go to Africa, but I've never had the chance. I've always read about Africa, though, and I've been particularly interested in witch doctors. The Lord has answered my prayers. I never dreamed I'd ever lay my hands on a real witch doctor! Wait till I tell my children!"

Wherever racism exists in any form, it justifies an oppressor. Racism allowed whites to love themselves and succeed as whites. It excused slavery in a land of freedom; oppression in a land of justice; disenfranchisement in a land of democracy; and victimization and brutality in a land of Christianity.

Racism is classic "blaming the victim." Since whites could never be guilty, they projected their guilt upon Negroes. Negroes were enslaved because they were inferior. They were a corrupting force, the reason for everything wrong in the South. As the stain on America, they were responsible for white atrocities. Whites kept Negroes from literacy and education and blamed them for being ignorant. In slavery, they took away incentive and any sense of responsibility, and blamed Negroes for being lazy. They bred slaves like cattle and blamed Negroes for sexual abandon. They blamed Negroes for white barbarity, saying, "It's the only thing the Negro understands." Southerners blamed Negroes for the Civil War — the South's loss of glory and aristocratic way of life. Whites, who used violence to control Negroes, condemned violence in Negroes.

During the 1950s, Negroes were never forgiven as the evidence of white evil. Whites "knew" about Negroes from folk knowledge passed down by word of mouth or by reading about the Negro experience. Southerners never accepted Negroes or changed their minds about them — no matter what Negroes did or didn't do.

In a political science class at Lincoln, Dr. Miller told us about an incident that happened to him and Dr. Savage. When they stopped for gas in Mississippi, the white teenage attendant said, "Hey, Boy! Niggers can't be drivin' a car like this. Where you come from?" Dr. Miller told him they were professors at Lincoln. After consulting with an old white man, the teenager said, "Prove it."

As Miller gave the teenager the university telephone number, he said, "What should I say?"

Miller coached, "Ask for Dr. Scruggs."

When President Scruggs came on the phone, he said, "Is something wrong with Dr. Miller and Dr. Savage?"

The teenager said, "Nothin' wrong with 'em, Suh [Sir]. They're on their way. Thank you, Suh."

Since I lived with President Scruggs that year, I asked him that night about it, "Why did he call you Sir?"

He said, "Benjamin, in this country, the vast majority of whites cannot think of a Negro being a college president. Educated whites may entertain the idea but never illiterate whites. The young man thought I was white. That's why he accepted my statement and addressed me as Sir."

Negroes were always suspect. At Fisk, I borrowed *Mein Kampf* from a German professor. Several days later, a guy who lived in my boarding house told me, "Ben, the landlord told me some FBI agents raided your room. They scattered everything around. They told him they'd be back."

When I got there, my landlord said, "They took *Mein Kampf.*"

I was waiting when they returned. They said, "We were looking for evidence. We suspect you're related to a subversive movement."

The Civil Rights Movement revealed that white attitudes hadn't changed. Southerners rejected Negroes. Northerners avoided them. The tragedies and troubles of the movement were all the fault of blacks. Martin Luther King Jr. was to blame for the racial turmoil. Race relations in the South were just fine until he riled blacks up.

A white friend who was a policeman in Washington, D.C., during the 1960s and 70s, told me, "Ben, racism was the essence of the police force in the D.C. area and I believe it was true for many parts of the country. In those days, the police force was white and male. Our training in the police academy was that you could never trust blacks. They were criminals unless they showed otherwise. Even then, they were just waiting for an opportunity to do something. If you saw any black man with a TV or tools, he was a thief. If you saw two or three blacks talking together, they were up to something. When civil rights brought about integration, the police force picked blacks that were big and strong. They put them in positions they weren't trained for. When they didn't do the work, whites said, 'You see? They're stupid.'"

In 1966, at Ohio University, when I became chairman of the sociology department, I took over from an old white man who had chaired the department for the past twenty-seven years. Bill had no filing system because he didn't even trust his secretaries. The year before, a Chinese sociology professor had taken over. Bill harassed him so much, he left the university. Two white sociologists begged me to take over.

Bill immediately sent for my transcript from Michigan State. When he saw a "D/F" on it, he called a department meeting, which included several deans. Before the group, he asked me, "In my entire academic career, I've never seen a D/F. This grade must be either a D or an F. Will you explain this please?"

Taken by surprise, I said, "Have you spoken with the people in my department at MSU? Or the president of the university?"

He said, "No. Your transcript tells me more than anyone can tell me."

I said, "Gentlemen, D/F stands for deferred grade. I had a final paper to turn in. Graduate students who teach at MSU can defer a paper for a quarter because of the pressures they face. I turned in the paper the next quarter. That's why there's an A after the D/F. If any of you don't believe me, you can call the university." I walked out. I was so angry I wanted to go back to MSU.

That evening, one of the white sociologists called and told me he called MSU and I was right. He requested it in writing to present it to Bill. After he did so at the next faculty meeting, I asked Bill, "Do you have any more questions about my qualifications?" He never looked me in the face. He just got up and walked out.

White suspicion hasn't lessened. In 1976, after class at the University of Michigan-Flint, one of my black students in law enforcement, told me, "Last night, I was off duty walking down Saginaw Street. An elderly white woman clutched her purse and hurried across the street." With tears in his eyes, he said, "Dr. Dennis, as a law enforcement officer, I would have given my life to save her. And there she was, terrified of me."

Whites were suspicious of Muhammad Ali's religious objection to the Vietnam War. They condemned Martin Luther King Jr. and Jesse Jackson for womanizing, but dismissed President Kennedy and President Clinton. Whites easily believed O.J. Simpson was guilty of murder and Michael Jackson, guilty of sexual abuse. When it came to the B.T.K. killer in Kansas, they found it hard to believe it was a white man.

In racial profiling, blacks are guilty of "driving while black." In 1999, white policemen in New York City shot a West African immigrant named Amadou Diallo because they thought he was reaching for a gun instead of his wallet. A black friend told me, "Whites think blacks are all criminals so that's all they arrest. And yet, the heavy weight crimes are committed by whites. When blacks are arrested, they're more often booked. Once you're booked, you're 'criminal.'" Most people arrested for drugs in America are white. More than half of those convicted are black. Whites assume black police are corrupt. Blacks have the same image. In 2004, black officers accidentally killed a black plainclothes policeman trying to help them.

In 1999, a black dean at Florida Gulf Coast University, told me, "Doc, I was at Wal-Mart the other day and a security guard followed me all over the place. All I had on was a tank top and shorts. Where could I hide anything?"

Racism continues to generate white callousness. Civil Rights has left a legacy of love and hate. Whites have more sympathy for civilians killed in warfare, and people denied their freedom around the world, than they do for blacks in their own communities suffering the inequities of racism. Concerning slavery, whites say to blacks, "Get over it. You're not the only ones. Other racial and ethnic groups have suffered oppression."

After Hurricane Katrina, a white woman told Anita, "How could they help those people when they were shooting at the helicopters?" Another said, "I don't think those people died from a lack of food or water. They died because they were old and frail." Racism makes whites blind to the needs of blacks. A white man said, "Hopefully all the rappers will kill one another. Then I won't have to listen to their garbage blaring from some punk's car that I'm stuck next to in traffic."

Since blacks are "guilty," they deserve whatever happens to them. When James Byrd was dragged to his death in Texas in 1998, whites said he was "no saint." The South is a guilt culture. Southerners say, "You hate to be around niggers cause you know what you done to 'em." The death of a black person is not as important or tragic as that of a white person, unless it's a famous public figure. When a white child is missing, there's a massive manhunt. If it's a black child, the response is low key.

Blacks continue to threaten whites because of white guilt and the need for status. Any time blacks reach a majority in a neighborhood, a school, or a social organization, whites flee. Any organization controlled by blacks is scrutinized. Any authentically black leader is seen as the enemy. Whites see black power as a threat to their power. White fear fuels the opposition to gun control.

The American society can't be freely assimilated because a full exchange of roles and leadership isn't possible. Race especially enters into politics. Whites fear genuine black political power because it implies clout. Black politicians are controlled by whites, for the most part. Since blacks are in the minority, black political candidates must cater to whites to have white support.

For the most part, blacks are leaders of their own people, their power relegated to the black community. Successful blacks can only do so much and there can only be so many of them. In a decision-making or profitable organization, whites passively accept a few token blacks. If blacks approach a majority, there's white hostility. In a voluntary social organization, blacks accept authority from whites. Whites won't accept authority from blacks.

Blacks remain America's scapegoat. The descendants of whites responsible for slavery are seen in a positive light. The descendants of slaves that served America are seen in a negative light. Despite their evil, whites are wanted in the American society. Despite their contributions, blacks are unwanted.

Whites hold blacks responsible for their limitations and poverty. They criticize them for what they made them. Whites judge black behavior as "stupidity." They say blacks don't succeed because they aren't motivated. Blacks don't value hard work and education. They're lazy and dependent on welfare. They destroy themselves in black on black crime. Their crippling fixation on victimization keeps them from accepting responsibility.

Whites say, "It's their fault we don't get along. They're too sensitive." In 2002, in Ft. Myers, a white teacher let the white students in his class ask a black girl why whites couldn't call her nigger, since blacks called each other that. When the girl objected, she was taken out of the class. The teacher was never reprimanded. In Tennessee, a white state legislator condemned the Black Legislative Caucus for being worse than the KKK because it rejected whites as members.

Blacks are still on the spot to fix themselves. They must change white hearts by earning equality — making themselves acceptable to white society. They must know their place, measure up, or fulfill some requirement. Whites say, "Get people ready first and then we can talk about Affirmative Action." Blacks must save themselves just as other minorities have done, as if to say, "After all, others have faced hardships and survived."

Blacks are expected to fail, and when they do, it's their fault. When a black child does well, there's always something wrong with his background. In the beginning, whites questioned Tiger Wood's ability. Books written by blacks are displayed in the African-American section of a bookstore, regardless of topic. The assumption is that whites wouldn't be interested in what blacks have to say about anything.

The Harlem Chess Club was touted because black kids excelled in a white game based on intelligence and strategy. If a black political candidate loses an election, it's his own fault. If he wins, it's because liberal whites supported him. White teachers are required to focus on black history one month of the year, as if it was a separate entity. Even black children are largely ignorant about the civil rights struggle.

Whites dilute black success by qualifying it. Colin Powell said that a white officer told him, "You're a pretty good lieutenant for a black." Blacks who are successful in the highest echelons are a black judge, a black artist, a black congressman, a black college president, etc. The classic comment to a successful black is, "You're different. You're not like the rest of 'em." Or it's, "Oh, I get it. You're 'Cosby show' black." The comment to a mulatto is, "You're not really black."

With integration, blacks must appeal to a white clientele. Black doctors and dentists have to be exceptionally qualified for whites to go to them. This applies to foreign doctors as well. A hospital with foreign doctors is called an "Ellis Island hospital." A hospital with white doctors is called a "Plymouth Rock" hospital. Racism limits blacks in trust occupations such as financial advisors and insurance men. Blacks have to offer more to compete with whites. I have a black friend who was successful as a realtor in Naples because he offered free real estate lectures on how to sell or buy a home.

In their distrust, whites don't think blacks should be leaders. If they are, whites have little confidence in them. Whites initially doubted Condoleezza Rice's ability. Colin Power has status and legitimacy because of white support. In 2003, in Ft. Myers, when a black friend's wife was slated to become Commodore of their boating club, she overheard a white man say, "We can't trust that woman." The members ignored the club's rules and elected a white man as commodore. Whites continue to doubt black competence. Black qualifications remain suspect. In 2008, Hilary Clinton's "3 a.m. phone call in the White House" was sufficient to raise doubt about Obama's qualifications because it didn't take much.

Blacks remain nobodies until proven otherwise. Muhammad Ali threw his boxing medals into the river when he was refused service in Louisville, Kentucky. Cornell West, in his book, *Race Matters*, tells in his introduction about his difficulty in hailing a cab in New York City. Blacks are expected to be janitors, laborers, farmers, or criminals — never anyone of substance or in authority.

A black friend told me, "This happened a lot to black managers. At work, I'd be standing in a group and everyone there worked for me. When someone came in, they addressed anyone but me, even though I was well dressed."

When blacks don't fit stereotype, white assumption must be corrected — if whites are able to receive it. I've shared the countless insults every black person continuously suffers — a situation whites will never understand unless they experience it. In white minds, there is never the slightest possibility that I have earned two doctorate degrees. If and when it becomes known, there's surprise and an element of doubt.

During the 1980s, at the University of Michigan-Flint, white students never assumed I was a professor. When students waited to see me and I walked into my office marked, "Dr. Dennis, Sociology," they just sat there. The secretary had to say, "Weren't you waiting for Dr. Dennis?" She would open my door and say, "Dr. Dennis, some people are here to see you." As I greeted them, their jaws dropped. Some of them tried to save face by saying they were expecting someone older. It hurt even more when black students did the same thing.

In 1990, when I was the Executive Assistant to the Chancellor for Minority Programs, I was downstairs getting a drink when three white businessmen came down the hallway. Although I was dressed in a suit and tie, one of them pointed to some candy wrappers on the floor and said, "You missed that!"

A while later, as I came out of my office, the registrar came down the hall with the men. He said, "Dr. Dennis! I'd like you to meet some people. Mr. Campbell here is interested in having his boy come to our school."

Their eyes widened as he continued, "Gentlemen, I'd like you to meet the man in charge of minority programs here. He has a Ph.D. in sociology and anthropology and he teaches in both areas."

In 2007, at Gold's gym in Ft. Myers, I was standing in the hall near three white retirees who were talking with each other. Chris, the young white manager of the gym, walked by and said, "Good morning, Dr. Dennis!"

The men stopped their conversation and stared at me. One of them looked at me sternly and said, "Aren't you the guy from Africa? You're a doctor? What kinda doctor are ya?

At this point, a young white girl who worked there, walked by and said, "Don't you know? This man is a retired college professor. He has so many degrees I can't even count 'em."

The man said to me, "Where'd ya get all those degrees? In Africa? Black people here can't even do this and you did it?"

Blacks are seen in the extreme — either as potential thieves or spectacular sports heroes like Michael Jordan or prominent political figures like Colin Powell. In entertainment, stereotype is where the money is. "Post Cosby" black TV shows that don't fulfill stereotype, don't last long. Blacks rescue whites as sidekicks, either as comics or magic Negroes. Tiger Woods and Barack Obama are seen as magic Negroes. Some sort of mystic force is guiding their success as if they can't succeed the same way as any other man. If Obama is elected, will he rescue America from its taint of racism?

The irony of white suspicion is that there's a valid reason for it. Since circumstantial inferiority in the black lower class fuels racist myth, white think, "We were right all along." Whites have spent so much time generating differences between blacks and whites that they've become reality.

Lower class blacks reinforce the worst stereotypes of blacks. In slavery, there were the Uncle Tom's. In freedom, the "Steppin' fetch-its." Today, gangsta rap reminds me of Negro minstrel shows where Negroes were forced to make fools of themselves. Rap utilizes "over the top" bad stuff for shock value, glorifying illicit sex, violence, and murder. Even well-meaning whites see blacks as inherently inferior. Although a few blacks succeed, the vast majority of lower class blacks never will. The liberal media treats poor blacks with condescension.

Whites equally resent successful blacks. They say they succeeded unfairly, "Black people can get away with anything because they can claim racism." They're itching to see prominent blacks fail. At the same time, the token black exonerates whites because, "If he can succeed, why can't they all?"

Blacks are expected to stay in their place — and only accepted in their place. They're offensive and defensive players in football, rarely the quarterback, the "brains" of football. In any white organization or corporation, the token black must not only be twice as qualified, he must fulfill his role. Whites don't like blacks who talk back to white people. They see black leaders, who flaunt their importance, as ludicrous parodies. They disparage Jesse Jackson and Al Sharpton, saying, "Who on earth listens to them anyway?"

It's especially gratifying when those you have oppressed, agree with you. Black agreement means whites were right all along. Since whites only promote like-minded blacks, diversity in America is squelched. Black conservatives, rightly or wrongly, justify whites. The black conservative columnist, Thomas Sowell, has pointed out that whites could never have accomplished the slave trade without the help of Africans.

A black friend told me, "There's an arrogance in corporate America that allows whites to feel that once a black attains a certain level in the corporate atmosphere, they're ignored as black. Once, a white senior manager said right before me that he was going to get a black guy who worked there because he was dating a white woman. The guy was a union official so they couldn't do anything to him. But the white manager acted as if I wasn't there. In essence, he was saying, 'I'm gonna get your brother but we own you. You have no significant bearing on what's going to happen.' "

In 2000, my white mother-in-law surprised me when she said she wanted to vote for Alan Keyes for president.

I said, "Why's that?"

She said, "Because he shares my views more than any of the other candidates. He's against abortion."

Racism continues to govern America as a cultural force. Slavery made racism a predominant cultural value — America's true religion and unwritten constitution. Racism governs mandatory social institutions such as government, education, and economics. It governs voluntary social institutions such as religion, social organizations, sports, and entertainment.

Because America was built on slavery, racism is woven into all of America's history. Everything in America is couched within the realm of racism including art, history, literature, children's literature, nursery rhymes, memorabilia, etc.

In 2004, when I was discussing my book with a white friend, he said, "Ben, have you ever heard of a niggerhead?"

I said, "What's that?"

He said, "It's the round steel ball on a boat deck they use to tie the boat to the dock. There's a ball on the boat deck and a ball on the dock. In the Navy, these steel balls were painted black to make them stand out from the grey boat deck. That's why they're called niggerhead."

Ruth recited to her boys, "This little nigger went to market, this little nigger stayed home." As a child, Anita listened to Amos and Andy on the radio with her parents. She read *Little Black Sambo*. In the grocery store, we still have Uncle Ben's rice, Aunt Jemima Pancake Mix, and a Negro porter on Cream of Wheat — comfortable images of the compliant and subservient Negro. Ships on the Great Lakes that carry dirty stuff are called "tar baby." One of our sons caught some of his white friends laughing at the line, "How many niggers does it take to tar a roof? It depends on how you slice 'em."

Whites inevitably participate in racism simply by living in white society. Racism gave whites a common interest, purpose, and experience as a racial group. Although whites may think and act in various ways when it comes to other things, they think and act as whites in the area of race. Racism is so integral to being a white American that it's naturally assumed. It doesn't have to be exhibited. Whites must show they're an exception.

Racism is a social force — a learned mentality that is renewed in each generation. Even when parents say nothing, children naturally absorb their societal attitudes. In 2005, in Ft. Myers, after church one Sunday, I tapped on the shoulder of a little white boy to show him an African finger trick. When he didn't respond, I tapped him again. Suddenly, he turned around and yelled, "Don't touch me!"

At Gold's Gym, I'm friendly to the children in the nursery. Two little Hispanic girls always wave to me. One day, when they ran up and hugged me, the little white girl with them stood watching with a blank look on her face. When I gave the kids candy, the Hispanic children immediately ran to me. The four little white girls stood back. When I beckoned them with my finger, and one girl ran up, the others followed.

As an overriding norm, racism has social power. Race remains the sole determinant of status in America. While whites can intellectually believe that racism is wrong, they remain governed by it emotionally. No one is neutral or impartial about race. Everyone has an opinion, whether or not it is expressed. Since the emotional need for status is very powerful, racism has no compromise. We all crave status in the eyes of others. We want status in the eyes of our peers and our status confirmed in the eyes of those below us.

Race supersedes social class in establishing status because racism gave race value — superiority or inferiority. That's why poor whites in the South had "status" and rich blacks today remain "niggers." This is why whites are somebody until proven otherwise and blacks are nobody. Because race determines status, race consciousness applies to every social setting and interaction. This includes working with someone, talking to them, sitting next to them, and even assessing them as they walk by. Everyone is seen as either belonging to your racial group or the other racial group.

White society has status. As a white nation, America has status in the world community. Social class is more than money. It's about family name and attitude, a particular sense of the world. White exclusivity includes a set of social rules. Those "in the know" follow proper etiquette and fashion; and many rules of etiquette are nothing more than tests to reveal something about class. Classism underlies racism. Whites don't want to identify with or associate with the poor.

Since whites are dominant and superior, everyone wants to be white. Most Hispanics list their race as white. Since there's no status in being black, no one wants to be black, including blacks. Skin color is preferred by its implication of status. Southern belles (like many categories of ladies) wanted pale skin because it indicated they didn't work outdoors. By contrast, in modern times many whites want a suntan because it implies the leisure that allows for sunbathing, if not exotic vacations. Suntanned whites, especially in winter, have status as whites even though some of them are darker than many mulattos.

Everyone wants status in the eyes of whites. Blacks want status in the eyes of whites, but they can only attain genuine status in the eyes of blacks. Since racism determines status, whites are racial conformists. Today, racism has gone underground — masked by sophistication, good will, and politeness. There's a broad continuum of racism that ranges from an intense hatred of blacks, such as the dragging death of James Byrd, to a great empathy for blacks such as the Southern Poverty Law Center.

Whites conform racially for the acceptance and approval of their peers. The classic phrase of peer pressure is, "What would the neighbors think?" As social creatures, we want to belong to the in-group, the inner circle of prestige and knowledge. Conformity makes whites inconsistent. During a worthy cause, they proudly associate with blacks. When they are with their peers, they are ashamed to be associated with blacks.

Whites qualify any black in a white social setting to justify his inclusion. My white mother-in-law always introduced me as Dr. Dennis when we visited her white church. My white pastor calls me "Dr. Ben." At the birthday party of a ninety-year-old German friend, he introduced me by saying, "This man is a professor."

Whites must be socially safe. In their fear of rejection as a nigger lover, they intentionally or unintentionally reject blacks, even though it doesn't seem right to them. Since blatant racism is taboo, whites keep their racial opinions to themselves since they don't know how other whites stand.

Being liberal has status. In any gathering of whites and blacks, some whites, to prove they're open-minded, fawn over the blacks there. When they say, "Some of my best friends are black," they aren't referring to an intimate friendship without reservation. Blacks are immediately aware of this race consciousness. Since whites want to believe they're good people, they're blind to their own racial conformity.

The greatest enemy of blacks isn't blatant racists. It's the vast majority of racial conformists. Passivity to racism is most damaging since it implies consent. It's significant that there's no term for a white person who actively rejects and opposes racism. "Liberal" is close, but it applies more to a general concern for the poor and disenfranchised. Whites don't speak out against racism as individuals, or as a racial group, because they know it will cost them power and advantage. It will result in the disapproval of their peers.

Despite social change, white racial attitudes have remained throughout America's history — although not in the same intensity. Racism has survived protests, legislation, sacrificial deaths, and community meetings. White compliance hasn't meant agreement. The law can't change how whites feel about race. Believing that discrimination and racism are wrong doesn't mean blacks are equal or worthy of being loved. A more tolerant America isn't the same thing as a society without racial assumptions. Although whites no longer express racism openly, it remains a secret in their hearts. Each time they feel threatened, it resurfaces.

All whites, regardless of where they stand, have racial stereotypes in their subconscious, even in their imagination and dreams. They're well aware of the myths of racism even if they don't subscribe to them. I would wager that every American could recite them to me.

In 2005, in Michigan, Anita and Julie, a teacher's aide, got on friendly terms. Julie told Anita that the teacher in her classroom mentioned that she had two Hispanics and a black in her classroom, but Julie hadn't noticed.

Several days later, Julie and Anita were joking and Julie asked if blacks could get sunburned. Anita said, "Yes, but not as easily." When Anita joked, "Ask me anything. I'm the answer lady," Julie laughed and said, "Is it true black men are more endowed?"

Even educated, well-meaning whites are ignorant about blacks. Liberals assume they know blacks because they have a black friend. In 2007, when I underwent a medical test, Anita visited with the white nurse and told her about our book. She wrote down the title and our names so she could look for it when it came out. A few minutes later, she came up to us and leaned in close, saying, "You're both educated so I can ask you this. What's all this fuss about the 'n' word? After all, blacks call each other that."

Racism influences every white person whether they are conscious of it or not. As the in-group, whites focus on positive things about themselves. They focus on negative things about blacks as the out-group. Racial stereotypes apply not only to poor blacks, but to blacks who flaunt their wealth and macho.

Blacks may assume they can be superior like whites, but whites don't assume that. While whites no longer believe that Negroes are brutish savages from the jungles of Africa, they see inner city problems as symbolic of blacks. Since a greater percentage of blacks are poor, blacks are the image of poverty — even though there are more poor whites than poor blacks in America. Whites ignore the fact that urban blacks are more educated than rural poor whites. Even when well-meaning whites see some evidence for racism, they automatically accept it rather than question it.

Today, most whites are racially ignorant. They have no genuine interest in blacks since they aren't their social equals and they have little or no personal contact with them. They don't care what they do as long as it doesn't affect their lives. Assumption continues to poison race relations — regardless of the status or qualities of those involved.

In the tragedy of racism, no one has satisfaction. Whites and blacks live in such separate cultural communities, they have different speech patterns. America's racial polarity has generated a fear of racial disloyalty. Racism and prejudice may be underground, but they are resilient. According to a Washington Post ABC news poll in 2008, nearly half of all Americans say race relations are in bad shape. Three in ten acknowledge feelings of racial prejudice.

Half the harm that is done in this world is due to people who want to feel important.

They don't mean to do harm — but the harm does not interest them. Or they do not see it, or they justify it because they are absorbed in the endless struggle to think well of themselves.
— T.S. Eliot

The Myth of Integration

Negroes migrated north, not only for opportunity, but to escape Jim Crow. There, they faced white passive aggression in discrimination and separate facilities. They had to find out what places were closed to them by word of mouth in the Negro community. They said, "At least in the South, you know what you can and can't do. In the North, you don't always know what you can't do until it's too late."

Northern whites had no intention of letting Negroes become an integral part of America. Negroes were ostracized, not considered a part of the public. They were ignored and made to wait if served. White professionals didn't serve Negroes. Negro professionals didn't serve whites.

To protect their status, whites were socially exclusive, their social organizations strictly segregated. Negroes worked with whites but they weren't allowed to mix socially with them. They could drink liquor with them but they couldn't go to a bar with them.

In 1956, at Washington University, one of my professors invited Ruth and me to a party at his home. I took Ruth to an exclusive dress shop. After I picked out a dress, I told the white sales clerk, "I'd like my wife to try on this dress."

She gave me a blank stare. She walked away and brought back another clerk who said, "That's an expensive dress."

I said, "Yes, I'll be paying cash. Please show her to the dressing room."

She called another clerk who said, "If you like it, you'll have to buy it. We don't let Negroes try on anything."

I said, "Do you buy clothes without trying them on?"

She paused and then said, "No, not me."

Whites in the North didn't want Negroes in their neighborhoods and they fought it tooth and nail. They excused their residential exclusivity by saying, "Why don't they want to live with their own kind?"

In 1957, when I went to Michigan State University to finish my doctorate, the foreign studies department arranged for me to rent a room. I told the white woman who answered to the door, "I've been assigned a room here. My name is Benjamin Dennis."

She said, "You're Benjamin Dennis? I don't think you'll be happy here. The other guests living here won't like it. They won't want you to use the bathroom."

I said, "You knew I was coming more than two months ago. Why didn't you write and tell me about all of these complications?"

She said, "We thought you were Irish. Could you find another place?"

I walked over to the campus and found President Hannah's house. I told him, "I don't have a place to stay. They refused me."

He said, "Go back there and tell them you'll take the room."

I walked back. This time the woman's husband said, "We had two students signed up for that room. Sometimes people don't show up. The other guy called yesterday and said he wants it."

I walked back to the president's house and told him what happened. He sent me to the housing department. The minute I walked in, the man at the desk said, "Mrs. Hannah just called. We'll have to nip this in the bud." He called the couple and told them, "If you can't accommodate this man, we'll take you off the housing roster." He sent me back over there.

This time the woman showed me the room and the bathroom. She told me the towels were changed each week and said, "We're happy to have you. You must be tired. Would you like a cup o'coffee?"

Integration benefited white realty companies. During the 1950s, in Kansas City, Kansas, and St. Louis, Missouri, white realtors told a radical Negro, "You're so educated, we can sell you a house in a white area." They selected a Negro couple and told them, "You've got children. It'll be better for you to live here." When these Negroes agreed, the white realtors told whites in the area, "Man, you're in something and we can't do anything about it. Some of your neighbors have broken the restricted covenant and sold to a Negro family. The guy who just moved in has lots of people behind him, including the NAACP. Your best bet is to move out before the value of your property goes down."

As whites moved out, white realtors sold the houses to Negroes at inflated prices. Since the price was high, Negroes thought they were really getting something. These houses were usually in an older neighborhood which meant Negro homeowners got stuck with repairs they couldn't afford. The interest rate was so high on the mortgage, they ended up paying two to three times what the house was worth. Whites bought up the remaining houses and rented them out. As they packed people into them, the neighborhood declined.

When I heard about these practices, I told Rev. Huntley, "This should be illegal."

He said, "When it's the white man, nothing is illegal."

Rev. Huntley preached to his congregation, "If you move in there, keep your house up. I know you have lots of children. Give them chores to do. Don't let us down. Do better than they have done."

One day, we were riding through a white area and he told me he could pick out the Negro homes. He pointed to a place and said, "This house looks nice. You see how the other houses have leaves all over the yard and even into the street? This yard is clean. This is a Negro home."

I said, "Prove it to me."

He said, "O.K. Let's stop and see."

As we walked up to the front door, I noticed that the porch was clean and the wood floor polished. When a young Negro girl opened the door, I said, "Rev. Huntley and I commend you for your house and yard."

She said, "Mama! Daddy! Someone wants to talk to you!" Rev. Huntley introduced himself. They knew him and invited us in, even though they were members of another church. The house was spotless. During our conversation, we learned that the man of the house had been a captain in the army during World War II and worked at the McDonnell-Douglas Corporation.

After Rev. Huntley introduced me as his "son from Africa," I asked the man, "Why don't the others rake their leaves?"

He said, "We're five Negro families dispersed in this white neighborhood. Whites say 'Niggers run down the place.' We're set to prove 'em wrong. Benjamin, white people talk a whole lot but they do very little. We don't talk much but we do a whole lot. Remember that, my friend."

The relationship between blacks and whites today is one of tolerance, not acceptance. Prohibiting discrimination and segregation doesn't mean whites accept integration and equal opportunity. Because our status is determined by who we associate with, blacks face the stigma of what Glenn Loury calls "petty apartheid," racial animus in daily life. The vast majority of whites don't hate blacks. They're indifferent to them. They not against them, but they're not for them either. In 2006, a white man in my church told me, "Ben, I don't have any personal hatred for blacks or Hispanics. I don't know them. But I do have the feeling that we'll never have anything in common."

Blacks are "they" not "us." Since whites think of blacks in negative terms, they're quietly suspicious of them. They don't want to talk to them. When they do, they're uneasy. They don't know how to respond to them since they don't know what they're thinking. During my life in the academic community, whites were always reserved until they realized I was a colleague.

Blacks are frustrated because it's harder to deal with subtle racism and microaggression. Whites don't care about offending blacks and there's no benefit in siding with them. As a result, liberals hope racism will go away by itself. They won't personally attack racism amongst their peers since they know the consequences. No one wants to be a social pariah. Since liberals can't talk to whites about racism, blacks have to solve the problem.

One of the last frontiers of racism is voluntary social association. Without freedom of association, America remains a captive country. Whites and blacks can belong to either racial community, but not both. Black and white families and communities have no relationship as equals. Friendships only go so far. Blacks and whites are acquaintances, not intimate friends. They don't confide in each other. They don't want their children to marry each other. Social separation begins in middle school at puberty. Until 2006, Georgia had segregated proms.

Blacks need complete assimilation, integration on all levels. However, when they moved to suburbs in the North, it was controlled integration, not assimilation. Closer contact only resulted in residual hostility.

Because race determines one's position in the American society, racism remains powerful. Whites must protect and preserve their image. They can't afford to identify with blacks as a racial group or as equals. In 2005, in Ft. Myers, Anita overhead a white teenage girl in the Penny's dressing room, ask her mother, "Does this look ghetto?" Whites go to great expense to adopt a white child overseas. Whites, who marry blacks, marry down. They're no longer fully accepted by whites or in white society.

Whites don't want to spend time with blacks because being socially associated with them always brings some form of shame and loss of status. They fraternize with them as co-workers or teammates, but the relationship isn't buddy-buddy. The token black is never part of the in-group. When white and black executives meet at a bar for happy hour, the token black isn't invited to someone's house after the meeting.

Whenever whites are in a social setting where blacks are the majority, their status as whites is jeopardized. A few blacks may visit a white home, if they're included in a group of whites. However, suspicion is aroused if a group of blacks regularly visit a white home. If whites do visit a black home, they don't reciprocate the invitation.

In 2005, a white woman told Anita, "My parents weren't racist. They told me to love everyone. But there weren't any black people around. I did have a black roommate my last two years of college. I got to know her pretty well."

Anita said, "Did you ever visit her home?

She said, "Oh, no. She came from California."

In any interaction with whites, blacks face the possibility of rejection. The unwritten rule is, "You're not welcome here." Blacks are excluded and ignored — "You don't belong."

Our white church in Ft. Myers has a parochial school. Elite whites enroll their children there because they don't want them in integrated schools with (lower class) blacks. In any given year, the school has one or two black or foreign students.

In 2001, the school instituted "Grandparents Day." The first two years, I served as an honorary grandfather for two white girls in the church that I knew. The third year, I volunteered to be an honorary grandfather for any child. They matched me with two white girls in the third grade. The first girl was receptive, but the second refused to walk into the gym with us. The youth director told me, "I'm sorry. I'll have to put those girls with someone else."

America is becoming re-segregated. In 2008, political analysts said demographics indicate that areas are becoming more homogenous in political affiliation. Where we live reflects our status. Lily-white neighborhoods have the highest status. Whites excuse themselves by saying, "The location of my neighborhood is an issue of safety. Black neighborhoods aren't safe." Whites say blacks never keep up their houses: "Blacks talk big but they never follow through." Those whites who can afford it gradually flee integrated neighborhoods. In 1970, Anita and I were the first "black" family to move into a white working class neighborhood in Flint, Michigan. Today, that neighborhood is completely black.

I am retired in Ft. Myers, Florida, the twelfth most segregated city in the United States according to a study by the University of Michigan in 1990. In 1992, Anita and I moved into the Villas, an older, tree-shaded neighborhood of affordable housing, in an excellent location just south of the city. When we moved in, the vast majority of residents were either white retirees or young couples. As homes become available, more blacks and Hispanics have moved in.

In 2004, as I was walking in the neighborhood, I heard some Haitians talking on their front porch. A few weeks later I saw a "For Sale" sign go up at the house next door where an elderly white couple lived. It was on the market a long time before it sold.

The black dean at Florida Gulf Coast University, whom I mentioned earlier, rented a luxurious home in Cape Coral in 1997. When the owner tried to sell it in 1999, there were no takers. Greg told me, "When whites see the decorations on the walls, they don't want to live in a house that 'blacks lived in.' "

Schools are becoming re-segregated. The Harvard Civil Rights Project found that in 2003 seventy per cent of black students attended segregated schools in comparison with sixty three per cent in 1980. The value of real estate depends on the school system. School choice is a response to forced integration. Private schools foster re-segregation since most blacks can't afford to attend them.

The Myth of Equal Opportunity

America has the image of an even playing field. White fairness is summed up in the expression, "It's a free country," which means that everyone can become capable of earning something and achieving some success. Such a belief discounts racism and the advantages of social class which include upbringing, educational and travel opportunities, character development, social connections, etc. Racism has made America a paradox of the most open and yet the most closed society in the world.

Because racial disadvantage doesn't apply to whites, they are optimistic about social change. They can't relate to black anger, but say, "Everything's open to them now. I know things were bad back then but we've come a long way. Blacks have equal rights. Government businesses have to be fair in hiring minorities. Blacks can make it if they try. It's time for them to take advantage of the new opportunities and not cross their arms over their chests and say, 'I hate whitey.' The problem with blacks is, they just don't do the right thing." Whites are oblivious to the effect of racism. A white woman asked Anita, "Wealthy blacks don't have self-hate, do they?"

At the same time, no white person wants to experience life in the United States as a black person. Whites are well aware that the rules of white supremacy and privilege still apply. Racism is less obvious but is perpetuated in a more subtle way. America's class system remains altered by racism. The gap between rich and poor is based on race. Although integration has given an illusion of equality, race still has something to do with all success or failure.

Blacks must compete at great disadvantage. The odds are against them being qualified. The poor don't have options. Whites assume blacks have equal access simply because they live in white society. In 2005, a white teacher told Anita, "Blacks have equal access to education today." If that were true, why did President Bush inaugurate "No Child Left Behind"? Why do colleges reach out to blacks who are the first in their family to go to college?

Racism is linked to power and wealth. In any genuine advantage to blacks, whites retreat from their lofty motives. Affirmative Action has been largely a failure. The poorest blacks don't have the qualifications to benefit from it. While Affirmative Action can give opportunity, it can't dispel destructive cultural mentalities — "You can take a horse to water but you can't make him drink."

Less opportunity means blacks face an even greater economic threat. There's no more frontier, no land rush or California Gold Rush. America's technological development requires a different work force. Technology only goes so far. Capitalism relies on maximum profit. The door is open for blacks and Hispanics to be exploited as cheap labor.

Workers' rights and universal health care are most crucial for blacks. They are the most difficult to achieve and maintain. In a society of increasing anonymity, there's no more common support for the poor. The homeless and mentally ill are made to fend for themselves, circulating in and out of prisons. Although more whites were on welfare, in absolute numbers, the curtailment of welfare hurt blacks more since they didn't have the racial advantage of whites.

The open marketplace is a myth. It's not just what you know. There may be a glut of "those who know." It's still very much who you know. Job searches require networking. In employment, racism makes blacks low on the likeability factor. Good jobs require sophistication and finesse — which lower class blacks lack. That's why there are programs to teach blacks common things that most whites learn growing up. Blacks in the ghetto are far from mainstream America. For example, most black kids in New York City have never been to Manhattan. They've never seen the Empire State Building.

Because of a few token blacks in a few key economic positions, blacks have the image of inclusion. The reality is that blacks haven't made it as a racial group. White businesses that cater to black or Hispanic customers profit their white owners, not the black or Hispanic community.

A black friend told me, "The only thing that affects corporate America is the bottom line. It's not about being fair. You can't expect people who have the advantage to be fair. Whites protested the set aside of ten per cent of the contracts for blacks while they had ninety per cent of the contracts. Whites don't want to share the system. How can blacks have an advantage with ten per cent? I have no problem understanding that whites hire and promote in their own image. But don't tell me whites are fair and honest."

The Myth of White Christianity

Racism made white Christianity organized religion that followed society rather than leading it. Accommodating slavery irrevocably weakened the Christian church. Slavery was resolved by a civil war, not by Christianity or white morality. It wasn't abolished simply because it was wrong. Lincoln used Emancipation as a strategy to punish the Confederate states to hasten the end of the war. The white Christian church has never seriously challenged racism. While the South is the Bible Belt, it's also the home of the KKK that used the cross of Christ to intimidate Negroes.

Slavery and racism transcended Christian unity. During slavery, Christian abolitionists opposed Christian slave masters. During the Civil War, Confederate Christians fought Union Christians. After Emancipation, white Christians lynched black Christians. During the Civil Rights Movement, white Christians opposed black Christians.

When I was at Lincoln, I was invited to speak at the final session of a tent revival of a white Baptist church in Denver, Colorado. I told the people, "The love of God is present everywhere, even in Africa. His love is for all and especially for those who believe in His name. When I pray I say 'Our' Father because he's my Father just as he's your Father. According to the Scriptures, we're all included in the family of God. We are one as God's children."

The pastor paused as he looked out over the crowd. He began his closing remarks by saying, "Do you all understand this? Say Amen!"

The crowd shouted, "Amen!"

With drama and increasing intensity, he said, "Brothers and sisters, our God's mercy reaches the farthest corners of the earth. To the east, ... and to the west, to the north, ... and to the south. God saw Benjamin and said, "I'm gonna send him not only to America, but to Colorado ... Not only to Colorado, but to Denver ... Not only to Denver, but to our church.... so we could hear him. Didn't our hearts burn within us as he spoke? Wasn't he like an angel sent from heaven? I want you all to listen carefully. I'm not speaking figuratively. Take a good look at him. Isn't he a nigger? The love of God surpasses anything. If Americans don't carry the Gospel, the Lord will claim for himself a man to do it.

"Benjamin's from the jungle. One day, he was walkin' there and a hungry lion started droolin', 'I'm gonna catch that sweet little soft thing.' And you know what happened? God said, 'Lion! Let my nigger go! Don't touch him! He's my Daniel, my messenger.' The leopard looked down and said, 'I'm gonna get him,' but God said, 'I know you're hungry, but not that nigger.' The giraffe started to step on him but God said, 'Don't move.' The elephant wanted to stand in his way but God said, 'You may be bigger but I made you. Benjamin may be little, but he's my nigger. Look how beautiful are Benjamin's feet! He'll go across the ocean and tell them of my love for all people.' God is no respecter of persons. Isn't he a NIGGER? And yet, the Lord sent him to us!"

Today, Christianity remains based on class and race. Capitalism and racism are primary cultural norms. White Christians, in their secular viewpoint, are primarily concerned about the opinions of whites. As the most conservative institution in society, the church maintains the status quo. The claim to fame of conservative Christians is their divine calling to preserve the purity of the church's teachings. Like the Pharisees of old, they own Christianity even though they fail in following it in the area of race.

The white Christian church functions primarily as a social club based on white elitism. Wealthy churches maintain the status of the rich. Churches in lower class neighborhoods minister to the poor. The rich don't want to attend a "poor" church nor are the poor welcomed into "rich" churches. Parochial schools have become synonymous with "white."

The church remains a bastion of segregation. During the Civil Rights Movement, Martin Luther King Jr. said, "Eleven o'clock on Sunday morning is still the most segregated hour in America." Malcolm X said, "America preaches integration and practices segregation." For the most part, whites remain socially exclusive. White Christianity in America is the only major religion that practices such a level of racial discrimination, albeit subtle.

Whether whites are Christian or not, they are ashamed of being associated with blacks. When neighborhoods changed, white churches refused to integrate.

Instead, they sold their church to a black congregation and moved to the suburbs. Their justification was that a black church would serve the area better.

In 1967, at Ohio University, I showed a documentary film in my race relations class, that was called, "A Time for Burning." A white Lutheran pastor in Omaha, Nebraska, attempted to cross the racial barrier by having his white members meet with black Christians in their homes. The initial participation was meager. It ultimately caused such an uproar, the pastor was forced to leave.

White Christians have no problem supporting foreign missions. They have a problem welcoming local blacks into their fold. My national church body considers itself integrated since it has black congregations. However, this sharing of ideology doesn't involve worshipping together. It doesn't entail intimate fellowship and friendships. White churches that have partner churches worldwide, share a long-distance fellowship with Christians who live in their own foreign enclave. An ethnic congregation within a white church doesn't threaten it because it's considered a separate ministry, a mission effort. Ethnic members are converts, not brothers and sisters in Christ. The language barriers excuse whites.

White urban churches, supported by the larger church body, are a second-class ministry that is expected to fail. Any church that becomes significantly integrated is touted in the church's magazine since it's such a novelty. The only truly interracial churches are those that serve as a refuge for the poor and homeless — blacks and whites that have no status to lose.

White Christians can't openly hate blacks, nor do they openly love them. Blacks who visit a white church are welcomed by the pastor and the token blacks, not the white congregation. If whites are friendly to black members, they don't invite them to their home. They don't form intimate friendships with them. They don't want their children to marry them.

Blacks are observed and then gradually accepted. Whites are accepted and then observed. Token blacks in a white church are novelties. They are in a white church, but not of it. In 1992, I visited my white in-laws' church in Bonita Springs, Florida. As we stood and sang the liturgy, I heard an elderly white woman behind me whisper loudly to her friend, "He knows the liturgy."

To prove they're not racist, whites welcome a few token upper or middle class blacks. At the same time, they don't want a large number of lower class blacks in their church because it would transform it and lower its status. In 1992, when Anita and I visited a white church in Ft. Myers, a white elder told us, "We're so glad you're here. We've been trying to get some coloreds in this church."

In 2004, Anita and I encouraged a young black teenager to attend our white church. The church subsidized him as part of a youth group mission trip to the Dominican Republic, to show the people there that our church was open-minded. White churches with token blacks are relieved that black visitors will see "one of their own kind." As a small cadre, token blacks become a congregation within a congregation as they support one another.

Whites are always in control. During slavery, Negroes left white churches in order to have their own say. Today, a black congregation may have a white pastor, but a white congregation will never have a black pastor. In 1983, in Flint, Michigan, Africans in the area initially formed the African Association of Greater Flint to support a black pastor from South Africa, who was called to integrate a declining white church. Within a month, the only members of the church were a few elderly white women.

White Christians are never accountable to black Christians. Any effort to combat racism in the church must be general and interdenominational so that individuals and congregations aren't personally indicted. The international Christian church can address racism since no country is specifically addressed.

Whites want to mold blacks, not treat them as equal partners. Blacks are second-class Christians in white churches. They're not a part of the leadership, the inner circle, unless it's an inner city church. When the black congregations in my national church body proposed their own hymnal, the white president insisted on reviewing the hymns for doctrinal purity.

The unity of race is greater than the unity of faith. White Christians don't love black Christians in a common way, much less a sacrificial way. Whites, Christian or not, align themselves against blacks, Christian or not. Christian whites are more comfortable with non-Christian whites than they are with Christian blacks. Christian whites and blacks live in parallel Christian realms. There's no unity except shared theology. Christian whites are more comfortable with their peers. The same is true for Christian blacks.

Racism is a sacrosanct topic in the white Christian church. It's a hot button topic since every white is indicted. The vast majority of white pastors are not only ignorant about blacks and blind to their own racial attitudes, they refuse to challenge their own people. Worldwide evangelists can attack racism. Pastors can address it in their radio ministry. But no white pastor will open racism's "can of worms" with his own congregation. He may touch upon it in a roundabout way, but he cannot preach a sermon solely on the evil of racism.

In 2003, in Ft. Myers, my white pastor took me, as his token black, to a community forum of black and white pastors. The purpose was to discuss race issues within a broad venue. During the course of the discussion, I told the group, "We're not addressing the real problem. The best thing you white pastors can do is to preach against racism within your own congregations." There was dead silence. After a long pause, one of the white pastors said, "If I did that, they'd crucify me. I'd end up being the preacher and the congregation."

When I suggested to my white pastor that he conduct a Bible class on racism, he suggested I do it. He gave me a Bible study book on racism written by whites.

Since blacks have no credibility or respect among whites, whites must address their peers. By their silence, white pastors honor their congregations more than they honor Christ. If white Christians don't fulfill God's purpose in history by challenging racism, revolutionary movements will win the hearts of the poor and disenfranchised. Racism continues to destroy any white witness to blacks and those of other cultures.

The Myth of White Benevolence

White benevolence, like everything else, serves white purpose. Whites have never acted as a racial group to serve Negro/black interest in a way that cost them anything. White do-gooders who publicly participate in a moral cause, enhance their status as someone good and moral. The Quakers who advocated abolition didn't benefit from slavery. While those in the Underground Railroad weren't generally known, they were known to their peers. White philanthropists in the American Colonization society exiled Negroes to Africa for their own good. Emancipation freed whites and America from any obligation to slaves. After the Civil War, Northern white missionaries who went to the South to educate Negroes, would never have welcomed them into their own communities. Whites supported Booker T. Washington because he trained the hands, not the brain.

During World War II, I told a white GI in Monrovia, "Whites in America must be good. They helped to win the war against Germany."

He said, "Not all of them are good. Even those who appear that way don't love or accept Negroes. You can't be openly good to Negroes unless you're a person of means. If you're poor and want to do something for them, you'll pay for it because you're not supposed to do that. Benevolent whites are as prejudiced as everyone else. They brand other whites as bad people because they're open about their prejudice. So-called good whites don't want a relationship with Negroes. They just want to be recognized and praised because they're stooping to help those lower than themselves."

During the 1950s, whether racist whites viewed Negroes with contempt or benevolent whites viewed them with condescension, whites expected Negroes to serve their purposes.

When I was a student at Lincoln, I spent the summer with Rev. Freeman and his family in Kansas City, Kansas. One day, as I rode my bike to Independence, Missouri, I changed a car tire for two women stranded by the road. When the elderly white passenger offered to pay me, I refused.

That evening, as I was returning by the same road, two white teenage girls called out, "Grandma wants to see you!" The girls were standing in front of a large iron gate that said "Hawthorne Estate." In the distance was an impressive house with a large manicured lawn and flower beds. The girls took me into the kitchen where I met the elderly white passenger from the car; she was now in a wheelchair. She said, "Come and have supper with me." As we ate, she said, "Tell me about yourself."

I said, "I'm from Liberia and I came to America by way of Queens College, Oxford University, where I studied pre-law. I'm now a sophomore at Lincoln."

She said, "Oxford? Our people originally came from Manchester. My grandfather built up this place. Folks here call us Yankees. You're a cultured young man. How do they treat you here?"

I said, "Well, you know how they treat Negroes."

She said, "That's a shame because we're all God's children. I'd like you to do yard work for me this summer." The first day, as I was mowing the lawn, one of the granddaughters told me, "Grandma wants to see you."

I said, "Let me finish this mowing."

She said, "Grandma wants to see you now."

When I went into the kitchen, Mrs. Gilmore said, "Let's talk." One afternoon, she said, "It's beastly hot. How about going swimming? The girls'll go with you." When I jumped into the community pool, everyone got out. The girls said, "Let's go. We're gonna tell Grandma."

Back at the house, Mrs. Gilmore said, "You're coming with me."

One of the granddaughters drove us to President Truman's home in Independence. As Mrs. Gilmore wheeled herself up the sidewalk to the house, a security guard said, "Ma'am, you can't go in there." She hit him with the cane she carried and said, "Get outta my way!" She called out, "Bessie! Is Harry in?"

Mrs. Truman came to the screen door and said, "Good afternoon, Mrs. Gilmore! Come right in."

Mrs. Gilmore said, "Where's Harry? I want to see Harry."

Mrs. Truman said, "Harry! Mrs. Gilmore's here. I think something's wrong."

President Truman came and said, "Come on in, Mrs. Gilmore."

Mrs. Gilmore said, "I'll get right to the point. This young man here is very cultured. He's from a very good family in Africa. He even attended Queens College at Oxford University. It's an honor that he's attending Lincoln. I sent him to the pool and when he got in, everyone got out. If you don't get everyone back in that pool, I'm going to have it closed and filled up."

President Truman whispered something to an aide. When we got back to the pool, Mrs. Gilmore watched from the car as we got into the water. At home, she asked me, "Did anyone ever get out of the pool?"

I said, "No."

She said, "That's my boy! That's it!"

From then on, my "work" was to go swimming. One day, I told Mrs. Gilmore's daughter that I didn't feel like swimming every day. She said, "I knew this was going to happen. That's why I didn't drive you over to the Truman's. You've hit her nerve. This is her campaign. She's going to miss your swimming when you go back to school."

In the Civil Rights Movement, Martin Luther King Jr. was a "savior" of whites as well as blacks, in bringing about a more equitable society. There were real causes for the movement. Negroes suffered abuse to do the ordinary. A few individual whites marched in the movement, publicly associating with blacks. After the march, they went back to their white lives and communities.

Today, whites can only be socially identified with blacks as do-gooders. Well-meaning whites see blacks and minorities as the downtrodden, not their peers. Throughout America's history, white politicians have had to cater to the majority. If they sided with blacks and the poor, there was nothing in it for them. They lost white support.

Whites do right only to a few select blacks — and those blacks must appreciate it. If blacks don't play the game the way whites want them to, whites get angry and pull out. Whatever whites do to make things right for blacks, it's only a small compensation for what whites have done to blacks and are still doing.

Benign neglect has the same effect as blatant oppression. Whites adopt a responsibility for the poor that have been made poor by racist practices. White goodness doesn't affect or alter these practices. Liberals display their goodness to show they're not like the rest. White losers gain status by working with those below them — the poor or criminals. Christian whites who can't fit into white society, become missionaries overseas with great status and privilege.

Social work is impersonal. Whites work in black communities to help blacks. The blacks they help aren't their personal friends. In 1999, in Ft. Myers, the whites who marched in the Martin Luther King parade didn't attend the black celebration at Centennial Park afterwards. Being noble towards blacks doesn't involve living with them, going to church with them, sending your children to school with them, or intermarrying with them. Whenever Anita is friendly to blacks or Hispanics, they ask me privately, "Where did you find her?"

Token blacks serve white purpose on an international level as well as a national level. They give America the image that if these blacks have made it, the door is open to all. America's promotion of democracy worldwide benefits her image more than examples of her flawed democracy at home.

In 2005, during Hurricane Katrina, CNN showcased white families who took in black families. It was unusual and portrayed an image whites want of themselves. This was a short-term help between strangers. It didn't mean these blacks became their neighbors or close friends. It didn't mean whites, as a racial group, identified with blacks.

The Myth of Assimilation

The doctrine of the antebellum South was the prevention of a mongrel race. If the white race was polluted, whites would no longer be genetically superior. As a result, whites defined racial purity. A white man improved the Negro race when he injected his "blood" into a Negro woman. Frederick Douglas' intelligence and capability were attributed to his white father. In contrast, a Negro deteriorated the white race when he injected his "blood" into a white woman. One drop of Negro blood 'kinked the hair and dulled the mind." Both sexual unions produced the same thing — a mulatto child. To keep the white race pure, mulattos were relegated to the Negro race.

During the 1950s, sexual taboos were rigid. When I was a student at Lincoln, I was invited to speak at a white independent Baptist church in Nebraska. When Rev. Allen picked me up from the bus station, he told me, "You'll eat all your meals with us but I'll put you up in a motel." That night at dinner with his family, I met his two very attractive daughters.

Later that evening, he took me into his study and told me, "You're new in America so you don't know our culture. As a friend and Christian brother, I'd like to explain some things to you. Besides preaching, my greatest job is to protect my daughters. I don't want 'em messing around with another race."

I said, "Rev. Allen, why do you assume they'll fall in love with a Negro or an Indian since there aren't many of them around here?"

He said, "God made us different and we should keep that separation. Let's go back to creation. Birds mate with their own kind. You don't see white birds mating with black birds or the other way around."

I said, "You're right. Birds and animals that belong to different species don't mate. That's not true for mankind. All human beings belong to the same species 'homo' and the same genus 'sapiens.' That's why, when whites and Negroes mate, they produce a mulatto child."

Rev. Allen stood and said, "It's time to take you to the motel. I still won't let my girls go to bed with niggers or Indians. It just don't seem right."

When I spent the summer with Rev. Freeman and his family in Kansas City, Kansas, I liked to sit on their front porch in the evening and read. Since their house overlooked the Negro neighborhood, I noticed that two white priests regularly visited the home of two attractive mulatto girls who were friendly to me.

One evening, when I visited the girls, I found the priests there. As we sat around talking, I said, "In Liberia, Catholic priests are celibate. Is your Catholicism different from ours?"

One of them said, "For us, that's not Scripture. The Bible says those who can't be celibate should marry. Peter was married before he met Jesus and Jesus accepted him."

I said, "You're not married to these women."

He said, "Who knows? We may end up marrying them."

During the Civil Rights Movement, there was a fear among whites that civil rights would lead to intermarriage. Despite any other laxness during the 1960s, sexual taboos were in force. While intermarriage could no longer be prevented, it was frowned upon. Whites told their teenage daughters, "You have to be careful with those blacks. That's all they want."

One of the last frontiers of racism is intermarriage. The greatest barrier to the full assimilation of blacks is the question, "Would you want your daughter to marry one?" No white father willingly gives his daughter to a black man regardless of the man's background, education, or accomplishments. When forced to comply, he considers such a marriage a tragedy.

In 1963, at Michigan State University, Ruth and I lived in University Village. Our next door neighbors were a newly married interracial couple. One day, the black husband told me his white in-laws were coming to visit and he wanted me there for moral support. After we all sat down, his white father-in-law said, "John, I'm in a position to help you. My wife and I have agreed to give you forty thousand dollars. If that's not enough, we'll give you fifty thousand to divorce our daughter. Whenever you need anything after that, you can always call on us."

The husband, stunned and angry, looked at me and said, "What would you do?"

I said, "Don't ask my opinion. Ask your wife. She's their child."

The wife, who was also angry, told her parents, "We've heard you clearly. Nothing's worth more to me than my husband."

The husband agreed, "You heard her. Nothing's worth more to me than my wife."

The parents stood up, the mother sobbing. They couldn't imagine anything good could come from such a marriage. Mulatto grandchildren would put them in a terrible social predicament.

White women were discouraged from an interracial relationship by the expression, "If you go with a black man, no white man will have you." Black men were equally discouraged. In 1961, President John F. Kennedy snubbed Sammy Davis Jr. for marrying May Britt, a white woman. Whenever a black man marries a white woman, his status is increased. Hers is decreased.

While intermarriage is more common, it's never desired or welcomed. It's still against the norm. In 2005, in Ft. Myers, a white woman said to Anita, "If you don't want your daughter to marry a black man because of what she'll face in life, does that mean you hate blacks?"

Intermarriage and intimate friendships between blacks and whites are still an aberration, something unexpected. Those who intermarry are still "rebels."

In 2006, in Ft. Myers, Anita and I attended a wedding at our white church. At the reception, as I stood in line at the buffet table, Anita was farther back in line talking with some friends. While I was waiting, I struck up a conversation with the white woman ahead of me who was a family minister in Marco Island. When she asked me about myself, I told her Anita and I were writing a book.

When she asked where Anita was, I pointed and said, "She's back in line, talking."

She said, "I don't see your wife anywhere."

I said, "She's right there."

She said, "I still don't see her."

When I called Anita up beside me, the first thing the woman said to her was, "You're a brave woman."

Because our marriage is a novelty, the first question we're asked is, "How did you two meet?" In Ft. Myers, we're never assumed to be together. We can stand side by side at a doctor's reception window and the receptionist will invariably ask Anita first, "May I help you?" Later on, she'll turn to me and say, "Do you need help?" When we walk the beach, we get dirty looks from white retirees. One of my white surgeons joked, "I wonder what your kids look like."

Whites equally oppose white men marrying black women. In 2006, at church, a white friend told us he had dated a black girl in college in the 1960s. He was interested in her and assumed there'd be no objection since his parents were open-minded. When his step-mother came to pick him up for the summer, he casually kissed the black girl good-bye. The entire trip home, his step mother never said one word to him. She was devastated that he would "ruin his life that way." He never married the girl.

Whites resent a white man marrying a black woman since it elevates her and gives legitimacy and honor to a degrading relationship historically kept secret. In 2003, in our neighborhood in Ft. Myers, a black woman married to a white man, confided in me, "This is a man's world. A black woman marrying a white man raises the wrath of the white man. They think we're not good enough for them. It raises the wrath of black men too. Black women have always been taken from them and they could do nothing. Now that they're in a position to do something, they feel whites are still taking their women."

Whites speculate about interracial marriage according to the lowest common denominator. If a black man marries an attractive white woman, whites think, "How could she give her life away like that?" If the woman is ugly or obese, they think, "No one else would have her." A white woman marries a black man for sex. A black man marries a white woman for prestige. A white man marries a black woman because he's either desperate or he marries her for sex. She marries him for prestige. Given the realities of racism, there's an element of truth in all of this.

Because of America's history of slavery and miscegenation, there's no such thing as a pure race in America. The ultimate racial contradiction is the mulatto who passes for white. Despite his white racial image, he is socially black. Some mulattos are lighter than some whites.

Race remains significant since we see color first. Racial blending poses a challenge — how to identify what race someone belongs to. Whites are uncomfortable when they meet someone, until they ask, "So what are you?" so they can put people in their proper racial and cultural box.

The Myth of White Superiority

Whites say, "John Hope Franklin's assertion that white Americans are 'the direct beneficiaries of slavery' is unbelievably grandiose." The truth is that slavery benefited all whites, past and present, since it benefited America as a whole. Slavery was the economic lifeblood of America. It was the pillar of capitalism that transformed America. The great profit of slavery not only "made" the South, it built up the nation, and thus "made" America.

Slavery wasn't an aberration practiced in secret. It was a national norm, an integral part of Southern daily life. It lasted hundreds of years and involved generations of Negroes. Whites say, "Not all whites in the South practiced slavery." Well, the ones who mattered, did. Slavery was practiced by America's elite, including those in the highest echelons of the national government. Slave masters were not renegades. They were well respected citizens in the South.

Slavery and racism made America a nation of hypocrisy. The real issue wasn't freedom, but who was free. The issue wasn't a rule of law, but who benefited from the law. America is the only country in the world that declared her ideals to the world and so obviously failed to lived up to them.

In the South, holders of morality bragged about their atrocities. Slavery was a two-edged sword that destroyed whites as well as Negroes. Emancipation fueled Southern depravity. In the South's rule of insecurity, whites brutally punished Negroes before they could do something to them.

The KKK, as "Southern law," enacted the "justice" white society couldn't legitimately do. In their callousness, whites had no shame. In their lynch mobs, where no one was individually responsible, they reverted to savagery. Pictures of lynchings show Southern citizens watching with pride and satisfaction. Whites castrated and burned alive a Negro on Saturday and attended church on Sunday. Lynching was an occasion for picnic lunches. Kids were let out of school. Postcards of mutilated corpses and pieces of charred flesh were sold door to door as souvenirs.

During the 1930s, the NAACP flew a banner from their New York office that said, "A man was lynched yesterday." While Nazi war criminals were hunted down, Southerners got away with murder. In 1955, two Southerners were acquitted of brutalizing and murdering Emmet Till, a fourteen year old boy, for whistling at a white woman. In the face of this and other bold atrocities, white Christians all over America kept silent.

Societies and nations ultimately bear the consequences of the sins of their people. Thomas Jefferson said, "I tremble for my country for justice cannot sleep forever." It wasn't all of the Germans who killed the Jewish people. It was Hitler leading some of them. Even so, Germany bears the guilt as a nation. The Germans were guilty of acquiescence. Not fighting evil is evil. The same is true for America.

America embodies political expediency. After the Revolutionary War, America's leaders ignored slavery entrenched in the Southern colonies, for the greater cause of national unity. Slavery was an irresolvable issue until the Civil War, because wherever it proved profitable, the powers that be ensured its continuation. While Thomas Jefferson condemned slavery, he never freed his slaves, even upon his death. The Emancipation Proclamation didn't initially apply to all slaves. President Ulysses S. Grant abandoned Reconstruction in 1877, letting the South solve its own problems. In 1955, President Dwight D. Eisenhower refused to answer a telegram from Emmet Till's mother after his white murderers confessed in LOOK magazine.

In the Civil Rights Movement, justice came to America in spite of whites. Whites had to be shamed into doing what was right. They accepted civil rights "kicking and screaming." The American system moved no farther than it was forced.

Whites didn't care what blacks thought of them. What they resented was America's world stage where white policemen beat fellow citizens peacefully marching for the rights every American should have. America's "horror movie" laid America's sins bare. People around the world said, "Isn't this the country that calls itself the moral policeman of the world?"

Civil rights were an abstract cause for Northerners until King took the movement to the North's backyard of Chicago. Southerners, who were personally threatened, used "any means necessary," which included bombing a Negro church, killing four little Negro girls early for Sunday school. Southerners protested school integration. Northerners protested busing. Throughout America's history, whites have acquiesced to all kinds of white atrocities because they were done to Negroes/blacks. Whites have shown power instead of demonstrating morality.

Whites, as a racial group, bear a national responsibility for racism. When slavery divided America, the Civil War was only a partial solution, because it united whites as a nation, not whites and blacks. Racism is America's continuing tragedy. No matter how congenial the gathering, racism is the undercurrent of every organization and relationship — whether whites are by themselves or with blacks. An instantaneous barrier arises each time a white person sees a black person until interaction takes place — if it does. Even if a black person is considered nice, there's reservation until a relationship is established. The dissolution of the racial barrier between two individuals or groups doesn't translate to blacks as a racial group. Racial barriers exist for blacks as well. Regardless of familiarity, they know racism is in the minds of all whites — if not on the surface, then underneath.

Racism made whites their own worst enemy, by generating a society of injustice and inequity they must live with. Racism impeded progress by keeping Negroes/blacks from contributing. When you diminish any member of a society, you diminish the society.

While America has an image of national unity, racism, as an undercurrent, generates disunity. America is a nation divided. Whites fight to retain their control and advantage. Blacks fight to be free to do their own thing. Racism has generated separate cultural entities. Whites participate in mainstream American culture. Lower class blacks participate in a sub-culture of the American culture. In America's history of violence and conflict, racism always results in fear and mistrust — hatred and injustice.

Part III. Conclusion

The greatest sin of our time is not the few who have destroyed,
but the vast majority who had sat idly by.
— Rev. Martin Luther King, Jr.

The story of racism is inevitably sad. The result has only been frustration and futility. Poverty and inequality are a recipe for disaster, wherever they exist. If the cries of human suffering don't move us, enlightened self-interest should. The white Eurocentric world view has made the rest of the world an insignificant periphery. The threat of terrorism has changed that balance considerably. In today's global interconnectedness, whites can no longer afford their cultural arrogance and hubris.

Technology is no longer the challenge. The real issue is the development of pluralistic societies within a world community where people can enjoy the sweetest kind of freedom from racism. Every culture has strengths and weaknesses. The key to cultural borrowing is to take the positive and leave the negative. Biracial, cross-cultural people can be tremendous assets in bridging the gap between races and cultures.

Arnold Toynbee said that some twenty-six civilizations have risen from the face of the earth. Their decline and fall were not caused by external invasions but by internal decay. Diffusing racism will not only benefit blacks, its greatest benefit will be for whites — and for America. Racism is America's unfinished business — her last frontier. Americans have conquered the West and outer space. Now they must conquer the "inner space" of racial attitudes. When whites share power and responsibility, joint leadership will benefit America.

Nothing will change until whites, as a racial group, own the problem. You can't conquer what you won't confront. In 2005, at a "white" party in Tampa, Florida, the hostess asked us what our book was about. When Anita said it was about racism and I filled in the details, suddenly we were the only voices in the room. Only when the subject changed, did things liven up and conversation resume. The hardest thing for any of us to do is face the truth about ourselves. Only the truth can save America. In 2006, the University of Michigan's theme for Martin Luther King Day was, "It's time to break the silence."

Since racism remains an integral part of the American society and culture, it must be combated on a societal and national level. What is needed is a national organization against racism. As long as the battle against racism remains on the fringe of white society, nothing will happen. It's not sufficient for blacks to fight against racism. Whites must take the lead in diffusing it among their peers. It will take a group of white leaders strong and influential enough to enforce a whole new cultural standard in America. A massive public effort is the only way to generate the agreement and momentum necessary to enact significant social change.

The Obama candidacy for president has heightened the need — and the opportunities — for a national dialogue on racism. The first step is a private dialogue among America's white and black leaders in a setting where they can be honest with each other. When conflict is handled correctly, people grow closer as they face and resolve their differences.

Throughout America's history white Christians, who did so much in the name of love, never loved Negroes. During the Civil Rights Movement, blacks couldn't count on white Christians for justice. They were forced to cry out to the legal system and the government. White hypocrisy remains the greatest challenge to the church to this day.

National church bodies should fill their own missing role in the fight against racism. A national consortium of white pastors, across denominational lines, could provide, in a spirit of honesty amongst themselves and with blacks, positive contributions of their own. They could at least support local pastors who speak out. If Christians made a real effort for Christian unity to supersede racial unity, it would help set the tone for the nation.

Only a lasting change in whites will bring about a lasting change in blacks. Blacks will be free to express their hurts and propose solutions. They will be empowered to face and attack the destructive cultural mentalities of the black community. Upper and middle class blacks will be energized to use their success for the good of their race. The focus must be on a national agenda. America will become a truly great nation when whites and blacks become allies, rather than competitors.

Liberia's tragedy can only be redeemed by learning from it. The key to Liberia's future is to understand what destroyed us and our country. We must face the truth because only the truth can save us. It's no shame to admit your limitations. It's a shame to do nothing about them. With a true and accurate history, Liberians must forge a new unity out of suffering. They must abandon their "every man for himself" mentality. Liberia's national focus must be the greatest good for the most people.

To paraphrase the words of John F. Kennedy, we must "ask not what Liberia can do for us, but what we can do for Liberia." Nothing will happen until we realize that we rise or fall together. No one can do for us what we must do for ourselves. We must be serious about morality because there's no substitute for it. We must take God seriously and humble ourselves before Him to heal our nation. To generate a new national standard of integrity, it will take a group of committed Liberians at the highest level.

We are not failures unless we make failure a way of life. Let's not let our crucible of suffering be for naught. For the sake of progress, we must see beyond ourselves. Only when we are serious, can Liberia claim its rightful place in the world. Let us aspire to that day when we can be proud to be called Liberians. May God help us and help Liberia.

There's a big difference between publicly saying something, privately thinking it, and doing something about it. The tragedy of racism should move all of us to action. None of us has chosen our race, our culture, or our life chances. However, we can choose our response to racism. The battle begins in the mind.

Rev. Martin Luther King, Jr. dreamed of a society where people were judged by the content of their character. Imagine what Christianity could be if it were free of racism. Imagine what the United States and Liberia could be. Finally, imagine one human family in the world community. In a core belief that racism must be ended, "What are you going to do about it?" The antidote to racism is love. Without love, we are all nothing.

Made in the USA
Middletown, DE
05 December 2019

80067531R00158